SPIES ON THE MEKONG

SPIES ON THE MEKONG

CIA Clandestine Operations in Laos

KEN CONBOY

CASEMATE

Philadelphia & Oxford

Published in the United States of America and Great Britain in 2021 by
CASEMATE PUBLISHERS
1950 Lawrence Road, Havertown, PA 19083, USA
and
The Old Music Hall, 106–108 Cowley Road, Oxford OX4 1JE, UK

Hardback Edition: ISBN 978-1-63624-019-0
Digital Edition: ISBN 978-1-63624-020-6

A CIP record for this book is available from the British Library

Printed and bound in the United States by Sheridan

For a complete list of Casemate titles, please contact:

CASEMATE PUBLISHERS (US)
Telephone (610) 853-9131
Fax (610) 853-9146
Email: casemate@casematepublishers.com
www.casematepublishers.com

CASEMATE PUBLISHERS (UK)
Telephone (01865) 241249
Email: casemate-uk@casematepublishers.co.uk
www.casematepublishers.co.uk

Contents

Acknowledgements

During the Cold War, the Central Intelligence Agency's largest and longest-running paramilitary operation was in the tiny kingdom of Laos. Hundreds of its advisors and support personnel trained and led guerrilla formations across the mountainous Laotian countryside, as well as ran smaller road-watch and agent teams that stretched from the Ho Chi Minh Trail to the Chinese frontier. Added to this number were hundreds of contract personnel providing covert aviation services.

It was dangerous work. On the Memorial Wall at the CIA headquarters in Langley, Virginia, nine stars are dedicated to officers who perished in Laos. Added to this are more than one hundred people from proprietary airlines killed in aviation mishaps between 1961 and 1973. Combined, this grim casualty figure is orders of magnitude larger than that of any other CIA paramilitary operation.

But for the foreign intelligence officers of the CIA, Laos was more than a paramilitary battleground. Because of its geographic location as a buffer state, as well as its trifurcated political structure, Laos was a unique Cold War melting pot. All three of the Lao political factions, including the communist Pathet Lao, had representation in Vientiane. The Soviet Union had an extremely active embassy in the capital, while the People's Republic of China—though in the throes of the Cultural Revolution—had multiple diplomatic outposts across the kingdom. So, too, did both North and South Vietnam.

All of that made for fertile ground for clandestine operations. This book details, for the first time, the cloak-and-dagger side of the war in Laos, from agent recruitments to servicing dead drops in Vientiane. It is important that this story be told for several reasons. First, clandestine operations in Laos were often in support of the wider Indochina campaign, and an analysis of these operations adds to a better understanding of the CIA's contribution during the Second Indochina War.

Second, some of these operations were tied to America's overarching Cold War struggle; for example, against the Soviet Union and Warsaw Pact. In one case, a recruitment started in Laos ranks among the most important CIA penetrations of the Soviet intelligence services. Understanding these operations in Laos allows for a fuller reading of the CIA's historical competition with its communist counterparts.

Finally, many of the CIA personalities in Laos went on to prominence within the Agency and factored in major operations outside of Southeast Asia. Understanding their experiences in Laos permits for a greater appreciation of what they accomplished elsewhere.

This book is based on both written sources and interviews. Special thanks go to Soutchay Vongsavanh, who was extremely generous with his time and extraordinary support. Thanks, too, go to Merle Pribbenow for his unparalleled insights into Vietnamese military history. I also extend my sincere gratitude to Dan Arnold, Barry Broman, Albert Grandolini, Peter Koret, Kevin McCarthy, Arya Panya, Song Ramawati, Martin Rathie, Ousa Sananikone, Veera Star, Christopher Tovar, James Tovar, and Maya Velesko. Finally, I owe a continuous debt to Charn Wisezjan—the ever-resourceful Albert—for his unwavering support and invaluable commentary.

Research for this book took place over more than a decade. Sadly, several of those who were instrumental in my research have passed away in the interim. I would like to draw attention to the help, and especially friendship, of the late Jim Dunn, Jim Morrison, Soui Sananikone, MacAlan Thompson, and B. Hugh Tovar. They are truly missed.

CHAPTER I

Growing Pains

Laos was a most improbable nation to transfix the superpowers of the mid-20th century. A landlocked patch of mountainous territory roughly the size of Great Britain, it had its heyday six hundred years earlier when local royalty rose to prominence under what was called Lan Xang, the Kingdom of a Million Elephants. Back then it had flourished as a center for the arts and Buddhist theology. Equally impressive was Lan Xang's military prowess, its warriors extending the kingdom's reach over most of current-day Laos, northern and central Thailand, and northern Cambodia.

By the 16th century, however, Lan Xang's fortunes began to wane as it was weakened in a series of wars with the Burmese. Three centuries later, continued foreign pressure, compounded by palace intrigue, split the kingdom in three.

Thus broken, the once-formidable Lan Xang was a sparsely populated backwater when the French traveled up the Mekong River in the latter half of the 19th century. Though the fractured principalities had few economic benefits to offer, France needed a buffer to shield its lucrative Vietnamese holdings from the expansionist Thai and the British in Burma. The French, then, fused the landlocked realms back together into a single protectorate and created Laos. As its titular leader, the king in Luang Prabang was elevated as the unified Lao monarch.

Under French rule, Laos barely developed beyond its frontier status. A handful of dirt roads, passable only in the dry season, were cut on an east–west axis to the Vietnamese coast. A single north–south road,

Route 13, was not completed until 1943. While Vietnamese laborers were imported to mine tin, and coffee and corn were grown on the Bolovens Plateau, products from Laos never represented more than 1 percent of total French exports from its Southeast Asian colonies.

With few resources to exploit, the Lao population was all but ignored by the French. And while the king of Laos was allowed to retain nominal control around Luang Prabang, in practice the French ruled Laos as would a benign and indifferent absentee landlord, retaining the existing traditional village structure and introducing hundreds of educated Vietnamese to run the country on a daily basis.

As for the apolitical Lao peasantry, most of whom had little interest in events outside their village, French indifference was matched in kind. Indeed, only two disturbances of any significance—both involving hill tribes—broke the peace during nearly a half century of French rule. These relatively minor events aside, Laos was as close as the French got to a perfect protectorate. At little cost, they had a nearly trouble-free buffer—until World War II.

With the fall of France to Nazi Germany in June 1940, France's grip on its Southeast Asian colonies quickly degenerated to a toehold. The reason was that Germany's Axis partner, Japan, had grand plans for Asia that did not include European overlords. Accordingly, Japan's military forced its way into French Indochina three months after Paris fell. By August 1941, some 40,000 Japanese troops were stationed in France's Lao, Cambodian, and Vietnamese territories, giving Tokyo de facto control behind a veneer of pro-Axis French administrators.

Across Southeast Asia, the Japanese proved themselves mercurial masters. Initially brutal toward indigenous resistance, they quickly warmed to local nationalist movements when the war started going bad and the Allies looked poised to reenter Indochina. In Laos, they went so far as to kidnap Crown Prince Savang Vatthana in order to force King Sisavang Vong, a dedicated Francophile, to declare on 8 April 1945 an end to French protectorate status.

Taking a cue from the Japanese, the educated upper stratum of Lao society began to flirt with notions of nationalism and independence. Leading the pack of budding nationalists were three brothers from the junior branch of the royal family. The oldest, Prince Phetsarath, was a French-educated viceroy who had been a driving force behind establishment of the Lao civil service and judiciary before World War II; he was widely recognized as the second-most powerful man in Laos after the king. The second brother, Prince Souvanna Phouma, had earned two engineering degrees in France before returning to Vientiane as chief of the Architecture Bureau in the colonial Public Works Service. The third brother, Prince Souphanouvong, was, more correctly, the younger half brother of the other two. Ambitious, vain, and academically gifted, Souphanouvong had earned a reputation as a rebel, his resentment of authority fanned by childhood discrimination because his mother was a commoner.

With Phetsarath and Souvanna Phouma at the forefront, a young nationalist movement, the Lao Issara—or Free Lao—took shape. And with Tokyo's strong encouragement, it was this group that declared independence in the waning days of World War II.

Not having any of it, the French cobbled together an expeditionary force and rushed it back to Laos. As the French pushed their way into the panhandle in early 1946, the Lao Issara all but melted away. After southern Laos was liberated, on 24 April the French dropped an airborne battalion along the outskirts of Vientiane; the Lao Issara offered no resistance. Fifteen days later, a similar drop put Luang Prabang under French control. Three months after that, the French reincorporated Laos—along with Cambodia and the Vietnamese territories—into an Indochinese federation.

With French authority restored, the Lao Issara leadership regrouped in Thailand. Moping in Bangkok safe houses, the dispirited nationalists began to bicker endlessly among themselves.

That the Lao Issara remained toothless was welcome news for France, which had its hands full combating the fast-growing threat from communist Vietnamese guerrillas known as the Viet Minh. To free more assets for use against the Viet Minh, France transformed Laos in May 1947 into a constitutional monarchy with sufficient autonomy to inaugurate a national assembly in six months' time. Continuing in the same vein, a July 1949 Franco-Lao agreement granted the Royal Lao

Government (RLG) the right to raise a Lao National Army (Armée Nationale Laotienne, or ANL).

As the French now had Laos speeding down the road toward de facto independence, the Lao Issara all but lost its raison d'être. Thus, when the RLG dangled a promise of amnesty, many from the Lao Issara expressed interest. Prince Phetsarath, at odds with the king, chose to sulk in Thailand. Souphanouvong, long known for his unusually close ties to the Vietnamese, had been expelled from the mainstream Lao Issara in May 1949; predictably, he made his way to Vietnam to lobby support from the Viet Minh's revolutionary godfather, Ho Chi Minh. Alone among the brothers, Souvanna Phouma formally dissolved the Lao Issara in October and then led the bulk of his comrades across the Mekong in peace.

The RLG soon faced a threat from a different quarter. Since the opening of 1949, the Viet Minh had been quietly nurturing a sister wing composed of communist Lao guerrillas in the northeastern province of Sam Neua. Soon after creation of this movement's first 25-man guerrilla band, Souphanouvong, ousted from the Lao Issara, offered himself up as their ally. For the ambitious Souphanouvong, this guerrilla movement offered greater personal visibility—free of competition from other senior nationalists; for the communist guerrillas, the flamboyant prince was a good publicist, adding appeal and legitimacy to an otherwise obscure, Viet Minh-backed splinter movement.

With hill tribe recruits, Souphanouvong's imprimatur, and Viet Minh support, the movement made early gains. By August 1950, 150 of its members were on hand for a clandestine rally at Ho Chi Minh's mountain redoubt in Tuyen Quang, Vietnam. It was there that the resistance was cosmetically reshaped into the Neo Lao Issara (Free Lao Front). The meeting also saw the first use of the term Pathet Lao (Lao Nation), in reference to the Neo Lao Issara's armed wing; from that point forward, despite several official name changes over the years, the term Pathet Lao became synonymous with both the Lao communist military organization and its associated political front.

Meantime, the French war effort was not going well. By early 1952, the Viet Minh had seized most of the northern border region with China, leaving it free to make raids into northern Vietnam's fertile Red River delta. Hoping to turn the tide, French forces maneuvered into blocking positions. Rising to the challenge, the Viet Minh responded with some twenty-five thousand troops and grabbed even more swaths of territory by the second week of March.

For the French, things only got worse. Near year's end, colonial officials were convinced of an imminent Vietnamese invasion of Sam Neua. Garrisoned by two Lao battalions and three local guard companies, the province had already lost a pair of frontier outposts to encroaching elements of two Viet Minh regiments in early December.

Recognizing Sam Neua's vulnerability, the French high command dispatched Lao paratroopers to Sam Neua town, the provincial capital, during the third week of December 1952. But rising to the challenge once more, Vietnamese forays savaged the Lao paratroopers over the next three months. Then, in a defining moment for the Viet Minh, on 12 April 1953 a massive Vietnamese task force spilled across the Sam Neua frontier. Given less than a day's lead, the Franco-Lao garrison retreated southwest; only a fraction eventually reached safety on the Plain of Jars (Plaine des Jarres, or PDJ), a grassy plateau between Sam Neua and Vientiane.

As Sam Neua Province was being overwhelmed, a second Viet Minh invasion force massed in the Vietnamese valley of Dien Bien Phu. Composed of one regiment and Pathet Lao auxiliaries, this column crossed the border and pushed south toward Luang Prabang. As an emergency blocking force, a lone company of Lao commandos was parachuted halfway between Dien Bien Phu and Luang Prabang on 14 April. In addition, the French orchestrated a major airlift of reinforcements into the royal capital, pumping the town full of Foreign Legionnaires and Moroccan troops. Still, by 27 April the outlook for Luang Prabang looked grim as the isolated commando company was overrun in less than three hours.

From a purely military perspective, the French top brass would have been right to order a withdrawal from Luang Prabang. But greatly complicating matters, the king of Laos refused to vacate his throne, allegedly influenced by psychic premonitions of a local blind seer who said the Viet Minh would stop short of the town.

Their prestige tied to the monarch's welfare, the French had no choice but to rush in still more reinforcements. Continuing to roll south, the Viet Minh had moved to within 30 kilometers of Luang Prabang by 10 May. The French forces waited tensely for a final confrontation. The weather, however, proved their salvation as monsoon rains began two days later. With their extended supply lines quickly mired, the Viet Minh troops retraced their steps back toward Dien Bien Phu. Luang Prabang, against long odds, was saved.

As the French were scrambling to hold northern Laos, halfway around the world the United States was paying close attention. Whereas Laos had once been relegated to a footnote in discussions of Indochina, the US government was now breathlessly equating the kingdom's fate with that of the entire noncommunist bloc south of China. Said newly inaugurated President Dwight Eisenhower during a 28 April 1953 National Security Council meeting, if Laos is lost, we will "likely lose the rest of Southeast Asia and Indonesia. The gateway to India, Burma, and Thailand will be open."[1]

Matching this sentiment with action, the United States loaned six transport planes (with civilian aircrews) to conduct supply drops as the French rushed reinforcements to the PDJ. By the end of May, the augmented garrison surged forth, beating the Viet Minh column back toward the border. At the cost of 1,569 Lao and French Union soldiers, the Viet Minh offensive had at long last been stopped.

Though the French had won a temporary reprieve, Washington remained deeply concerned. The United States already had diplomatic outposts scattered across Indochina to help keep its finger on the pulse. In 1952, the modest-size legation in the southern Vietnamese city of Saigon had been upgraded to an embassy under Ambassador Donald Heath. This embassy, in turn, oversaw tiny legations in Vientiane and the Cambodian capital of Phnom Penh, as well as a consulate in the northern Vietnamese city of Hanoi.

To that time, the Vientiane legation, founded in 1950, was almost notional. Junior diplomats from elsewhere in Indochina were rotated through one or two at a time for short stints. Aside from a Thai consulate, they were the only foreign representatives in town.

Continuing the trend, the vice consul in Hanoi, 32-year-old Lloyd "Mike" Rives, was temporarily shifted to Vientiane in June 1953. Hailing from an affluent New Jersey family, Rives was up to the task. For one thing, he had majored in French at Princeton University and was thus fluent in the lingua franca of the kingdom. For another thing, he was more than familiar with hardship after four years in the Marines, much of it island-hopping in the Pacific.

Arriving at the same time was Ted Tanen, a 27-year-old California native who had just completed a tour as administrative clerk at the embassy in Burma. Tanen's role in Vientiane was as a proto–public affairs officer, gathering cultural material for use on Voice of America.

While the pair had prior experience in Southeast Asia—Rives in Hanoi, Tanen in Rangoon—Vientiane made those two venues look positively cosmopolitan by comparison. The Lao capital had no running water and only intermittent electricity from generators. Tropical diseases, especially amoebic dysentery, were rampant. Roads had yet to be paved.

The legation itself was located in a spacious French-style villa on the bank of the Mekong. Rives and Tanen, both bachelors, had bedrooms in the villa, setting aside another room to function as the chancery for official business and repurposing an adjacent lavatory as a code room. Electricity was provided by a generator that was used only in the evenings; gasoline was hauled across the Mekong in jerry cans. Water was hand-pumped to a tank on the roof, allowing gravity to funnel it through the shower and toilet.

Making the most of his French language skills, Rives quickly net-worked across Vientiane's upper echelon of French administrators and, to a lesser extent, Lao elites. He would then take his notes back to the lavatory-cum-code-room, where he would encrypt them—old school—using one-time pads. The resultant number groups were then brought to the central post office and transmitted either to Saigon or directly to Washington. Reversing the process, each evening a messenger from the post office would arrive with the day's incoming telegrams, which Rives would decrypt while sitting on the toilet with a one-time pad.

As the State Department had now sent two officers to Laos, the CIA felt compelled to follow suit. Though just six years old, the Agency had inherited an impressive roster of experienced Asia hands from the Office of Strategic Services (OSS) and the other military intelligence outfits that had flourished during the war. The tiny legation in Laos, however, did not rate such a seasoned veteran. Instead, they looked among their recent hires of young bachelors full of postwar optimism and willing to endure a hardship posting.

Getting the nod was 27-year-old Theodore "Ted" Korbin. Serving in the Naval Air Corps during the war, he had graduated on the GI Bill from the University of Michigan in 1949. During his college days he had been a standout on the school's baseball team. Contemplating a career in sports, he continued for another two years in the minor leagues. When that did not work out, the Agency was his runner up.

In mid-September 1953, Korbin arrived in Vientiane and was ostensibly assigned as the vice consul. Due to the legation's spartan amenities, he bunked in the villa with Rives and Tanen. For the time being, he even was forced to share a filing cabinet with Rives. This led to an embarrassing incident that poisoned relations within the legation from the outset. As Rives remembered it,

> We shared a filing cabinet at one time, when [Korbin] first got there before his own things came. One day I went down there…his drawer was open, and I did something which I shouldn't have done, but the yellow pad was sitting there, and I read it. It was a report about me, which they weren't allowed to do, were not supposed to do, and swore they never did. So I said to the Ambassador in Saigon, "Either he goes or I go." So he went.[2]

Tanen corroborates the tale:

> Our relationship with the CIA got off to a very bad start…. Mike [Rives] discovered that Korbin was writing reports on us, which drove him right up the wall. So, we notified Washington, and I think Korbin got slapped on the wrist, but we felt that if he is here to report on something, he should be reporting on the political situation, and not on the staff, the two of us.[3]

For his indiscretion, Korbin was temporarily shifted to Saigon, only to return to Vientiane in mid-1954. By that time, a protracted siege against the French garrison at Dien Bien Phu in northern Vietnam had been settled in favor of the Viet Minh. Facing a growing anti-war movement on the home front and having suffered the tremendous psychological blow of losing Dien Bien Phu, the French ventured to Geneva to begin negotiating in earnest an end to their colonial rule in Southeast Asia. The ink to this agreement was soon dry, with a ceasefire scheduled for 6 August.

★ ★ ★

As Laos would now be gaining true independence, the US legation braced for a major boost. On 18 August, seasoned diplomat Charles Yost was appointed as America's first ambassador to the kingdom. Soon joined by his wife and three children, Yost opened the spigot to a steady stream of fellow Foreign Service officers, aid workers, clerks, and secretaries. Having collectively outgrown its villa, the legation had a US Army field tent set up on the front lawn as a makeshift annex. In addition, two further villas were rented, one for single men and the other for single women.

What Yost and the rest of the legation found was a kingdom that, on a superficial level, appeared to have emerged from the war in good shape. After all, the Geneva accords foisted a mantle of diplomatic neutrality upon Laos, theoretically exempting it from Cold War rivalries.

Beneath the surface, however, Laos was left exceedingly vulnerable. Landlocked at a geographic crossroads, each of its twelve provinces bordered a foreign nation, two of which—the People's Republic of China (PRC) and the Democratic Republic of Vietnam (DRV)—were openly sympathetic to the Pathet Lao.[4] Even its capital, Vientiane, faced foreign—Thai—territory, on the opposite bank of the Mekong.

Politically, Laos was equally challenged. Although US government assessments at the time noted that the kingdom—given its sparse, rural, politically apathetic population—was not particularly susceptible to internal rebellion resulting from social, economic, or political grievances, there was fertile ground for future strife.[5] First, the Geneva agreement's call for an immediate departure of all Viet Minh from Laos was never carried out in full. In fact, an advisory group from the People's Army of Vietnam (PAVN) was retained at the Pathet Lao headquarters in the mountains of Sam Neua.[6]

Second, the ANL was still not up to the task of defending the kingdom. As noted in a pessimistic French assessment one month before the ceasefire, more than 500 French officers and non-commissioned officers—including all cadre from ANL technical and support units—were set for immediate repatriation. Moreover, half the 35,000-man ANL was volunteers whose enlistments were up.[7] As a much-needed stopgap, Geneva had authorized a continued presence of 1,500 French advisors, plus 3,500 French Union combat troops grouped into a half brigade. By December 1954, however, the half brigade was disbanded for budgetary reasons, and only a token battalion was maintained at Seno airbase in the panhandle.[8] The French stopgap all but gone, the ANL was on its own.

Third, Geneva had dictated (with, in Souvanna Phouma's words, a "dangerous lack of precision") that the Pathet Lao could regroup unmolested for four months in two northern provinces—Sam Neua and Phongsaly—before reintegrating into the RLG. Pathet Lao officials, however, announced three months into the grace period that they intended to keep permanent control over both provinces. Immediately, they began appointing local officials and establishing schools, printshops, and a military academy.

Fourth, mandated with overseeing this imperfect peace was Geneva's most heinous of pitfalls, the International Control Commission (ICC). Comprising military delegates from pro-Western Canada, communist Poland, and nonaligned India, the ICC theoretically was expected to rush tripartite teams to the scene of ceasefire violations and, with the weight of its office, make objective observations that would presumably lead to peace. In reality the ICC was a paper tiger from the start. Undermanned, short of transportation, and crippled by the need for unanimity among its three politically diverse delegations, the ICC did not assemble in Laos until October 1954, fully two months after the ceasefire and halfway into the Pathet Lao grace period. Once in Laos, it was repeatedly stonewalled by the Pathet Lao in requests for access to northern hot spots. On the rare occasion that an ICC team reached a ceasefire violation and attempted to adjudicate, it lacked means of enforcement.

Fifth, though faced with an impotent ICC and communist insurgents consolidating their hold over two provinces, the RLG focused an inordinate amount of its attention on Vientiane politics. There, intrigue was in abundance with a National Assembly torn by feuds between diehard Francophiles and equally strident nationalists.

Meantime, not five months had passed after the end of the French Indochina War before the ANL, alone, faced its first major test. The Pathet Lao, its four-month integration period having expired, refused to peacefully relinquish control of the two northern provinces. A confrontation looming, RLG and Pathet Lao negotiators met on the PDJ in January 1955. As their talks deadlocked, clashes broke out later that month around Moung Peun, the only RLG-held town in Sam Neua Province. With sporadic fighting continuing through the spring, the ANL ordered two reinforcement battalions to Moung Peun in June.

By the first week of July, with Moung Peun surrounded, the ANL general staff directed more infantry reinforcements to the PDJ. After these marched north to Moung Peun, they were joined by the ANL's airborne battalion in its first post-ceasefire combat jump.[9] It was only when summer monsoon rains bogged down the opposing sides in August that fighting around Moung Peun subsided.

Just before the confrontation in Sam Neua went into remission, the CIA decided to ratchet up its representation in Vientiane. After an extended home leave over Christmas of 1954, Korbin had returned to Laos in February 1955 to start a second tour. But with the legation scheduled to be upgraded to embassy status in August, the Agency wanted to add a relatively more senior officer to head a proper station.

Selected for the job was Milton J. Clark, a square-jawed All-American who was six years Korbin's senior. One of nine siblings born in New York, Clark had left college to enter the US Army in 1942. Directed to the Pacific theater, he was in China at war's end and, in a moment that left a lasting impression, had the opportunity to peer briefly into the steppes of Inner Mongolia.[10]

Returning stateside with the rank of captain, Clark reentered college and completed his degree in 1947. Without pause, he shifted to Harvard University for graduate studies. Completing this in 1951, he became one of the many Ivy Leaguers who answered an early recruitment drive by the CIA.

Before he could start his career as an intelligence officer, however, Clark chanced upon a newspaper article about Kazakh refugees making an arduous one-year trek from China's Xinjiang to sanctuary in India's Kashmir.[11] Recalling his fleeting glimpse into Mongolia at war's end, and judging the Kazakh to be an intriguing subject for a doctorate, he got a deferment from the Agency and a research fellowship from the Washington-based Middle East Institute.

The following summer, in August 1952, Clark arrived in Kashmir for a year of field study among the displaced Kazakh. Returning to Cambridge in late 1953, he published an account of his travels in *National Geographic*, hammered out a fourteen thousand–word English-Kazakh dictionary, and completed his doctoral thesis on Kazakh refugee society. He successfully defended his dissertation in January 1955.[12]

At last ready to join the Agency, Clark partook in expedited training and was in Vientiane by June 1955. As with the rest of the embassy, he was immediately confronted by two limiting factors. First, though Laos was independent on paper, it remained firmly under the French thumb. As of March 1955, there were still upwards of 150 French civilians assigned to RLG cabinet ministries, down only 50 from the 1953 number. In addition, 780 French combat troops were stationed at Seno, and on top of that, a French military mission as of 1955 had 1,192 advisors with the ANL and police.

Second, despite the clashes at Moung Peun, some of the Lao political elite remained convinced they could accommodate the Pathet Lao. This was especially true of Souvanna Phouma, who was named prime minister in March 1956. Fixated on creating a coalition government with his communist brethren, he spent much of his first year in office courting his half brother Souphanouvong.

This all came at a time when Washington was advocating a more aggressive stance against communism. In June 1955, the same month Clark arrived in Laos, Secretary of State John Foster Dulles had delivered a pivotal speech in which he labeled diplomatic neutrality "an immoral and shortsighted conception." His younger brother Allen Dulles, who headed the CIA, was inclined to implement policies—especially covert operations—that supported this world view. Bottom line: While

Washington paid lip service to the neutrality extended to Laos in the Geneva agreement, it wanted the RLG free from communist taint. The CIA—through Clark's two-man station—was to seek ways to achieve that outcome.

All of that put Clark in a quandary. As was customary when operating in a friendly nation, his first choice was to work in conjunction with an RLG counterpart. Preferably, that local counterpart would be a civilian intelligence organization. Just one month after he arrived the RLG had, in fact, created a quasi-civilian counterpart known as the Special Service for Political Propaganda (Service Special de Propagande Politique, or SSPP).

Trouble was, the SSPP was hardly an optimal partner. For one thing, it was small, had almost no budget, and was not privy to intelligence from existing ANL and police networks.[13] For another, it saw its prime mandate as a coordination office for disseminating white propaganda to counter the Pathet Lao message. Its biggest claim to fame was capitalizing on the September 1955 defection of a Pathet Lao official named Kavinh Keonakhone, organizing a press conference for him in Bangkok with several dozen foreign journalists. With this kind of overt focus, the SSPP sought liaison with the public affairs officers at the US embassy, not the CIA.[14]

Shifting tack, Clark looked toward the Lao National Police. Specifically, there was a fledgling Police Spéciale section that encompassed investigations and counterintelligence. Helping Clark with introductions was his new deputy station chief, Kinloch Bull. A consummate gentleman of the South, Bull hailed from a prominent family that included the last British governor of South Carolina. He had spent two years at the Sorbonne, lending a much-needed French linguistic ability to Vientiane Station when he arrived in May 1956 to replace Ted Korbin.

During their approach to the Police Spéciale, Clark and Bull were soon to get help from another quarter. Ever since 1951, the CIA had established an exceptionally close relationship with Thai Police Director General Phao Siyanon, one of that country's three strongmen. Fearful that the PRC might blitz mainland Southeast Asia, as well as of the latent threat posed by the Communist Party of Thailand in the countryside, the CIA sought to boost the abilities of Phao's forces.

To channel assistance, the CIA used a Miami-based proprietary known as the Southeast Asia Supply Company, popularly known as Sea Supply. The bulk of Sea Supply's activities were aimed at raising a Thai gendarmerie, later known as the Border Patrol Police (BPP). By the end of 1953, ninety-four BPP platoons, each averaging forty-five men, had been trained by Sea Supply's cadre of twenty paramilitary advisors and deployed along the Thai frontier. In a testament to the close US-Thai coordination in this effort, three Sea Supply members were officially commissioned as Thai police officers.

Besides the BPP, Sea Supply also raised a special police commando outfit for both offensive and defensive missions, to include CIA-sanctioned cross-border forays. This outfit, based at the southern Thai town of Hua Hin, was soon tapped for several Lao projects. In 1955, for example, some of its members rigged parachutes at Udorn airbase for US-piloted planes making food drops into Laos. Also during that year, a contingent of thirty ANL officers were sent to their base at Hua Hin for a month of heavy-weapons instruction. General Phao even envisioned a broader strategic role, boldly offering in June 1955 to deploy a contingent of his border police (pending an official RLG request) for combat in northeastern Laos.[15]

As there was now a readily available cadre of seasoned Sea Supply advisors sitting across the border, Clark received permission in mid-1956 to bring one Sea Supply officer to Vientiane to seek avenues of cooperation with the Police Spéciale. Chosen for the assignment was Jack Shirley, one of the three Sea Supply members who had been commissioned in the Thai police. Shirley recalled,

> I spoke some French, so I was sent to Vientiane to be liaison with the head of the Special Police, Captain Vattha Phankham. He was a diehard Francophile and, being honest, not much was accomplished. I was only there for a short period, and then they replaced me with another Sea Supply officer, Phil Montgomery.

Faring poorly with the SSPP and police, Clark turned toward the ANL. Specifically, he made contact with Lieutenant Colonel Ouane Rathikoun, 37, the commander of Military Region One encompassing the north and northwestern reaches of the kingdom. A favorite of the royal family, Ouane had made a habit of staying close to Luang Prabang ever since the French colonial era. Back in June 1955, with strong support from Crown Prince Savang Vatthana, he had been the driving force behind creation of the ANL's Auto-Défense (AD) program, intended as a militia network that would infiltrate across the two Pathet Lao–held provinces. Using ANL cadre and local recruits, Ouane had established the first AD forces during the second half of 1955 in Phongsaly Province. He had correctly predicted that communist control was weak in Phongsaly; by year's end there were some three thousand AD irregulars conducting raids and cutting communist supply lines on a north–south salient west of the provincial capital.

Finding the AD program worthy of support, Clark was already lending covert funding to Ouane's pet project by early 1956. The Pentagon got wind of this and, also finding merit, signed on to a CIA proposal that the ANL hand over its non-US firearms to the AD militia, with the ANL stocks to be replenished with standardized US weaponry. Clark passed word of this promise to top RLG officials at the beginning of March, with a transfer of five thousand US carbines and submachine guns to the ANL authorized at the end of May.[16]

Meantime, much to the consternation of Washington, Souvanna Phouma's flirtations with Souphanouvong were making headway. At the former's invitation, on 1 August 1956 a Pathet Lao delegation ventured to Vientiane. Within the week, the half brothers issued a statement announcing that the Pathet Lao were now permitted to become a legal political entity and participate in future elections. Another week after that, the pair issued a second statement in which they agreed in principle to a government of national union with participation of the Pathet Lao. Immediately thereafter, Souvanna Phouma flew to Beijing for a ten-day trip, concluding it with joint communiques about increasing Sino-Lao economic and cultural ties.

Predictably, warning bells were screaming across Washington. CIA chief Allen Dulles, commenting on the first communique, said it could be the "first step in Communist penetration of the Laotian Government."[17]

In Vientiane, J. Graham "Jeff" Parsons, a rather frosty New Englander who arrived as the new US ambassador in late July 1956, was in charge of penning a counterstrategy.[18] Like the Dulles brothers, he was staunchly opposed to neutralism and reflexively equated it with anti-Americanism.

On 7 August, barely two weeks into the job, Parsons recommended to Washington a Laos strategy blending aid and subterfuge. Part of this involved discreet lobbying of key RLG officials to create doubts and reservations about Souvanna's machinations. Washington lent its approval on 10 September.[19]

Later that September, CIA Director Allen Dulles saw such urgency in the Laos situation that he made a trip to Bangkok to rendezvous with Parsons for an afternoon of consultations. The anxiety level in both men was through the roof. "Laos remains the piece of real estate most vulnerable to Communists anywhere in the world," Dulles concluded. To his mind, Laos was first on the "totem pole for Communist political takeover, with vast consequences to the security of Vietnam, Cambodia, and Thailand."[20]

Returning to Vientiane, Parsons redoubled his efforts via personal appeals to Souvanna Phouma. He emphasized to the prime minister that Washington would undoubtedly rethink its support of the kingdom—which amounted to underwriting nearly the entire RLG budget—if flirtations with the Pathet Lao persisted. But the two had gotten off to a bad start and, unmoved by Parson's pleadings, Souvanna Phouma joined his half brother on 28 December in issuing yet another joint communique. This one reiterated what was stated in August, adding that they intended to move forward with forming a coalition government. The stage was set, with a showdown all but certain for 1957.

CHAPTER 2

The Young Turks

While Ambassador Parsons was quick to decry the softness of Souvanna Phouma, the United States was still capable of finding the occasional kernel of positivity about the prince's governance. Such was the case at the opening of January 1957 when the prime minister, after hinting for months that he would make a push in the area of rural development, issued a decree establishing an ambitious civic action program under his direct control.

At its core, Souvanna Phouma's take on civic action was envisioned as a self-help program designed to stimulate rural populations to draw upon their own resources and talents for basic improvements in health, education, public works, and agriculture, among others. Mobile civic-action teams under an envisioned Commissariat for Civic Action, comprising experts drawn from seven different ministries, would put the self-help program into motion. AD militia would then move in to ensure the programs were implemented, thus allowing the civic-action teams to move to other areas. Well aware that neighboring countries like South Vietnam and the Philippines had already embarked on civic-action programs of their own, the prime minister envisioned from the outset sending officers abroad to study existing programs.

Hearing of the decree, representatives from across the US embassy gathered on 5 January to consider special support for the new program. As Souvanna appeared determined to hold elections with Pathet Lao participation sooner rather than later, the embassy had its eye on the clock in getting civic action off the ground to expand rural support for the RLG. Moreover, while it determined that civic-action aid would ultimately get phased into existing village development programs overseen by the Department of State, an emergency preelection phase of assistance would need to be administered via a different route. Tied to this, Ambassador Parsons believed that an initial funding surge of $300,000 should not come from State Department funds but rather from a different "pertinent agency."[1]

All of that was diplomat-speak for the CIA. Not by coincidence, the Agency had already prepared a young officer with relevant civic action experience in South Vietnam. Rufus Phillips, 29, had been recruited by the CIA back in 1951 from one of its favorite recruiting grounds, Yale University.[2] As his first assignment, he had been sent to South Vietnam in August 1954 and was placed in the Saigon Military Mission (SMM) commanded by the highly unorthodox Colonel Edward Lansdale.

Despite its name, Lansdale's SMM was wholly controlled by the CIA, not the Pentagon. It was initially focused on preparing a stay-behind resistance in northern Vietnam and—just in case—the south as well. The mission's mandate also came to encompass psychological warfare, political warfare to prop up the young administration of Ngo Dinh Diem, and civic action.

It was in this latter category that Phillips was heavily involved. The South Vietnamese civic-action program, for which Lansdale had funneled seed money, sought to provide public services to villages so the communists would not fill the void. While not normally a CIA core business, the SMM took on this assignment because of Lansdale's ability to cut through red tape and fast-track assistance more efficiently than the more plodding official channels used by the State Department.

After a year of this, Phillips extended his time in South Vietnam through 1956. By then Lansdale's mission had largely outlived its welcome, as it had been repeatedly stepping on the toes of the regular CIA station and the expanding efforts of both the Pentagon and State Department. Shortly before the end of 1956, Lansdale got word that Laos might be interested in its own version of civic action. Thinking this was well suited for Phillips, Lansdale arranged for him to fly up to Vientiane for a long weekend to meet Station Chief Clark and Ouane to discuss the existing AD efforts.[3]

Fast forward a couple of months to February 1957, when Phillips returned to Vientiane as the CIA's point man for the Souvanna Phouma–backed program. It was now understood that the Lao civic-action teams would each consist of eleven men, and two teams would be assigned to each province. Each team would spend no more than two weeks in one village before getting replaced by AD militia. During those two weeks the teams would provide minor medical treatment, sanitation instruction, assistance with local construction projects and education, and training for volunteers to act as information agents.

After taking this in, Philipps met his Lao counterpart, Lieutenant Colonel Oudone Sananikone, one of the younger standouts from the powerful Sananikone clan. Though not royalty, this extended family held considerably sway as its numbers included a raft of influential politicians and army officers. Oudone, originally part of the ANL's tiny armor squadron, had spent the previous year as director for the ANL's own civic-action efforts and was therefore well prepared to fast-track a similar campaign under the prime minister's office. Very quickly, however, Souvanna Phouma became distracted by a cabinet crisis, and it was another two months before he got around to signing off on details of the commissariat meant to oversee the program.[4]

With civic action not looking to pay dividends any time soon, Clark and Bull spent their time discreetly lobbying key Lao officials in the National Assembly and elsewhere. Much attention was focused on the sickly and shifty Katay Don Sasorith, an aging nationalist who had served as prime minister just before Souvanna Phouma, at which time he had made all the right protestations about the dangers of communism. The aim of the CIA station was to sow just enough doubt so that Katay and members of the legislative wing would take the easier route of kicking the can down the road and not taking up Souvanna's 28 December communique before the National Assembly closed its session in mid-March.

Which is exactly what happened. On 15 March, a relieved Parsons cabled Washington and declared a tactical victory after the assembly concluded its session without touching on Sovuanna's controversial proposal.[5] Six days later the ambassador penned a memo to CIA Director Dulles, noting the "indispensable contribution" of Clark and his station.[6]

Despite this praise, however, not all was well between Parsons and Clark. Of all things, Parsons was seething about Clark's choice of housing. The background to this came about as the ever-expanding US embassy had a housing compound built near the That Luang temple in January 1957. This had been done in haste, with dozens of prefabricated cottages flown in from Japan. On account of their shiny metallic exteriors, the compound was dubbed Silver City.

Except for the ambassador and a few privileged others, American diplomats were directed to the new housing at Silver City. As Clark was considered the equivalent of a second secretary in rank, and the State Department's bona fide second secretary was given a Silver City cottage, it was expected that Clark would follow suit. But dipping into the station's generous coffers, Clark opted instead to rent an opulent villa with an exorbitant lease.

Of course, there may have been legitimate operational reasons for Clark to reside outside Silver City. Still, this incident irked Parsons on two counts. First, he claimed it was raising eyebrows within the embassy and diplomatic corps, as they could not reconcile how a mere second secretary rated such a luxurious abode.[7] Second, and unstated, Clark's blatant display of CIA spending power was sending a signal to the RLG that the CIA—rather than the State Department—had considerable funds at its disposal and therefore was the true powerbroker at the embassy.

With this housing episode leaving a bad aftertaste, Clark's tour came to a close in August 1957 and he was replaced by Henry Hecksher. Born in Hamburg, Hecksher had attended three different Germany universities before getting a law degree and starting work as an attorney in 1932. It was not until 1937, when Adolf Hitler made his infamous speech declaring that Nazi Germany was too small to guarantee its food supply—thus telegraphing the imminent annexation of Austria—that Hecksher voted with his feet and emigrated to the United States.

Unfortunately for Hecksher, his arrival in the United States came at a most inopportune time. Already within the grim setting of the Great Depression, the American economy was experiencing a further downturn. Still, he was able to eke out a wage as a bank accountant.[8]

All this changed at the close of 1941 with the entry of the United States into World War II. Still a year short of becoming a naturalized American, Hecksher volunteered for the US Army. Due to his German background, he was posted as an instructor at the Military Intelligence School at Camp Ritchie, Maryland. In 1944, he was transferred overseas and participated in the Normandy Invasion. At that point, Lieutenant Hecksher's linguistic skills (he was obviously fluent in German, as well as French and Russian) were put to use when he was assigned to the interrogation center of General George Patton's Third Army. In short order, he became known as a specialist in the interrogation of Nazi officials.[9]

Following the unconditional German surrender in May 1945 was a confusing phase in which several US intelligence units took shape and later merged in postwar Europe. Hecksher remained on hand throughout, serving there as the United States made a strategic pivot: where he had earlier sought information about possible Nazi resistance, now he interviewed the internally displaced to identify key people such as nuclear scientists and potential penetration agents for use behind the emergent Iron Curtain. After becoming a civilian employee in May 1946, he joined the fledgling CIA the next year and went on to become deputy head of Berlin Station.

By the time he left West Germany in 1954, Hecksher had already gotten the attention of the CIA leadership as a skilled clandestine operator. Brought back to Washington, he was assigned to the team scheming to overthrow President Jacobo Arbenz of Guatemala. Bribing Arbenz's military commanders to shift loyalties, the CIA would use a rebel army and a healthy dose of psychological warfare to unseat Arbenz within a month and replace him with a pro-US authoritarian regime. President Eisenhower was reportedly so pleased that he invited Allen Dulles and several other key officers—including Hecksher—for a personal debriefing at the White House.

It was with this weighty résumé that Hecksher arrived in Vientiane with the expectation that he could rub off some of his Guatemalan magic in Laos. To be sure, the contrast with his predecessor, Milton Clark, was glaring. For one thing, Hecksher was a full decade older, and his cover was as first secretary in the Political Section, a significant boost in stature over Clark. For another thing, they had diametrically opposed personalities. As Phillips explained,

> Milt Clark had been very laid back in his dealings with the Lao and with me. He loved to puff on his pipe and philosophize about what could or couldn't be done in Laos and with the Lao. His soft and restrained approach went down well with the senior Lao with whom he was on good terms.... Hecksher on the other hand had a peppery, impatient and sometimes peremptory personality.[10]

From the start, Hecksher's impatience was on full display. Following some early meetings with senior Lao officials, he came back enraged with their lackadaisical approach. "It was like punching pillows," he complained to Phillips.

Especially frustrating was the intransigence of Souvanna Phouma. On multiple occasions during October 1957, the embassy tried to convince him of the folly of pursuing compromise with the Pathet Lao. He was even given French-language case studies about similar communist subversion efforts in Czechoslovakia, Italy, and Guatemala. To this, Souvanna Phouma insisted that the Pathet Lao, at their core, were neither communists nor communist-controlled. Such naïve sentiment would not age well.[11]

In the face of Souvanna Phouma's obstinance, Hecksher carried on with a multifaceted approach to blunt Pathet Lao inroads. First, he revisited the possibility of cooperating with RLG counterparts. In this area, he was pleasantly surprised. In April 1957, the Police Spéciale had gotten around to organizing a sub-unit called the Special Branch. This was focused on gathering intelligence for the police, ANL, and Immigration Service so that Lao subversives could be neutralized and foreign agents deported. Despite the large number of Chinese and Vietnamese residents in Laos—some no doubt working in conjunction with the Pathet Lao—the Special Branch had yet to unearth any foreign subversives through the end of 1957.[12] Still, the CIA had its liaison officer attached to the Police Spéciale, and there was always the possibility that performances could pick up.

More promising, the RLG had finally established a true intelligence agency. Created in May 1956 from the core of the earlier SSPP, it was now known as the Inter-Ministerial Service for Social and Political Action (Service Interministeriel d'Action Sociale et Politique, or SIDASP). But more than a mere rebranding, SIDASP differed from SSPP in several key respects. For one, it drew about half its members from the ANL. For another, they had been officially mandated with surveilling communist threats from the PRC, the DRV, and Poles in the ICC, in that order. In November 1956, Souvanna Phoumi had even authorized them to conduct surveillance against Pathet Lao officials.[13]

Encouraged with this aggressive stance, Hecksher had opened channels with SIDASP to propose training. SIDASP took up the offer, sending six members for tradecraft and paramilitary instruction at the CIA base on the island of Saipan.[14] In July 1957, the CIA had also extended financial and advisory assistance for a new SIDASP sub-unit called Bureau d'Ordre de Bataille de la Subversion (Order-of-Battle and Subversion Bureau), which was specifically charged with clandestine operations.[15]

A second part of Hecksher's multipronged strategy involved recruiting more sources within the upper crust of RLG society. In this, he made maximum use of a new arrival at the Station, 29-year-old R. Campbell James. Himself born into New York high society, James had been sent off to prep schools since the age of 6, picking up mannerisms and an accent that—to Americans at least—came off as terribly British.[16] He went on to attend the Sorbonne for a year before getting a degree in the Classics from Yale in 1950.[17]

Drafted immediately after graduation during the onset of the Korean War, James had completed basic army training in California and was shipped off to the Far East. Instead of landing in Korea, however, he ended up in the Republic of China on Taiwan. There he was seconded to the CIA in 1953, working under the Agency's local proprietary, Western Enterprises. Though ostensibly an import-export company, Western Enterprises was actually charged with training, advising, and providing logistical support to the thousands of guerrillas on the Nationalist-held offshore islands. James would spend three years on Taiwan, much of it under constant PRC shelling on Quemoy island.

From Taiwan, James returned stateside to attend Officer Candidate School.[18] Upon completion, he promptly resigned from the army, officially joined the CIA, and in September 1957 was posted to Vientiane.[19] From the start, James alternatively delighted and perplexed his colleagues.[20] Phillips recalls,

> I remember staying in Laos for Christmas, and Campbell giving a large party with caviar and buckets of champagne which he had paid for and had flown in commercial from Hong Kong through Bangkok to Vientiane. He was a very generous but eccentric guy. One true story is that while in Vientiane he visited Saigon without notifying the Saigon Station Chief, Nick Natsios, that he was coming. He arranged to meet Natsios at his embassy office, introduced himself as simply Campbell James from Vientiane. In the conversation he talked about Agency operational matters. Because of Campbell's fruity high society accent, Natsios thought he was British and sent a rocket cable to Henry Hecksher asking who the hell is this Britisher involved in Agency matters.[21]

With his target audience—the upper-crust Lao—James got along swimmingly. Despite the prime minister's often contentious relations with the US embassy, James drew especially close to Souvanna Phouma. Importing expensive Cuban cigars to satisfy the prime minister's vice, James would end up being invited on elephant-borne hunting expeditions alongside the prince.

In the end, however, Campbell's soft approach was no more effective in altering Souvanna's trajectory. On 18 November 1957, two Pathet Lao officials were accepted into an enlarged cabinet. This included Souphanouvong, who was now minister for Reconstruction and Urbanism, and Phoumi Vongvichit, who, ironically for a member of a communist organization, was now minister for Religion and Fine Arts. Three weeks later, it was announced that supplemental elections for twenty additional legislative seats would be held in May 1958.

With an election date now fixed, Vientiane Station went into overdrive. Some of its more innovative advances were taken in conjunction with SIDASP. One project involved a notional secret society called Sinxay, named after an epic poem from the Lan Xang era. According to propaganda crafted by SIDASP, the Sinxay movement stood for traditional values and Buddhism; conversely, it took a hard stance against communist revolutionaries. SIDASP agents were tasked with discreetly using graffiti and posters to make it appear as though Sinxay was omnipresent at the village level. They even began a clandestine station called Radio Mekong that purported to be operated by Sinxay; the Pathet Lao were reportedly so vexed by its transmissions that they issued an internal order to find the broadcasting station.[22]

Far less successful was the civic-action program, despite the best efforts of Rufus Phillips. By the close of 1957, twelve civic-action teams had been trained and deployed. But with five thousand villages in all of Laos, this paltry number of teams could hardly make a dent.[23]

Realizing that there was not enough time for the teams to reach critical mass before the polls, Vientiane Station brainstormed other ways of helping the RLG win rural voters. Its leading idea was to airdrop relief aid directly onto villages on a massive scale. Ambassador Parsons liked the concept, which he outlined in a 3 January 1958 cable to Washington.

Once again, aid of this sort was not one of the CIA's core businesses. Normal State Department channels, however, promised bureaucratic delays of a year or more. The State Department owned up to their shortcoming and on 15 February sent a letter to CIA Director Dulles asking the CIA to fund, organize, and manage the emergency program of village-level "political impact projects."[24] The codename for the program was, appropriately, Booster Shot.

Switching hats, Rufus Phillips was placed in operational charge of Booster Shot. Helping him was a five-man CIA task force seconded from Sea Supply in Thailand.[25] Beyond just airdrops, Booster Shot began on 8 March with more than ninety work projects, including digging wells, repairing roads and airfields, and constructing hospitals. The centerpiece, however, was an impressive airlift using planes from the CIA proprietary Civil Air Transport (CAT) as well as the US Air Force. Aircraft from the latter were to carry especially heavy loads, including two bulldozers earmarked for the two former Pathet Lao–held provinces. All Booster Shoot drops were concluded by 27 April; village work projects continued through the elections and ended on 23 May.[26]

In the end, all was for naught. The Pathet Lao and an allied leftist party wound up winning thirteen of twenty-one contested seats. Many were won by just pluralities, a result of the pro-government parties failing to agree on a single national slate and thus splitting their vote. There had been seventy-five pro-government candidates for the twenty-one seats;

the leftists, by comparison, fielded only twenty-four candidates. Though still a minority in the National Assembly, the Pathet Lao had gained much credibility and momentum. Concluded CIA Director Dulles, "[We] have a great deal to fear in the 1959 general elections."[27]

If there was any silver lining for the US embassy, it was that Souvanna Phouma had been fully discredited by the poor showing of the noncommunist slate. At the same time, some of the younger generation of civil servants and army officers, impatient with the ineffectual older generation of noncommunist politicians, were itching to make an impact. Philipps had picked up on this early, as his counterpart Oudone Sananikone was counted among their number. So was Inpeng Suryadhay, a former political officer at the Lao Legation in Washington and now the director of SIDASP,[28] as well as Khamphan Panya, an outspoken advisor to Crown Prince Savang Vatthana.

Impressed with their energy and vision, Phillips had introduced Hecksher to some of these Young Turks. The famously impatient station chief saw in them kindred spirits. When they formally coalesced in mid-June 1958 into a grassroots organization known as Comité pour la Défense des Intérêts Nationaux (Committee for the Defense of National Interests, or CDNI), Vientiane Station was an early fan. Word of the CDNI quickly filtered back to Washington, with Allen Dulles referring to them in July as a "new dynamic group" being quietly supported by the United States.[29]

Though Vientiane Station was excited about the advent of the CDNI, they also realized that the group did not have enough National Assembly votes to remove Souvanna Phouma. As the cabinet crisis extended through the second quarter, Washington decided to intervene directly.[30] Dipping into the station's funds, Hecksher packed dollars into a suitcase earmarked for the prime minister. He then turned to a French-speaking second secretary from the Political Section, John Gunter Dean:

> One day, Hecksher asked me whether I could take a suitcase to the Prime Minister. The suitcase contained money, but I did not know that. Since I had easy access to most Lao, I complied. Whereupon, I received an official reprimand from the Secretary of State that I had abused my functions as a Foreign Service Officer, since a State Department Officer is not allowed "to pass funds." What I did find out was that not only a suitcase was taken to the Prime Minister, but

several suitcases full of money were being ferried over to [Foreign Minister] Phoui Sananikone, who was much more in line with the official American position on Laos. But the delivery of these suitcases was not entrusted to me.[31]

The payoffs worked. In August, Souvanna Phouma decided that an ambassadorship in France was more to his liking. At the same time, the noncommunist bloc suddenly coalesced around the shrewd, aristocratic Phoui Sananikone as prime minister. Recognizing the fast-growing might of the CDNI, Phoui included four members in his cabinet.

The United States should have seen reason for cheer with this new lineup. After all, Phoui Sananikone was by far the most pro-American politician among the older generation. Also, the pair of Pathet Lao ministers under the prior cabinet had been shown the door. But there were some problematic underlying issues. First, there was only a year until general elections (according to the constitution, they had to be held in late 1959 or early 1960), and the noncommunists showed no progress in unifying behind a single slate for provincial seats.

Second, the progressive CDNI firebrands had smelled blood in the water and were hungry for substantive reforms. Specifically, they wanted a strong executive—like Thailand got—and were eager for the older pro-French politicians to retire. The end result was a widening political divide on the right and an extended period of paralysis, leading a frustrated Phoui to appeal successfully to the National Assembly in January 1959 for a year of rule-by-decree. Uncomfortable with the RLG's conservative tilt, most of the Pathet Lao assemblymen took this as their opportunity to flee the capital for safer climes in Sam Neua.

With the Pathet Lao gone, political infighting between Phoui's older clique and the CDNI Young Turks only intensified over the course of 1959. Even when Phoui attempted to placate them by adding three more CDNI cabinet members in March, tensions barely abated.

Tied to this, a de facto civil war was brewing in the US embassy. Some context is necessary. Back in March 1958, Ambassador Parsons had been replaced by Horace Smith, a career diplomat with a background in China affairs. From the outset, Smith proved adept at burning bridges. The Booster Shot project was already in motion when he arrived, and he immediately criticized the way it was being organized. This no doubt would not have gone down well with Parsons, who was now his immediate boss as assistant secretary of state for Far Eastern Affairs. Then Smith insisted that openly marked US Air Force planes be used for the airdrops, ignoring the advice of both Parsons and Station Chief Hecksher that this would undercut efforts to give credit to the RLG.[32]

Following that, Smith became a staunch supporter of Phoui Sananikone once the latter formed his cabinet in August 1958. This carried into the following year, with Smith advocating a delay in the general elections and championing Phoui's efforts to extend his rule-by-decree for another year.

By contrast, Hecksher had grown disillusioned with Phoui and the Francophile gerontocracy in Phoui's cabinet.[33] Instead, he had hitched the station's wagon to the CDNI. Brought in to manage relations with these Young Turks was case officer Stuart Methven. Born in Hawaii, Methven had joined the CIA in 1952 and had already served two consecutive tours infiltrating anti-American labor unions in Japan. Though he spoke barely passable French, he answered Hecksher's call in May 1959 for a French-speaking officer to serve as liaison with a national "rice-roots" political organization.[34]

Once introduced to the CDNI leadership, the language barrier wafted away as the easygoing Methven developed solid rapport. He was soon joining the group on village tours across the countryside aimed at ginning up support for the organization ahead of the polls. A typical campaign stop involved handing out a pistol to the village chief, a single radio set to the villagers at large, a medical kit to the local shaman, boxes of school supplies, a pig for a barbeque feast, and copious amounts of CDNI pins that became popular as earrings and hair ornaments. The CIA was underwriting the costs of this barnstorming, including fifty thousand of the CDNI pins manufactured in Bangkok.[35]

While Methven dealt primarily with the civilian leaders in the CDNI, the organization also had a strong presence in the ANL, especially its younger officers. To get a better handle on the military, Hecksher had already brought in two more case officers who were directly paired with the ANL. The first was Jack F. Mathews, a former Montana smokejumper who had spent several years with Western Enterprises on Taiwan. He was assigned to Vientiane in September 1958 and ostensibly placed under the embassy's military mission (which, because of the Geneva prohibition against foreign advisors, was given the innocuous title of Programs Evaluation Office, or PEO). As a forerunner to the hundreds of CIA paramilitary officers that would later serve in Southeast Asia over the coming two decades, Mathews was matched up with the ANL's paratroopers and followed them into the field as they spearheaded the RLG's resumed skirmishes with the Pathet Lao.

The second officer was Ralph W. Johnson, a former CAT pilot who was in-country as of January 1959. Like Mathews, Johnson was under PEO cover. He spent most of his time attached to the ANL's intelligence staff.

Arriving, too, was Gerald "Jerry" Steiner. In many respects, Steiner was Hecksher's British doppelganger. Both were born overseas (Hecksher in Germany, Steiner in England) during the same year, and both had emigrated and become naturalized citizens in 1942.[36] Facing the Depression economy, Steiner had made ends meet by becoming a car salesman, then had entered the US Army during World War II and risen to the rank of captain. Joining the CIA in 1950, he had already served a tour in Austria. Cross-posted to Laos in November 1958, he was assigned as Hecksher's deputy.

While Hecksher was overseeing this expansion in the station, Ambassador Smith had been quietly stewing. He had taken an intense dislike to the CDNI, seeing them as little more than petulant children, and bristled at what he saw as Hecksher's insubordinate support for the group. This culminated in a pair of verbose cables to Washington in which he alternately whined about CDNI's "wrecking ball diplomacy" and Hecksher's role as their "self-appointed strategist."[37]

All of which came to a head in early December 1959. Overplaying his hand, Phoui moved to demote one of his CDNI ministers. In a show of solidarity, all seven CDNI ministers took this as their cue to resign in unison. Refusing to blink, Phoui formed a new cabinet on 15 December, this one devoid of CDNI participation.

Although Phoui had seemingly won the battle, it was as Pyrrhic as they come. Sensing this, Smith persisted in his shrill complaints, demanding to Allen Dulles that Hecksher be withdrawn. This was something of a nonstarter, as the station chief was already scheduled to conclude his tour at the start of 1960.

During the final two days of the year, the inevitable happened. His hold becoming increasingly tenuous, Phoui submitted his resignation on 30 December. That evening, tanks and troops mobilized around key installations in Vientiane. With the support of King Savang Vatthana (who assumed the crown after his father had succumbed to an extended illness two months earlier), top army officers tied to the CDNI were given his blessing to maintain order until a caretaker government was chosen for the run-up to the polls.[38]

It had taken two years, but Hecksher at long last had his Guatemala moment.[39]

CHAPTER 3

Hell is a City

Field Marshal Sarit Thanarat was the kind of authoritarian ruler Washington liked. To be sure, he had more than his share of blemishes: ever since grabbing power in a 1957 coup d'état, he had abolished parliament, censored newspapers, banned political parties, and detained hundreds that opposed his dictatorial bent. But Washington was more than happy to turn a blind eye to all that given Sarit's staunch anti-communism and pro-US foreign policy. And his government was fast to expel Soviet diplomats if there was even a whiff they were dabbling in espionage.

In point of fact, Sarit was more nuanced than your typical Third World strongman. At his core, he was a populist. That was probably because, unlike the normal Thai elite, his mother hailed from Isan, the impoverished northeastern quarter of the country. Growing up there, Sarit came to identify strongly with the rural poor in general and the Isan populace in particular.

The Isan, of course, were ethnic and linguistic first cousins of the lowland Lao on the opposite side of the Mekong. And as luck would have it, Sarit's mother was related to a Lao army officer who, not by coincidence, bore striking parallels to her own son.

That relative, Phoumi Nosavan, was born in Savannakhet in 1920. The son of low-ranking civil servants, he followed them into the civil service before the onset of World War II. He then joined the French police during the war, only to make a lateral shift to the Lao Issara when the Japanese prepared to capitulate.

In 1950, as the French dangled increased autonomy to the Lao, Phoumi joined the ANL as an officer. Though not intellectually gifted or in any way a military standout, he rose within the ranks on account of two powerful patrons. First, as he hailed from the Lao panhandle, he had grown close to Prince Boun Oum. Tall and heavyset, Boun Oum was the heir to the former king of Champassac in southern Laos. Accordingly, he held considerable sway in the south. Second, Phoumi, through insinuation if not fact, was seen to have the backing of his cousin Sarit, who by 1954 had already risen to become commander of the Royal Thai Army.

As the protégé of these heavyweights, Colonel Phoumi was chosen in 1957 as the first Lao to attend the École Supérieure de Guerre, the French War College. Correctly assessing that Phoumi was on the fast track for further promotion, while in Paris the CIA saw to it that he was befriended by one of their case officers.

Also while in Paris, Phoumi closely followed political developments back in Laos, especially the establishment of the CDNI. Not only was there strong support for that organization among ANL officers, but one of Boun Oum's other protégés, his nephew Sisouk na Champassak, had returned from a position at the United Nations to parlay his CDNI membership into a cabinet seat.[1]

Not wanting to miss out on an opportunity, Phoumi rushed back to Laos in August 1958 and immediately made his mark within the CDNI. Alternately shrewd and ambitious, he had consolidated power within that organization within one year and, in return, was named deputy minister of defense in mid-1959.

On a parallel course, Phoumi also continued to climb within the army. In July 1959, while facing a renewed Pathet Lao threat in Sam Neua, the military jurisdictions were rearranged and a new capital region was carved out around Vientiane; Phoumi, by then sporting the stars of a brigadier general, was named the first commander of this strategic post.

Not surprisingly given Ambassador Smith's pronounced bias against the CDNI, the State Department took a strong dislike to Phoumi. This was in evidence during the latter's tour of Washington in November 1959, when department officials sounded the alarm about his advocacy for a democratic *dirigée*—a strong executive—which they somehow found far less palatable than Smith's own support for Phoui's ongoing rule-by-decree.[2]

Not surprisingly, Vientiane Station, along with the Pentagon, viewed Phoumi's rise with guarded optimism. One could not help but compare the outspoken anti-communist to American favorite Sarit in Bangkok. Thus, there was little heartburn in these quarters when Phoumi was promoted to minister of defense in the caretaker government that took a seat in March 1960 during the run-up to the April polls.

It was with a strong sense of *déjà vu* that the US embassy looked for ways of bolstering the RLG's hand ahead of the 1960 national elections. While there had been a strong consensus back in 1958 that Booster Shot was ineffective at best and counterproductive at worst, no better ideas came to the fore this time around. As a result, the embassy elected to go with a modest reprise of Booster Shot as the centerpiece to its latest political support campaign.

As before, the CIA arranged for its proprietary air unit to take the lead. Now going by the corporate name Air America, its planes staged supply drops across the countryside. And the US Air Force offered use of C-130 transports for heavier loads, as it had in 1958. On 20 April, four days before election day, C-130s arrived in Vientiane with two trucks and a D-4 bulldozer; all three vehicles were successfully parachuted into Phongsaly on 26 April. Three days later, however, the cargo parachutes on a second D-4 did not deploy properly, splashing 9 tons of steel alongside the Phongsaly airfield.

As scheduled, the elections took place on 24 April. When the ballots were counted, however, the embassy's civic-action blitz hardly proved necessary. Phoumi had put security of the election headquarters in the hands of his loyal adjutant, Captain Siho Lamphoutacoul. Born of Chinese-Lao parents from Khong Island along the Cambodian border, Siho had briefly studied law before entering military service in 1953 as an ANL reserve officer. Posted to a staff position, he eventually came to the attention of Phoumi, who in 1957 selected him as his personal aide during Phoumi's year of study in Paris. The ruthlessly ambitious Siho had remained with Phoumi as the latter returned to Vientiane and ultimately took command of the Defense Ministry.

As head of electoral security, Siho made a farce of the democratic voting process. When CIA officer Methven visited the election headquarters on the day of the polls, he found the captain literally conjuring figures out of the air to give an unbelievable advantage to noncommunist candidates. So extensive was the ballot stuffing that the Pathet Lao candidate in the Pathet Lao stronghold of Sam Neua got only four votes. To nobody's surprise, CDNI members came out on top, taking thirty-two of the fifty-nine seats in the National Assembly. Over the remaining twenty-seven seats, the leftists got none.[3]

Although this latest National Assembly took its seats and gave the nod to a civilian prime minister, there was no mistaking that Phoumi Nosavan—who remained as minister of defense in the new cabinet—was the one pulling strings from behind. As this bore more than a passing resemblance to Sarit in Bangkok, Washington was willing to accept the tainted results with little more than a collective eye roll. If anything, the Eisenhower administration was convinced the situation was an improvement over Souvanna Phouma's limp neutralism prior to August 1958.

Facing this dynamic scenario was a new cast at Vientiane Station. Arriving in June 1960 as station chief was 48-year-old Gordon Jorgenson. Born in Japan of American parents, Jorgenson had gotten a degree from Harvard and worked as a newspaper editor before joining the US Army on the eve of World War II. He went on to serve fifteen years in the military, rising to lieutenant colonel. For his last assignment, he had been seconded to the CIA in 1955 to serve as Lansdale's deputy in the Saigon Military Mission. After formally transferring to the CIA, Laos was his first overseas posting.

The new deputy station chief, who arrived at the close of 1959, was Clifton "Cliff" Strathern. Following a spell in the US Navy at the end of World War II, Strathern had gotten two degrees from Boston University before joining the CIA in 1951. He had been cross-posted to Laos after a tour in Surabaya, Indonesia.[4]

Significantly, instead of the poisonous antagonism that had character-ized ties between Ambassador Smith and Vientiane Station, Jorgenson and Strathern got off to an exceptionally good start with the new US ambassador, Winthrop Brown. "[Jorgenson] was a man of exceptionally moral character, of great professional ability, and a very wise person," gushed Brown. "I relied on Jorgenson as my political advisor much more heavily than any member of my State Department section."[5]

As the ambassador's favored counselor, Jorgenson was initially focused on the growing clout of Phoumi Nosavan. To help manage its relationship with the emergent Lao strongman, the CIA had assigned John F. "Jack" Hasey to Vientiane Station in May 1960. Just short of his forty-fourth birthday, Hasey had led an exceptionally colorful life. Born in Massachusetts, he had gone to Colombia University for a year before deciding to shift to Paris with the idea of enrolling at the Sorbonne.[6] Unable to pay the school's tuition, however, he instead took a job as a Cartier jewel salesman traveling across France.

In late 1939, Hasey's Cartier career was put on hold. Hearing news of the Winter War, he instantly empathized with the Finnish resistance combatting the Soviet Union. Seeking to help, he served as an ambulance driver for French troops supporting the Finns. Wounded during that conflict, he returned to France to recuperate. But when Nazi Germany invaded a few short months later in May 1940, he had no choice but to flee across the English Channel to London.

While the United States was still more than a year away from formally joining the war, Hasey was itching to assist the beleaguered French. He opted to join the Free French Foreign Legion, serving as an officer in Africa and the Middle East. It was while participating in a harrowing bayonet charge outside Damascus that machine-gun fire ripped off part of his right jaw and larynx. Left with a whisper of a voice, Hasey otherwise managed a remarkably strong recovery. Posted back to London, where he was lauded by Free French leader Charles de Gaulle as the first American to shed blood for the liberation of France, Hasey ultimately went on to serve as liaison officer between de Gaulle and then-General Eisenhower. He was one of only four Americans (including Eisenhower) named Compagnon de la Libération, France's highest World War II honor.

Following the war, Hasey briefly returned to the jewelry sector. But on account of his unique relationship with the French, he came to the attention of the CIA and it recruited him in 1951. In fact, it was Hasey who in 1957 was dispatched to Paris to befriend Phoumi Nosavan. Now seeking to capitalize on that relationship, he was returning to Vientiane to re-ingratiate himself with the general.

Such was the situation as Laos entered the month of August 1960. In a relative sense, the kingdom was beginning to show signs of normalcy after three chaotic years. Even the astrologers in Luang Prabang seemed to agree, as they passed word to King Savang Vatthana that it was an auspicious time to begin discussions about the cremation ceremony for his father, King Sisavang Vong, who had died ten months earlier. Savang Vatthana had informed Vientiane of this, and on 8 August the entire upper echelon of the RLG duly ventured up to Luang Prabang for consultations. It was then, with Vientiane temporarily stripped of leadership, that the Lao soap opera irrevocably veered off script.

★ ★ ★

Jack Mathews, the CIA's first paramilitary officer in Laos, had an inkling there would be trouble. Ever since arriving in Laos in September 1958, he had been embedded with the ANL's airborne command. Over the next two years he had traveled with the paratroopers to hot spots across the country, giving him an unparalleled vantage point to view their abilities and shortcomings.

Assessing the two battalions within the airborne command, Mathews rated 2e Bataillon Parachutiste (2 BP) the most competent. Within that battalion, the key personality was its second-in-command, Captain Kong Le. In a kingdom where military promotion was often based on pedigree, Kong Le upended the stereotype. Born in 1934 to hill tribe peasants, Kong Le's minority heritage was reflected in his dark skin, wide cheekbones, and short, wiry frame. Taking to the rice paddies after his father's death in 1940, he had paused briefly for formal schooling at the Savannakhet Lycée and then, at age 17, enlisted in the ANL's original parachute battalion as a private.

There his military career might have plateaued, except for the fact that Kong Le left enough of an impression on the French to earn a coveted berth at Officer Candidate School. With limited formal education, he just got by, graduating third from the bottom in his class.

Now a newly minted second lieutenant, Kong Le went to Luang Prabang and was posted to an infantry battalion headed by then-Captain Ouane Rathikoun, the ANL officer who would later pioneer the AD militia. The two got on well and ratcheted up their comradery when Kong Le, who had pronounced libido, took Ouane's niece as his third and latest wife.

After the 1954 Geneva accords, Kong Le remained in the army and four years later transferred back to the paratroopers. The 2 BP, based next to Vientiane's Wattay airport, had recently been formed as part of the ANL's strategic reserve. Kong Le was named its executive officer and, with the battalion commander rarely present, led them for the next year as they focused on training.

All that changed in the summer of 1959, when the renewed Pathet Lao threat in Sam Neua demanded the battalion's emergency dispatch to that province. The panic over Sam Neua, Kong Le quickly found, was largely unwarranted; moreover, he was angered that his men were not paid during their combat deployment.

In December 1959, when the CDNI-backed army putsch put a definitive end to the Phoui Sananikone government, it was 2 BP that handled the sensitive assignment of seizing key installations in Vientiane. As the battalion commander was off touring the United States, it was acting commander Kong Le who led his paratroopers on behalf of the Young Turks. "I was a Phoumi and Ouane man," he later noted.[7]

Through this timely support, Kong Le counted himself in good graces with the CDNI and the upper echelon of the army. Under the surface, however, the CIA's Mathews had noticed grievances were snowballing. In March 1960, for example, Kong Le and his men had been sent on a sweep in southernmost Laos. When they accidentally strayed across the unmarked border into Cambodia, the generals in Vientiane were indifferent to calls for an emergency airdrop of food and ammunition.[8]

Two months later, 2 BP was yanked from retraining to head a failed attempt to recapture Souphanouvong. The background to this was as follows. Though under increased harassment from the rightists, Souphanouvong, along with fifteen other Pathet Lao officials, had stubbornly remained in Vientiane during the onset of Phoui's rule-by-decree. But in July 1959, after the renewed outbreak of fighting in Sam Neua, Phoui had ordered all sixteen to be imprisoned at the Phone Kheng gendarmerie camp in Vientiane. Eleven months later, in May 1960, a commando team of undercover Pathet Lao and North Vietnamese soldiers enticed the Phone Kheng guards into letting their Pathet Lao captives escape into the night. A tardy search by the Lao army, led by 2 BP, turned up no sign of the escapees.[9]

Exhausted and frustrated by all this, Kong Le began contemplating a coup. But the final straw came on 8 August, when new instructions called for him to lead the battalion on a sweep north of Vientiane along Route 13. In the field for most of the year, the exhausted paratroopers did not take kindly to their latest assignment.

Sensing that tension was building in the battalion, Mathews that evening took a Land Rover out to the 2 BP staging base. When he arrived at the jungle camp, he found security measures more rigid than usual. Moreover, Kong Le, who had tended to be upbeat around Mathews over the prior two years, appeared tense and distracted.[10]

The reason became apparent during the predawn hours of the next day. At exactly 0300 on 9 August, the battalion swung into action. One platoon took the army headquarters, guarded by just two sentries. Others took Wattay airport, the bank, the telephone exchange, and the radio station. Kong Le could make these moves knowing that his absentee battalion commander was once more touring the United States, while the bulk of RLG leadership was in Luang Prabang to discuss the royal cremation ceremony.

Within four hours, 2 BP was in total control of Vientiane and its population of 100,000. Resistance had been minimal; only six people were killed. Throughout the ordeal, Kong Le patrolled in his jeep, coordinating movements via a walkie-talkie net.

As an upstart national—and soon international—figure, Kong Le displayed political innocence commensurate with his simple upbringing.

Ideologues and opportunists were soon jockeying for influence to take advantage of his naiveté. Among the ideologues was Quinim Pholsena, a Chinese-Lao intellectual and ward of the Souvanna Phouma household who led a left-leaning political party.[11]

Receptive to advice, Kong Le heeded Quinim's call for Souvanna Phouma to take up the mantle of prime minister for the third time. Souvanna had earlier returned as ambassador in Paris to run (unopposed) in the April elections and got elected to the National Assembly seat from Luang Prabang. Now invited by the coup-maker to lead a new government, Souvanna obliged.

While 2 BP was consolidating control in Vientiane, most RLG and army officials were fuming in Luang Prabang. Jumping to the offense, General Phoumi rushed to Bangkok, where on 10 August he met his relative, Field Marshal Sarit. Kong Le's rhetoric deeply disturbed both men, as did the fact that the Pathet Lao had pledged cooperation with 2 BP paratroopers within a day of the coup. Convinced that harsh methods were needed, Phoumi outlined his plans to retake Vientiane by an airborne assault, and asked Sarit to underwrite the operation with planes, supplies, and funds. For the time being, the Thai leader remained noncommittal as his cousin returned to Savannakhet.

Back in Vientiane, Kong Le spent the ensuing week using hints of intimidation to whip his coup group into a full-fledged government. On 13 August, paratroopers and armored cars surrounded the National Assembly, which obediently voted the CDNI-dominated cabinet (most of which was still in Luang Prabang) out of office. Four days later, the assembly approved a new cabinet with Souvanna Phouma as prime minister.

On an apparent collision course, Phoumi gathered twenty-one cabinet members and assemblymen who had escaped Vientiane in Savannakhet on 14 August. Two days later, he arranged for a C-47 to buzz the capital, dropping leaflets announcing that his Savannakhet countercoup group would retake the capital by force. By 18 August, a Savannakhet transmitter was in operation and directing barbs at Kong Le over the airwaves.

For a time, the United States tried to walk a tightrope between the two sides. Ambassador Brown made no secret of his sympathies toward

Souvanna Phouma, and Voice of America on 19 August said that Washington would back the king, who was apparently leaning toward Kong Le. On a more discreet level, the CIA's Campbell James was instructed to revive his earlier cordial ties with Souvanna.

Brown and the embassy had good reason for guarded optimism. Two weeks after the coup, Souvanna had flown down to Savannakhet and reached agreement with Phoumi for the National Assembly to reunite in neutral Luang Prabang. Accordingly, the assembly factions linked up, the king officially confirmed Souvanna prime minister, and a roster for a new cabinet, including some pre-coup officials, was formed with the king's blessing.

All appeared settled by 2 September, the day the new officials were to take their oath of office. Then, as smoothly as the warring factions had come together, they spun hopelessly apart, triggered largely by a series of anti-Phoumi broadcasts by Kong Le. Afflicted by second thoughts, Phoumi flew back to Savannakhet, scrubbing the progress made at Luang Prabang.

Meantime, Souvanna was complicating matters on an international level. During the Phoui government, diplomatic recognition had been extended to South Vietnam and the Republic of China on Taiwan.[12] Souvanna, demanding balance, began courting supporters from the communist bloc. Heeding the call were the Soviets, who on 13 October dispatched their ambassador to Cambodia, Aleksandr Abramov, to open an embassy. Kong Le pulled out the stops for Abramov, dropping a company of his paratroopers at Wattay in an elaborate reception.[13]

Against all this, Vientiane Station was torn, literally. While Jorgenson, Strathern, and James remained in the capital, the remaining officers had been flown across the Mekong in mid-August and put on hold at the Erawan Hotel in Bangkok.[14] But hedging its bets almost as quickly, Jack Hasey was redirected to Savannakhet, where he moved into a house next to Phoumi.[15]

For five weeks, Phoumi received little more than moral support from Washington. Then, during the second week of September, Hasey was instructed by the CIA's Bangkok Station to prepare a makeshift runway near Savannakhet (away from the prying eyes of the French at Seno airbase). Clearing a crude strip, pro-Phoumi soldiers lined it with flashlights as an Air America Helio Courier flew in by night from Thailand. Piled aboard the plane were C-ration boxes crammed with US dollars. With a war chest suddenly full, Phoumi instantly commanded greater respect from among his fellow officers.

Shortly thereafter, Stuart Methven was dispatched from Bangkok to Luang Prabang. There he was ordered to monitor support for Phoumi, both in the palace and among some of the fence-sitting generals in the north.

For more than two months, Phoumi's countercoup plans progressed with fits and starts. Not until mid-November did he begin his march on Vientiane in earnest. Proceeding at a glacial pace up Route 13, pro-Phoumi forces rounded the panhandle at the opening of December and converged on Paksane, the last major town before Vientiane.

With a final showdown perhaps days away, Methven hopped aboard an Air America light plane heading from Luang Prabang to Vientiane. His main mission was to discreetly pass word for any remaining pro-Phoumi assemblymen in Vientiane to make their way to Luang Prabang, where Phoumi was looking to gather a quorum so they could deliver a vote of no confidence against Souvanna Phouma.

Methven had a second mission as well. Khamphan Panya, the CDNI vice president and foreign minister up until the Kong Le coup, had remained at Phoumi's side since August. However, his wife and son Arya were still in Vientiane and he feared for their safety.

Quickly locating the pair, Methven whisked them back to Wattay and the waiting Air America plane. As Arya remembers it,

> As we took off, we could see a pair of planes approaching Vientiane. They were Li-2s, the Soviet copy of the C-47. The Soviets were coming to help Kong Le's troops.[16]

It was true. For weeks, a desperate Souvanna Phouma had been lobbying the Soviets for material assistance. Not until 3 December did this begin, sort of, when a string of Soviet transport planes from Hanoi landed at Wattay. They were empty, however, as the pilots were merely conducting familiarization flights.[17]

By 9 December, the situation was increasingly grim. With Paksane firmly in Phoumi's hands, Air America planes dropped several sticks of paratroopers throughout the afternoon into Chinaimo, a military encampment located on the southeastern outskirts of Vientiane. Hearing of this, Souvanna dispatched a loyal general to Chinaimo to make a last-ditch appeal for peace. After being rebuffed, Souvanna and six of his cabinet ministers headed for Wattay. Before boarding an Air Laos Stratoliner for safe haven in Cambodia, the embattled prime minister ran into Campbell James. Over the previous four months, the CIA officer had consistently managed to convey sympathy as he shadowed the prime minister. "*La politique et la politique, mais l'amite est l'amite,*" he called out to James. Politics is politics, but a friend is a friend.[18]

On the following morning, 10 December, the senior remaining cabinet official, Quinim Pholsena, boarded an Air Laos DC-3 at 1030 hours and flew to Hanoi. Quinim's plea was direct: he would formalize a pact between the Pathet Lao and Kong Le's self-styled Neutralist Armed Forces (Forces Armées Neutralistes, or FAN) in exchange for a Soviet airlift of arms and supplies. Quinim, in fact, was repeating what already was reality: Soviet planes had been landing nonmilitary supplies at Wattay for nearly a week, and the Pathet Lao and FAN had been cooperating for months.

At 0900 the next morning, the first of six Soviet Il-14s landed at Wattay. Inside were four 105mm howitzers, six 4.2-inch mortars, and a dozen PAVN artillerymen, all part of the initial tranche of Soviet military assistance to FAN and the Pathet Lao. The North Vietnamese gunners quickly deployed their artillery pieces around the airport and pointed the tubes southeast.

It was too little, too late. On 12 December, the National Assembly quorum in Luang Prabang delivered its vote of censure against Souvanna Phouma. With this veneer of legitimacy, Phoumi formally was handed government powers.

At 1320 hours on 13 December, the storm finally broke in Vientiane. The main body of Phoumi's forces, identified by green and yellow scarves, linked up with pro-Phoumi troops in Chinaimo and dispatched a column toward the capital. As it reached the town proper, Kong Le's PAVN gunners unleashed a volley of 105mm fire, arcing over the advancing columns and hitting near the kilometer 3 marker, 2 kilometers short of Chinaimo.

After an eerie calm engulfed the capital overnight, the battle resumed the next morning. A pro-Phoumi tank, aiming at the army headquarters (which had been appropriated by Kong Le), fired a round through that building and hit the US embassy located across the street.

Inside the embassy, a meeting had just adjourned for lunch within the new, cell-like cement CIA wing when the round hit, igniting the wooden roof of the old chancellery building. CIA officers ran back to burn documents and destroy communications gear as flames engulfed the structure. Jorgenson's office was left in ruins.[19]

As of the morning of 16 December, the battle for Vientiane was fast approaching a climax. With few recognizable front lines, opposing sides traded control over streets and blocks. By shortly after midday, the outnumbered rebel paratroopers were pushed back to Wattay. There Kong Le ordered 1,200 of his faithful to load into trucks and begin a phased withdrawal north along Route 13.

By dusk, Phoumi's countercoup forces spread triumphantly through the capital. Their prize, they found, had taken some brutal punishment. Initial estimates put the number of civilians killed at up to 600. In addition, at least 600 houses were destroyed and 7,000 people made homeless. On top of that, a cholera epidemic had broken out.

More troubling for Phoumi was the fact that Kong Le had withdrawn with his fighting capability intact. Leaving behind pockets of resistance along Route 13, Kong Le's column had continued north to the Sala Phou Khoun crossroads, then veered east along Route 7. From there they spilled onto the strategic PDJ, routing the far larger but disorganized Phoumi defenders on the last day of the year.

As the dust cleared on New Year's Day 1961, Laos was hanging precariously in the balance. Besides the PDJ, the combined FAN/Pathet Lao forces had cemented their grip on Sam Neua. Too, the provincial army leadership in Phongsaly was leaning heavily in their direction.[20] Phoumi, meantime, was more focused on consolidating his political control over the capital than on seriously pursuing his opponents. Taking their lead from him, the majority of the RLG's soldiery was showing little appetite for combat.

There was a notable exception, however. In the hills of Xieng Khouang province ringing the PDJ, members of the fiercely independent Hmong hill tribe, led by Lieutenant Colonel Vang Pao, had both a natural flair for guerrilla warfare and a visceral distaste for the Pathet Lao and its PAVN mentors. Harnessing these qualities, the CIA began a paramilitary program in January 1961 to equip and manage these partisans. By early the following month, some 3,500 out of an authorized 4,000 Hmong were armed. To manage them, a cluster of paramilitary support offices were set up at Wattay. It was a portent of things to come.

★ ★ ★

In 1961, CIA stations around the world were primarily populated by officers from the agency's clandestine wing, what was then known as the Directorate of Plans. As Methven explained, that directorate had a de facto caste structure:

> The top layer is made up of the Brahmins, the foreign intelligence (FI) officers. Real spies. The next layer is composed of the Shudras, the political action/ psychological warfare (PP) officers. The bottom layer consists of the Untouchables, paramilitary (PM) officers.[21]

In Vientiane Station, with the advent of the Hmong program, this arrangement had been turned on its head. As guerrilla recruitment soon spread among minority hill tribes elsewhere in the kingdom, Laos overnight became a major CIA paramilitary theater. The bottom caste, the so-called "untouchables," vaulted to the forefront and were transformed into a major growth industry. Members of Sea Supply dominated the initial wave of these blue-collar officers, joined by veterans from previous covert paramilitary projects in places like Indonesia and Tibet. Even a case officer earmarked for a desk job in Vientiane was rebadged as a guerrilla advisor and sent into the mountains.[22]

Vientiane Station also had its share of the middle caste, the politi-cal-action types. These were the likes of Phillips, Hasey, and even James, looking to mold the Laotian political landscape by subtly changing perceptions with mental bullets. It remained part of the station's mandate heading into 1961, with Hasey retained in Vientiane as the liaison officer with Phoumi[23] and James shifting to Luang Prabang in March 1961 to ensconce himself with the royals.[24]

But compared to these, the highest caste, the Brahmins, had thus far been relegated to an afterthought. Though this was the top of the clandestine totem pole, the buttoned-up, white-collar FI officers who did clandestine operations had barely been active in Laos, probably because backwater Vientiane had few in the way of proper Cold War adversaries.[25]

That was about to change.

CHAPTER 4

Apéritif

During the first quarter of 1961, Laos hovered on the cusp of becoming a superpower flashpoint. Then as suddenly as it started, the war was put on hold on 1 May as the Pathet Lao—eager for a ceasefire that would codify its gains—dispatched a representative to meet Phoumi Nosavan's forces to discuss terms for a local truce. Two days later, Pathet Lao and FAN commanders ordered their men to stop firing; Phoumi issued an identical decree to his rightist troops.

For a civil war involving three factions spanning the political spectrum, the peace process made surprisingly good headway. On 12 May, Canadian, Indian, and Polish officials from a quickly reconstituted ICC flew north to the PDJ and established an office at the village of Khang Khay. Four days later, international peace talks opened in Geneva.[1]

During all this, strong verbal support for a political settlement was offered by the new administration of President John F. Kennedy. Following the Geneva meeting in May, delegates from all three Lao factions met intermittently in Europe and Laos through the summer. By September 1961, agreement was reached for Souvanna Phouma to head a new coalition that would bring together the rightists, communists, and his neutralists. Over the remainder of the year, however, further negotiations to divide cabinet posts in the upcoming coalition achieved little progress. Although all three factions shared responsibility for the deadlock, Kennedy's assistant secretary of state for Far Eastern Affairs, Averell Harriman, pinned the bulk of blame on an uncooperative Phoumi.

By the opening of 1962, Harriman had run out of patience with the general. To pressure Phoumi, Washington cut cash grants to the RLG in early February. Then in mid-March, Harriman ventured to Nong Khai, the Thai town opposite Vientiane, where he lectured Phoumi and his Thai cousin, Sarit. Harriman's heavy-handedness continued during subsequent meetings in Vientiane, at which time he demanded the removal of Jack Hasey, Phoumi's CIA confidant.

The pressure seemed to work. By mid-June 1962, all three factions had agreed in principle to a division of power along tripartite lines. According to their compromise, Souvanna Phouma would be prime minister, Souphanouvong would be deputy prime minister and minister of economic planning, and Phoumi Nosavan would be deputy prime minister and minister of finance. To flesh out this understanding, the fourteen Geneva conference participants reconvened on 2 July, three weeks later ratifying the Geneva Declaration and Protocol on the Neutrality of Laos.

According to the new Geneva agreement—largely a repeat of the 1954 document, including its glaring shortcomings—all foreign military personnel (save for accredited military attachés) had to leave the kingdom by 6 October. Living up to the letter of this, the Pentagon withdrew military advisors from Lao soil during September. Living up to the spirit—and nearly the letter—the CIA removed almost all of its up-country paramilitary officers and shifted its paramilitary support offices from Wattay across the Mekong to Nong Khai.

Matching Washington's good faith, Moscow halted its ongoing airlift in early November and then turned over a dozen of its planes (with Soviet instructors) to the coalition government during a December ceremony at Wattay.

Despite superpower compliance, post-Geneva Laos still played host to some 100,000 soldiers divided among the three factions. The largest of these was Phoumi Nosavan's 51,000-man rightist army, which the previous year had been renamed the Royal Armed Forces (Forces Armées Royales, or FAR).

Much smaller than FAR were the 8,000-strong FAN neutralists. Leadership still rested with the mercurial, idealistic Kong Le, who, now sporting stars of a self-promoted major general, spent most of his time at the FAN headquarters in Khang Khay. The bulk of his troops were distributed around the PDJ, though his semi-loyal subordinate in Phongsaly, Khamouane Boupha, had three ill-equipped, understrength battalions under his charge.

Rounding out the Lao factions was the Pathet Lao. Estimated at 19,500 men, the Pathet Lao was deployed primarily in Sam Neua and Xieng Khouang, with a sprinkling of smaller pockets elsewhere.

Adding backbone to the Pathet Lao were North Vietnamese advisors and combat formations. By the late summer of 1962, the CIA was tracking an estimated twelve PAVN battalions stationed across Laos. These troops, plus an additional 3,000 advisors, support personnel, and cadres assigned to Pathet Lao units, put total North Vietnamese military strength in Laos at 9,000 men. Out of this sizable number, only 40 North Vietnamese "technicians" appeared before ICC representatives by the 6 October Geneva deadline for withdrawal of foreign military forces.

Though outnumbered in the field, the Pathet Lao immediately made its presence felt in Vientiane. The same month the Geneva accords were signed, it pushed Souvanna Phouma to establish diplomatic relations with a wide range of communist nations. The Soviet Union, of course, had already had an ambassador accredited since October 1960. During the ensuing year, the Soviets had shifted their diplomatic personnel to the PDJ. Now with a coalition government in place, they returned to Vientiane and opened a proper embassy along Rue Say Lom.[2]

For China, its move to Vientiane followed a similar progression. In March 1961, the left-leaning Quinim Pholsena (whose wife was ethnic Chinese and had close ties with Beijing) had proposed an exchange of economic and cultural missions. Near the end of that year, China made good on this offer and opened an economic and cultural center on the PDJ. In addition, consulates had been exchanged with Souvanna Phouma's blessing in Kunming and Phongsaly.

Upgrading these ties under the coalition government, the head of China's center on the PDJ, Liu Chun, shifted to Vientiane on 12 July 1962. Now elevated to ambassador, Chun set up shop across from the Vientiane sports stadium, just one block from the new Soviet embassy.

Conversely, the Republic of China on Taiwan, which had manned a consulate in Vientiane since 1959, severed relations with Laos in September and went packing.[3]

Finally, North Vietnam opened its embassy in November 1962. It chose a more isolated site, to the west of town just off the airport road to Wattay. Chosen as ambassador was Le Van Hien, a close acquaintance of both Ho Chi Minh and Souphanouvong's Vietnamese wife. Taking its lead from Taiwan, an enraged South Vietnam, which had an embassy in Laos since 1959, yanked its ambassador and threatened to cut ties; in the end they maintained relations but with only a *chargé d'affaires*.[4]

Not surprisingly, many of these communist missions contained intelligence personnel. Within the initial roster at the North Vietnamese embassy, for example, was a first secretary named Phan Dinh. Two years earlier, he had been part of the underground military intelligence cell that broke Souphanouvong out of the Phone Kheng jail. He had also been in Vientiane during the deadly street fighting of December 1960, shuttling messages between Kong Le and a PAVN advisory team.[5]

Similarly, the Soviets had assigned TASS news agency representative Yuriy Trushin to Laos when they dispatched an ambassador in 1960; prior to that, Trushin had been expelled from Thailand for a clumsy attempt to bribe a Thai journalist for political information.[6]

Three years later, in late 1963, Soviet intelligence efforts were again on display. Casting an especially wide net, one diplomat in Vientiane sent out a form letter to a multitude of officers across the FAR and FAN. It read,

> We are here to help the coalition government. We will be able to do so only if we are informed in detail about this country that we know little or nothing about. Help us. You will be serving your country and your cause. I am in my office every day. You will obviously be compensated for your time and effort.[7]

At least one FAN intelligence officer took up the offer and showed up at the Soviet embassy, whereupon he was paid the princely sum of $250 (equal to a lieutenant's annual wage). Once alone with the Soviet diplomat, he was quizzed about China's inroads in Laos, as well as the activities of the British, Americans, and French. Curiously, he also asked probing questions about North Vietnam, hinting that Moscow might not have been fully confident in their ties with Hanoi.[8]

The Soviet diplomat then wasted no time shifting to clandestine mode. For their next meeting, he proposed that the Lao officer walk alone on a quiet stretch of the airport road, where he would be met by a car bearing Soviet diplomatic plates. Uncomfortable with this turn, the FAN officer declined and reported the overture back to Souvanna Phouma.[9]

Among the most aggressive in its intelligence efforts was the reconstituted ICC, specifically its dozens of Polish officers that were shilling for the Soviets.[10] Recalled Frank Burnet, a political officer at the US embassy in 1963,

> The Poles had a large delegation and worked hard at gaining intelligence from Western embassies. Some of its members appeared to be targeted on some of us. For a long time, it was common knowledge that one of the handsomer Poles had befriended and was perhaps sleeping with the Canadian Commissioner's secretary. One day she was sent back to Ottawa very suddenly. Thereafter we irreverently referred to this episode as the Polish "penetration" of the Canadian delegation.[11]

★ ★ ★

In the face of this increasingly crowded, competitive landscape, Vientiane Station had a new cast on hand. Since the third quarter of 1962, the station had been headed by Charles Whitehurst, a former US Army captain who had served with the OSS, the intelligence agency during World War II. Whitehurst had been scheduled to jump into northern Vietnam to assist anti-Japanese guerrillas, only to have the mission scrubbed when the war ended. Shifting to the CIA, he had served with Western Enterprises on Taiwan, then headed the Indochina desk during the late 1950s before a stint as Singapore station chief.[12]

His deputy, arriving at the close of 1962, was George Kalaris. A Greek-American, Kalaris had been attending university in Athens when the Axis powers invaded and occupied Greece for most of the war. In the early 1950s, Kalaris had earned his law degree and served as an attorney for the Labor Department before shifting to the CIA. He had a tour in Indonesia at the close of that decade, ostensibly as an economic officer.

Both Whitehurst and Kalaris had arrived in Vientiane just as the Station had seen its extensive paramilitary operation uprooted and put on ice to abide by the Geneva agreement. As paramilitary activity went on the backburner, and the number of diplomatic targets packed into Vientiane mushroomed, this looked like a windfall for the CIA's foreign intelligence types.

Enter Serge Taube. Though born in New York City, Taube was a proud Volga German. This referred to the group of ethnic Germans who had emigrated to Russia in the 18th century, then were displaced in 1917 with the onset of the Russian Revolution. Most of Taube's family had made its way to France, and as a result he had spent a good part of his childhood among relatives still living there. Consequently, his French and Russian were at the level of native speaker.

Returning to the United States for college, Taube began studies at Georgetown in 1953 but soon left to fulfill his draft obligation as a US Army paratrooper. Upon completing his military service in 1955, his linguistic skills drew the attention of a CIA recruiter. Joining the Agency, he did a tour in Indonesia at the end of that decade. There he caught the eye of a female cryptographer at the embassy and came back to Washington with a wife.

After returning to Georgetown to complete his degree, Taube was once more dispatched to the Far East, this time to Laos at the close of 1962. Not since Henry Hecksher did Vientiane Station have an officer with fluency in Russian; now with an entire Soviet embassy in the station's sights, there were high expectations for Taube.

Before any significant results, however, Laos fell back to its familiar script of political upheaval. All the factions were culpable: FAR kidnapped the FAN intelligence chief in November 1962, the Pathet Lao killed a FAN colonel in February 1963, Kong Le's men retaliated by assassinating the left-leaning Minister of Foreign Affairs Quinim Pholsena in April, two days later a FAN intelligence officer was killed in a reprisal to that, and the FAN intelligence chief was gunned down by FAR in December 1963. Slamming the FAR for inadequate security in Vientiane, all senior Pathet Lao officials abandoned the capital for Sam Neua, leaving behind only a small representative office.

While the Pathet Lao had not been blameless, it did have a point. Fanning the flames in Vientiane was Brigadier General Siho, the Luca Brasi to Phoumi Nosavan's Don Corleone.[13] Belying his cherubic face, Siho had displayed a propensity for wanton violence from the moment the rightists had retaken Vientiane. In May 1961, for example, it was an open secret that he had set up a honey trap for a rival FAR lieutenant colonel, then placed a bullet in his head while the latter was parked alongside a road for a nocturnal dalliance.[14]

Once Siho reestablished himself in the capital, his vehicle for intimidation was an organization he created and led called the Directorate of National Coordination (DNC), under which he had absorbed the entirety of the National Police, the immigration service, and army intelligence. To give the DNC added punch, he also raised three crack airborne battalions that were rated as good as any unit in the FAR.[15]

Moving beyond mere intimidation, Siho spearheaded a full-blown coup in April 1964 that quickly succeeded in securing Vientiane. Phoumi Nosavan was informed of the putsch only after it was a fait accompli, but he quickly lent his support. Washington was having none of it, however, and it had the US ambassador give a tongue-lashing to the coup leaders. As a result, Souvanna Phouma, one of several prominent figures who had been detained, was quietly released and allowed to retake his seat as prime minister atop the bickering generals.

In the countryside, predictably, the war returned with a vengeance. CIA paramilitary operations in Laos not only ramped back up, but exceeded what had been in place prior to Geneva. Keeping pace, the paramilitary support headquarters shifted from Nong Khai to more spacious accommodations at an abandoned civil aviation compound at the Royal Thai Air Force Base in Udorn.

Back in restive Vientiane, January 1965 brought not just one but two more coup attempts. These were intra-army affairs, with the end result of both Siho and Phoumi being driven into Thai exile. Phoumi would ultimately live out his days on Thai soil. Siho made the mistake of returning in 1966 after an encouraging prediction from a fortune teller; the soothsayer had apparently read the wrong tea leaves, however, as Siho was quickly jailed and—so said the guards—shot dead while trying to escape.[16]

Kong Le, for his part, was fast growing irrelevant.[17] His FAN had withered over time, not helped by the fact that a large chunk had defected from his command and sided with the Pathet Lao. What remained became dependent on aid provided by the RLG, and in time that devolved into little more than a minor appendage of the FAR.[18]

In the midst of this diplomatic migraine, Washington had an epiphany. Though Souvanna Phouma had been vilified by senior US officials in years past, he had proven not only resilient, but also rather comfortable working alongside the cabal of FAR generals. And unlike the mercurial Norodom Sihanouk in neighboring Cambodia, who delighted in tweaking America's nose, Souvanna had come to accept a decidedly pro-Western form of diplomatic neutrality. Consequently, the United States realized Souvanna was about as good as they were going to get, and their wagon would remain firmly hitched to him.

Tied to this was another critical factor weighing on minds in Washington. Prior to 1963, Laos had repeatedly been the focus of attention in Southeast Asia. But after the 1964 Gulf of Tonkin incidents, and especially after US Marines landed in Danang in March 1965, South Vietnam grabbed center stage from then forward and relegated Laos to a supporting role.

This subordination was readily apparent when William Sullivan arrived as the new ambassador in December 1964. Sullivan brought with him an especially brash take on realpolitik, and from the start of his tour, he advocated an über-aggressive stance by the RLG to assist Washington's intervention in South Vietnam. Prone to micromanaging this effort—getting involved in airstrike targeting, for instance—he was facetiously dubbed "Field Marshal Sullivan" by US generals in Saigon.

Preceding Sullivan's arrival by seven months was a new head of Vientiane Station, Douglas Blaufarb. A newspaper editor and field reporter in London during World War II, Blaufarb later joined the State Department on a writing contract. Transferring to the CIA, he served on the Operations Coordinating Board, an Eisenhower-era interdepartmental committee that oversaw covert operations, then did tours in Saigon and Singapore before coming back to head the Laos desk at headquarters.

Perhaps not by coincidence, Sullivan's predecessor, Leonard Unger, had been Blaufarb's classmate at Harvard. To be fair, Blaufarb's measured, professorial approach was a good match with Unger's own understated demeanor. Sullivan's larger-than-life persona, however, seemingly demanded a more dynamic CIA chief who could ratchet up operations to the next level.

That is what they got when Theodore Shackley arrived to replace Blaufarb in July 1966. As a child, Shackley had been raised by his immigrant Polish mother in Florida's West Palm Beach; from her he learned to speak Polish as his second tongue. Enlisting just as World War II came to a close, his bilingual background earned him entry into the Counterintelligence Corps and a posting to occupied Germany.

Eyeing academic potential in Shackley, the army soon sent him back to the states to earn a degree at the University of Maryland. Graduating in early 1951 and now badged as a second lieutenant, he returned to Europe and was seconded to the CIA. Again making use of his linguistic talents, he was sent to Nuremburg and assigned to a unit running agent networks into Poland and Czechoslovakia.

When Shackley's obligation to the army ended in 1953, the CIA offered Shackley a full-time slot. Staying in West Germany, he was posted to the agency's Berlin Base. He would remain there for the rest of the decade, then return to headquarters as head of the Czech section in the CIA's Eastern Europe division.

In early 1962, Shackley was taken out of his European comfort zone and targeted against Cuba. The agency had been reeling over the previous year as a result of the Bay of Pigs invasion debacle, but was now persisting with a robust menu of agent operations, psychological feints, and commando strikes to undercut the Fidel Castro regime. Based out of Miami, Shackley was named chief of operations for this diversified effort for the next three years.

In the summer of 1965, Shackley's Latin America interlude came to an end. He was next sent back to his old haunt, this time as head of Berlin Base.[19] By now he had earned a reputation as a hardnosed manager of clandestine operations, something that did not go unnoticed by Desmond Fitzgerald, the CIA's deputy director of plans, responsible for the worldwide collection of foreign intelligence. When it came time to select a replacement for Blaufarb in mid-1966, Shackley topped Fitzgerald's short list. Recalled a case officer in Laos at the time,

> Shackley was assigned to Laos by Des Fitzgerald and was told, in effect, "Take that thing over and run it! You're the man who did the Berlin operation. You're the man who handled the Cuban Missile Crisis and got us out of the Bay of Pigs fiasco. I want you in Laos and I want you to get on top of that situation. You're in charge!"[20]

Fitzgerald did not appear overly concerned that Shackley had no background in Southeast Asia, much less the nuances of Laos. In that respect, Shackley was cut from the same cloth as the hyper-caffeinated Henry Hecksher: early career spent in Germany, an assignment in Latin America, then put in charge of Vientiane. Doing Hecksher one better, Shackley brought along several of his old Cuban and German crowd to the station, none of whom had prior Southeast Asia experience.[21]

Shackley could do so knowing that his deputy, James Lilley, more than compensated with a diverse Asia background. Born in China to American parents, Lilley had spent most of his formative years there until advancing Imperial Japanese forced an evacuation in the fall of 1940. Graduating from Yale and entering the CIA, his unique upbringing earned him an assignment to Taiwan where he was tasked with dropping agents into mainland China. Success proved elusive, however, as his first team came on the radio for a single transmission before going silent. A subsequent assignment running agents from Hong Kong was equally unrewarding when he was burned by information merchants selling fraudulent intelligence.[22]

Switching to Southeast Asia, Lilley's hard-luck tours continued. After French language training, he was sent to Phnom Penh in September 1961.[23] A large part of his attention focused on running ethnic Chinese agents, but he was forced to cut his tour short when the Cambodian authorities, seemingly wise to the CIA efforts, enacted a citywide crackdown that netted many of the Agency's sources. Lilley next went to Bangkok, but again had to cut short his tour, this time due to a bout of hepatitis.

Looking to break his string of bad luck, Lilley arrived in Vientiane in May 1965. After a year under Blaufarb, he experienced whiplash as the station chiefs rotated. Mandated to increase efforts exponentially to support military operations in Vietnam, Shackley thoroughly changed the complexion of the Laos operation. By Lilley's estimation, the station went from about 30 people in 1966 to more than eight times that number within two years.

To be sure, the vast majority was there to support CYHOPE, the crypt given to the agency's paramilitary effort in the Lao countryside. But Shackley had spent most of his career recruiting and running agents, and it was there that he also sought to make a mark. Moreover, given his own family history, it was no surprise that he would eye the Polish community as a target.

The only Poles in Vientiane, of course, were in the ICC. By that time, the commission was fast teetering toward irrelevancy. Prior to mid-1962, the Canadians had been performing a holding action as the Indian and Polish delegates more often than not sided with the Pathet Lao. For a brief period after their humiliation in the 1962 Sino-Indian War, the Indians soured toward the communists and began seeking common ground with the Canadians. But by 1965, the Indians were again foot-dragging. The deadlocked commission, as a result, rarely met. It produced only sporadic reports about its internal finances, but none about violations.

That left the Poles—a shrinking community of about two dozen civilians and military officers—with an exorbitant amount of free time on their hands. Eying the idle Poles at their compound near Wattay, the four Polish speakers at the US embassy—including Shackley—approached the bored ICC delegates with an offer to play volleyball against a US team. The Poles gladly accepted, and a successful initial outing quickly turned into weekly games at various venues, including Shackley's own residence, as well as postgame drinks and luncheon socials.

This continued for some fourteen months, during which time Vientiane Station analyzed candidates for potential recruitment. Lilley claims that the station actually pitched one, but he demanded too much in compensation.[24]

Shackley remembers it somewhat differently. Just as he had narrowed down his targeting to two possible candidates, the Poles unilaterally ceased all further social contact. He surmises that the delegation did a belated name trace that turned up Shackley's true employer.[25]

Despite these middling results, the ICC project whetted Shackley's appetite. If Vientiane Station was to support military operations in South Vietnam, Shackley interpreted that to include clandestine operations against the North Vietnamese embassy and the Pathet Lao representative office. Moreover, CIA stations around the world had a standing order to operate against their respective Soviet embassies.

All of these targets, it turned out, were soon to be on the station's menu.

CHAPTER 5

The Teams

At first glance, Thai national Pratheong Sorapan seemed a most unlikely covert operative. Bespectacled and diminutive, Pratheong was born in 1937 just outside the Bangkok city limits. After completing vocational high school in the Thai capital, he joined classes at Thamasat near the Grand Palace, which at the time was still a free-entry open university. He also took a conversational English course and, showing a flair for the language, got a job as a translator for the US military at the Southeast Asia Treaty Organization headquarters in Bangkok.

Five years on, Pratheong had an urge to continue his studies in the United States. With only $200 in his pocket, he flew to Washington and enrolled at George Washington University while working odd jobs to make ends meet.[1] To better fit in, he Westernized his name to Paul Seema.

Just shy of graduating, Seema decided to cut short his studies and return to Bangkok to resume his translation work. By that time, he had come to the attention of the CIA, which saw him as a self-starter with a healthy dose of street smarts. Recruited as a local asset, he was more than game to take on Agency tasks geared to test his competence.

Fast forward to April 1966, and a decision was made to provide Vientiane Station with a surveillance team to operate against communist targets in Laos. Since the team would operate unilaterally—without the knowledge of the host Lao government—it was felt that members recruited from Thailand would be beneficial for two reasons. First, Vientiane was inundated by Thai merchants, offering plentiful cover.

Second, Thai recruits promised a lesser chance of loyalties getting entangled in the confused Lao political landscape.

That is where Seema came into the picture. Asked by Bangkok Station if he could recruit six Thai men who might be willing to operate in Vientiane, he was up to the challenge. Reaching back to his days in the vocational high school, he recalled a schoolmate two years his junior who hailed from Isan, the northeastern quadrant of Thailand whose residents are close cousins of the Lao. That schoolmate, the soft-spoken, contemplative Somkit, was working at the Port Authority of Thailand. When approached by Seema with a tantalizing offer of better pay for a secret assignment in Laos, he quit his job and signed on as the team's first member.

Somkit offered up something else to Seema. He noted that two more of their schoolmates from the vocational school were working at the Port Authority. The first, the shy Ruangsak, also hailed from Isan. The second, Kriangsak, was a tall, chain-smoker from Thailand's deep south. Pitched by Seema, both resigned from the Port Authority and joined the team.

For the next candidates, Seema networked through a family friend who was a lieutenant in the Royal Thai Navy. From this lieutenant, Seema was recommended two sailors. The first, Sergeant Pyrot, was a 37-year-old radioman. The second, Sergeant Boungpoo, also 37, was a flag signaler. Both took up Seema's offer and left the navy.

For the sixth and last candidate, the navy lieutenant recommended Chan, a resourceful 26-year-old who was the son of a Royal Thai Army major general.[2] Rather than follow in his father's martial footsteps, Chan had worked for five years as a waiter at the Erawan Hotel. He had recently made the lateral move to bartender at the riverfront Oriental Hotel when Seema saddled up to the counter and dangled his offer. Chan flashed a wide grin and asked where to sign up.

Meeting his quota of six recruits, Seema reported back to Bangkok Station and was told to bring the group to Chiang Mai. As Thailand's second-largest city, it was felt that Chiang Mai more closely approximated Vientiane in terms of population density and layout.

Upon arrival, the six were introduced to their two CIA instructors. The first was a short officer named John. The second was Pat Dailey, a towering Denver native who had spent much of the prior two decades on sensitive assignments in Asia. As an OSS sergeant during World War II, Dailey had been attached to an airborne team that infiltrated northern Vietnam in 1945 to interdict Japanese lines of communication. Linking up with French Foreign Legionnaires on the run, they got dispersed by the Japanese and went back to China at war's end.[3]

In 1951, Dailey joined the CIA and was sent that September to Western Enterprises on Taiwan. There he spent a couple of years retraining the Nationalist Chinese airborne regiment along with civilian intelligence teams that were being sent back to the mainland.

Following a posting to CIA headquarters, Dailey next was assigned as an instructor at the Agency's training center at Camp Peary. In April 1959, he was again named an instructor, this time at the Agency's Far East training site on Saipan. In a secluded corner of that remote island he trained a wide range of Asian contingents, including Khampa tribesmen from Tibet. In 1961, he was back in Taiwan for a second tour coaching teams set to infiltrate the PRC.

With this impressive breadth of Asian training experience, Dailey, assisted by John and with Seema providing translations, began the classroom phase for the six Thai students. After sitting through several days of lectures on the basics—how to rotate an eye on the target, for instance, and how to detect countersurveillance—the six were taken out into Chiang Mai to practice extended static surveillance on a range of targets, such as hostels and police posts. After that, they graduated to mobile surveillance using motorbikes.

Three months later, the team was deemed sufficiently skilled to trade the placid setting of Chiang Mai for the urban chaos of Bangkok. For four weeks they were put through the paces along the streets and alleys of the Thai capital, often with Dailey acting as the rabbit they had to discreetly keep under watch.

By the opening of September 1966, the team was deemed ready to shift to Laos. In pairs they crossed the Mekong for what would prove an inauspicious start. Due to weeks of exceptionally heavy downpours to close out the rainy season, Vientiane was experiencing its worst flooding in decades. With most of the downtown area inundated, the team picked their way 6 kilometers northeast of the city. This was the location of the main residential compound for the ever-expanding US embassy. The compound—dubbed Six Clicks City—resembled a miniature American town, replete with an international school, sports facilities, and seventy-five Western-style homes, each with their own fenced yards.

Opposite Six Clicks City, the American houses gave way to local architecture. There, nestled along a quiet back street, the CIA rented a spacious Lao villa to serve as the team's safe house. As the first order of business, John rendezvoused with the six and told them they needed Western names for use in all future reporting. Feeling a bit cosmopolitan, Chan picked the first name Alberto and paired it with a fancy French last name. "Good," said John, "from now on you are Albert."

John then selected names for the remaining five. Somkit, the first to be recruited, became Dick. The second Isan member, Ruangsak, was Tim from that point forward. Pyrot, the navy radioman, became Tom. Boungpoo, the navy signaler, was dubbed Jack. And the tall, self-confident Kriangsak became Bob; he was also made the overall team leader.[4]

Once the flood waters receded, the six began familiarization drills around Vientiane in early October. Each was given a small Honda motorcycle, with the exception of Bob, whose large frame was matched with a larger bike. But once again their schedule was interrupted when Brigadier General Thao Ma, the disgruntled Royal Lao Air Force commander, lashed out at his fellow generals in Vientiane during a 21 October coup attempt that culminated in a dawn bombing run against the capital. Nearly two dozen were killed on the ground. One twisted body was still at roadside when the team made its way across the city that noon.

Through year's end and into January 1967, familiarization drills continued. After that, Dailey and John declared their work done and prepared to withdraw from the project. Seema, too, took leave of Laos and headed to the United States; there he was sworn in as a US citizen and, after being inducted as a CIA officer, began his own formal training.

Within Vientiane Station, the team was placed under a new External Branch that was to focus on the full range of communist targets in Laos. This included the Soviets, the Chinese, the Poles in the ICC, the North

Vietnamese embassy, and the Pathet Lao. Brought in to head the branch was William Center, a Harvard-educated officer who had already served two tours in Tokyo.[5]

To provide cover, the branch was separated from the embassy and placed in a two-story building at the sprawling Vientiane compound for the US Agency for International Development (USAID), the body created under the State Department in 1961 to administer foreign aid and developmental assistance. That compound was near the city center, just a block away from the Arc de Triomphe clone that the RLG was slowly erecting at the top of Avenue Lane Xang.[6] As administrative camouflage, the two-floor building was said to house USAID's Research and Management Branch (RMB). Accordingly, case officers assigned to the External Branch were mostly given RMB titles.

Among the first intake at the RMB office were two fresh case officers. The first, Bernard "Bernie" D'Ambrosio, had been a US Marine during the Korean War before getting a degree at the University of Southern California and then completing graduate studies at the Fletcher School at Tufts University. He had joined the CIA in 1959 and had served a tour in Burma before shifting to Laos in January 1967.

The second, John LeClair, was a devout Catholic who had arrived with his wife and seven children in May.

It was this pair—D'Ambrosio and LeClair—who were given control over the six Thai. To test their new team's abilities, they were weaned over the first half of 1967 on a relatively easy slate of static projects against the North Vietnamese embassy. This was accomplished without incident, with the team rotating members close enough to the embassy to record who came and went on a regular basis.

The team then switched to a schedule of mobile surveillance, tailing North Vietnamese diplomats on their motorbikes to establish patterns of life. Said Albert,

> We never used radios or walkie-talkies to communicate with each other. We had no sophisticated gadgets at all. We just kept it simple, rotating the motorcyclist at point every few minutes when we were following someone. Our bikes were different colors, and we kept different color shirts and caps to change our appearance.

By the close of 1967, the case officers ratcheted up the difficulty level by shifting the team against the Pathet Lao representative office in Vientiane. That office had fluctuated greatly in size over the years. During the first coalition government in late 1957, the Pathet Lao had sent several dozen members—including two ministers—into the capital. Under increasing pressure, however, all had either fled or been jailed by 1959.[7]

In 1962 during the second coalition government, a far larger Pathet Lao contingent had returned to Vientiane. This contingent was spread among five houses around Vientiane. They were protected by their own Pathet Lao bodyguards, 120 of whom had been flown into the capital aboard ICC aircraft.

This expanded presence proved short-lived, however. Soon after Quinim Pholsena was assassinated in 1963, most of the Pathet Lao voted with their feet and withdrew to Sam Neua.[8] Half of its bodyguard company was flown back to the PDJ.[9]

Still, the Pathet Lao had insisted on the ongoing legality of the 1962 coalition and doggedly maintained a small residual presence in the capital. Of the previous five houses they had earlier occupied, their reduced delegation kept just two. The first, which housed their chief representative in Vientiane, was a two-floor, mustard-colored colonial building one block south of the vast Morning Market complex and behind the Ministry of Post Offices and Telecommunications. The second, formerly Souphanouvong's residence, was a similar-size building in the That Dam residential area, only 300 meters from the US embassy.

As the Pathet Lao delegation did not have diplomatic immunity of any kind, and the hardline rightists within the RLG saw it as an affront, the two outposts were highly vulnerable to harassment. And the FAR did not disappoint, often driving loud trucks in front of the buildings late at night and firing salvos into the air. After especially embarrassing defeats to the communists on the battlefield, it was even prone to pelting them with grenades.[10]

Under this kind of pressure, a sense of paranoia consumed the Pathet Lao delegation. For example, the top Pathet Lao representative, Soth Petrasy, forbid members of his security force not just from interacting with outsiders, but even from listening to RLG radio stations. And to help minimize contact and increase self-sufficiency, he had the delegation turn its compound lawns into vegetable patches. For the same reason, chickens, geese, and pigs roamed the walled grounds.[11]

Such was the situation when D'Ambrosio and LeClair attempted to get a clandestine foothold within the Pathet Lao enclaves. As a first step, they got word that a villa next to Souphanouvong's former residence had come up for rent. Discretely grabbing it on a long-term lease, they handed it over to John Allen, a second-generation CIA employee who had arrived in 1967 to fill a support slot at Vientiane Station. This worked out exceedingly well for both parties. For Allen, he got a spacious dwelling above his pay grade. And as he was a young bachelor with an active social life, the villa was a hive of activity that provided plenty of cover for External Branch officers to peer into the adjoining property; on an infrequent basis, they even engaged the Pathet Lao guards in conversation.[12]

As a second step, they brought in the Thai team. Very quickly the team learned that the Lao police and FAR maintained a close watch on both premises, making it hard to maintain a vigil for any length of time without drawing unwanted attention from the authorities. As a workaround, the team procured a noodle cart for Jack and let him spend several hours a day across from the chief representative's house.

The team took another step to bolster its cover when in 1968 it added its first female member. Bouakeo—who took the Western callsign Becky—was a 25-year-old college graduate and businesswoman from Songkla in southern Thailand. She immediately proved her worth when she paired up with Albert and masqueraded as a couple on dates. "Police would come by when we were loitering near the Pathet Lao office," said Albert, "but when they saw we were 'dating' they ignored us."

Eventually, the External Branch began to show progress. On the occasions when Pathet Lao members made the rounds of social events and diplomatic functions, they were sometimes accompanied by a former monk named Maha Bounyok. Sensing he might be able to open doors, D'Ambrosio found opportunities to meet and befriend Bounyok. In relatively short order, D'Ambrosio recruited him.

With the help of the ex-monk, the CIA was able to start fleshing out biographic profiles for the occupants of the two Pathet Lao houses. One member in particular stood out: a senior delegate named Phonsai, who was not actually a Pathet Lao ideologue linked back to Sam Neua, but rather traced his roots to the Patriotic Neutralist splinter faction from Phongsaly province. Although the Patriotic Neutralists were useful allies of the Pathet Lao in the anti-RLG front, they were sometimes seen as lesser revolutionaries. Because of this slightly tainted pedigree, the External Branch felt there might be an underlying grievance that could be exploited.

Those instincts were right. Using Maha Bounyok as an intermediary, Phonsai was indirectly sounded out over a period of months and was amenable to forging a clandestine relationship.

Enter the Thai team. After extended static surveillance, it had managed to piece together the daily routine of the occupants of the two Pathet Lao houses. The team noticed that despite the best efforts of the Pathet Lao to achieve food self-sufficiency, every day at dawn around half a dozen of them would file out of each residence, march to the Morning Market, and work their way through its maze of stalls while haggling over vegetables and meat. They normally stayed in a tight pack, though occasionally there would be stragglers that walked alone.

The team noticed that Phonsai was often one of the stragglers, probably by design. Taking advantage of this, D'Ambrosio prepared messages for Phonsai, which members of the team would slip to him as he belatedly exited the market.

Eventually, however, fate caught up. As Phonsai headed out of the market one morning, Albert used the brief window of opportunity to instruct him to go to the wall of his compound that evening at 2100 hours. The reason was because the CIA's Technical Services, whose primary focus was technical support of CIA case officers in the field, had fitted a microphone into the sole of a shoe for use as a listening device. Earlier this had been provided to Phonsai to place inside the Pathet Lao residence, but the device had stopped working. Phonsai was to hand over the shoe that evening for repairs.

As planned, three team members—Albert, Dick, and Tom—made their way to the compound that night. Not knowing which part of the perimeter Phonsai would approach, they spread out down the alley that ran alongside the residence.

Recalled Albert,

> The Pathet Lao compound usually had five geese, which were kept as watchdogs because they quacked very loudly whenever someone came near. But that night only two were alive. The others were gone, maybe poisoned but not sure by who. At the right time, I heard someone come near the other side of the wall, and after that a shoe was thrown over to my side. But then all of a sudden, the lights went on in the compound and there were voices. We all ran.

Not long thereafter, Maha Bounyok passed on the grim news that Phonsai had fallen under suspicion and had been recalled to Phongsaly for consultations. He never returned.

Another operation the team handled was a proverbial needle in a haystack. Through a confidential source close to the Pathet Lao office, the CIA learned that there was a Thai carpenter in Vientiane named Chamlong who had done some repair work at the representative office and appeared to be sympathetic to the leftist cause. If he could be recruited, this kind of target appealed to the External Branch. After all, carpenters theoretically had the access and ability to hide technical devices inside woodwork.

The problem was, the CIA knew only his name and occupation. The obvious solution was to have the team start working the streets. "I spoke Lao fluently," said Dick, "and I spent an entire week visiting every construction site I could find to ask if they heard of a Chamlong."

His persistence paid off. At a house being built along Rue That Khao near the riverfront, he found his man. After watching him for five days, Dick and Albert made a joint approach. Chamlong, they found, was cagey but eventually agreed to meet them for dinner. Two more dinners followed, washed down with liberal doses of alcohol. When asked at the end of the third if he would like to consider ways of earning a bigger paycheck, Chamlong indicated interest.

To bring it to the next level, a safe house was rented along the road to the airport. On the agreed day, Chamlong showed up and was met by John LeClair. Their tryst, however, ultimately fizzled. "He was not the brightest of the bright," assessed LeClair. "He would have been a low-level asset at best."

Chamlong, for his part, was highly intimidated by the American officer. "John had taken out a pen knife to clean his nails," explained Albert. "Chamlong got really scared by this, even with such a small blade."

"We never saw him again."

* * *

One operation undertaken by the Thai team was extremely successful, albeit not in abetting a recruitment within the Pathet Lao office but in averting a potentially serious loss of Agency lives and property. It began when the station received vague details about an RLG court messenger who exhibited strong leftist leanings. "The messenger had a good cover job because he was able to visit many different ministries," said Albert, "so Bernie told us to follow him for a couple of weeks."

This was easier said than done. Every afternoon, the messenger would depart the courthouse on his bicycle and pedal 22 kilometers west of the city to his home village. The journey would take hours as he worked his way past endless rice paddies. Far to the rear, team members Dick, Tim, and Albert tailed in their motorcycles, remaining nearly out of eyeshot so as not to arouse suspicion.

After they reported the results back to D'Ambrosio, the case officer told them to change tack and begin their tail in the morning from the messenger's village. As instructed, they were outside the village before first light as the messenger emerged for the laborious trek into town.

Halfway to the city limits, there was a payoff. The three team members watched from afar as the messenger paused at roadside and approached another bicyclist, this one with a caged rooster strapped to the back of his bike. They conversed for several minutes before heading their separate ways.

The following morning, the two bicyclists again had a roadside meeting en route to Vientiane. This time the team members noted that the mystery man on the second bike wore gray coveralls.

For the third day, the team was instructed to shift focus solely to the second bicyclist. It did so, following him to Wattay airport and confirming he was a ground staff employee of Air America.

After the team reported its results, D'Ambrosio was both ecstatic and concerned. Knowing the messenger's sympathies, a cloud of suspicion automatically fell on the Air America employee. As it turned out, those fears were well founded. Brought in by the Air America security officer for questioning, the ground staffer broke almost immediately. He admitted befriending the court messenger during cockfights and, following half a dozen meetings with other Pathet Lao sympathizers, had been recruited to place a bomb at Air America's Wattay office. The plan had been thwarted, he confessed, just days before its planned execution date.

★ ★ ★

In August 1968, Vientiane Station saw the arrival of Lawrence Devlin as the latest in a line of high-octane chiefs. The son of a US Army colonel, the New Hampshire-born Devlin had followed in his father's footsteps and enlisted in 1942. He impressed his superiors enough to earn a quick berth at Officer Candidate School and as a newly minted lieutenant was shipped off to see action in the Mediterranean and European theaters during World War II.

Leaving the army in 1946 at the rank of major, Devlin lost no time in getting his undergraduate degree in San Diego, then earning a graduate diploma at Harvard. He was planning to forge ahead for a doctorate were it not for a fateful meeting with a professor in late 1948 where the prospect of CIA employment was floated. Devlin was intrigued, signing on as an Agency contract officer under non-official cover (he posed as an editor) in Europe.[13]

After several years on contract, Devlin in 1953 converted to a fulltime Agency employee. Following another four years at headquarters, he was assigned to the embassy in Belgium in 1957. This prepared him for his next assignment, where he was to be station chief in the Belgian Congo.

The Congo promised to be a hardship tour, but it soon got far harder. When Devlin arrived in Leopoldville in July 1960, it was ten days after Congo had been granted independence from Belgium and five days after its nascent army mutinied. The city descended into chaos during that short interval, with Prime Minister Patrice Lumumba ultimately appealing to the Soviet Union for support against secessionists in the mineral-rich south. The mayhem continued through the end of Devlin's tour in 1963, during which time Lumumba was deposed and executed and the secessionist revolt was crushed by a United Nations intervention.

After a brief respite as chief of the East Africa branch at headquarters, Devlin returned to the Congo in 1965 for a second tour as station chief. If anything, the stakes had risen in the interim. A brutal communist-backed rebel movement had overtaken large swaths of the country during the first half of 1964, with thousands of Europeans and Congolese taken hostage. The Congolese army had largely folded, forcing the recruitment of hundreds of white mercenaries in Rhodesia and South Africa to prop up the government.[14]

Just prior to Devlin's arrival, the Agency had launched a diverse and extremely successful paramilitary operation that, together with the mercenaries and a Belgian airborne task force, had rescued the majority of foreign hostages (including CIA Chief of Base David Grinwis and two communicators at the US consulate in Stanleyville) and hobbled the rebels. That paramilitary program included use of Cubans—veterans of the Bay of Pigs—who manned CIA planes, spearheaded a ground commando force, and piloted Swift boats interdicting rebel supplies coming across Lake Tanganyika. Devlin maintained this paramilitary operation through his tour, crushing the final pockets of rebel resistance.

By the end of 1967, Devlin was back at Langley for a short stint at headquarters. By the time he landed in Vientiane to replace Shackley, those in the station could not help but feel a sense of *déjà vu*. Like Shackley before him, Devlin had no prior Far East experience. Also like his predecessor, he brought several of his colleagues (from the Congo) in tow. Among them was Eugene "Gene" Jeffers, who overlapped with Devlin during his first tour in Leopoldville, and Adger Player, who overlapped during his second.[15]

Also like Shackley, Devlin took over the station secure in the knowledge that his deputy chief was a seasoned Asia hand. That deputy, Clyde McAvoy, was a savvy New Yorker who had entered the CIA in 1953 and was quickly posted to Tokyo. There he showed a rare gift for recruitment when he befriended—and channeled covert financial support to—conservative Japanese politician Kishi Nobosuke. That support made McAvoy in no small part responsible for helping Nobosuke land the job of prime minister in 1957. When the US ambassador belatedly learned that a junior CIA case officer was "handling" Nobosuke, he was not amused; his shrill complaints led to a directive that from then forward the CIA station had to clear with the local ambassador any clandestine relationship with a head of state.

Back at headquarters, McAvoy obviously earned kudos for his feat in Tokyo. He did so again in 1961 after he was assigned to Jakarta. As the mercurial President Sukarno drew closer to Indonesia's communist party, McAvoy befriended Adam Malik, a journalist, politician, and diplomat who was one of the few senior Indonesian officials brave enough to eschew the communist tilt. This relationship would reap benefits in later years—after the Indonesian military crushed the communists in 1965—when Malik went on to become the foreign minister, speaker of the legislative branch, and vice president.

It was this strong Asia foundation that McAvoy took to Vientiane when he arrived in early 1968 to take over the deputy chief slot. As during Shackley's term, the marching orders given to Devlin and him were to maximize paramilitary activity against the North Vietnamese military to divert pressure off the South Vietnamese battlefield. Devlin would go on to do this with particular gusto, even earning internal detractors for his propensity to personally micromanage the paramilitary campaign.

Within Vientiane itself, the External Branch kept up its schedule of operations against communist targets. It had developed a particular fixation on the North Vietnamese embassy, which was understandable on two counts. First, there was an extremely vibrant Vietnamese population across Laos, a holdover from the waves of ethnic Vietnamese that arrived in the wake of World War I as France increased economic activity in its colonies. Even after Lao independence, Vietnamese still liberally peppered the civil service and commercial sector. As the North Vietnamese embassy appeared successful in winning over the loyalty of a substantial portion of this well-connected expatriate population, the CIA was weary of a fifth column.[16]

Second, the North Vietnamese embassy in Laos was one of North Vietnam's more important diplomatic outposts. Given difficulties in reaching Hanoi, it was often the default destination for everyone from journalists to wives of downed American pilots.[17] And in the first half of 1968, it was a critical conduit for confidential messages passed to the US embassy when Washington and Hanoi began exploring sites for possible peace talks.

The North Vietnamese embassy itself was on the western edge of town, a block away from where Rue Sam Sen Thai merged into the airport road to Wattay. It was an area called Nong Douang, Lao for "Beetle Pond." Appropriately, the embassy abutted an expansive catchment area that formed a shallow lake in the rainy season, a fetid swamp during the rest of the year.

During the Shackley era, North Vietnam's embassy had been an occasional target of the External Branch. After all, the Thai surveillance team had cut its teeth with static surveillance at Nong Douang during its first months in-country.

The team—or at least one of its members, Albert—was again targeted against the embassy in 1968. This had come about six months after the Paris peace talks began that May. As North Vietnam's embassy in Vientiane was being kept in the loop and sensitive telegrams were no doubt passing through its code room, the station contemplated a covert entry into that room to install technical gear that could ascertain the codes. If Hanoi's codes could be broken, this would give Washington a tremendous leg up in the peace talks.

The station knew the approximate location of the code room, which faced the rear of the embassy. But it needed to know if the room was vacant during the evening hours. Specifically, it wanted to know information like when its lights went on and off, and how many people were around it at night.

This is where Albert came into the picture. By that time, Albert had proven himself the team's most energetic and daring member. "He was one of those rare, marvelous agents who see Superman when they look in a mirror," remarked one of the branch's case officers. "That was why he became the *chouchou* of the entire Station. There was nothing he wouldn't do."

Problem was, the North Vietnamese embassy backed up to the Nong Douang—and the Nong Douang was in its swampy phase of the year.

Ever the trooper, Albert did not back down. The case officers wanted him to spend seven consecutive nights in the swamp, each visit lasting about four hours. As cover, he purchased a basket full of fish and frogs at the Morning Market; in the event he encountered anyone behind the embassy, he would display these as proof he was night-fishing.

On the first day of the assignment, Albert parked his motorcycle on the far north side of Nong Douang. It was a moonless night and nobody was in sight. Removing his sandals, he stepped into the slimy water. It was not deep, just over his knee. He remembered,

> I was all alone the whole time. The only thing I saw were snakes, but they left me alone. I got close to the rear wall of the embassy and noticed that there were several German Shepherds—probably around five—that were active inside the compound. I stayed for the four hours, made my observations, and then went back across the swamp. When I stepped out, there were ten huge leeches gorging on my legs.

On the second night, Albert retraced his path through the swamp. This time, he kept scraping his legs to dislodge any hitchhikers.

This continued for the rest of the week. Each time, he noted which lights went on and off. For the seventh and final night, a CIA officer impressed on him the need to focus on one particular room—the code room—and determine how many people were inside.

Albert did as he was instructed. He also attempted to catch some of the conversations in the compound. As he was dating a Vietnamese girl at the time—she was from Saigon, working at a Vientiane nightclub—he spoke a smattering of Vietnamese. However, while he could hear voices, he could not discern any of what was being said.

On that anticlimactic note, the swamp operation concluded, and Albert's legs made a speedy recovery. Given the fact that the compound appeared fairly busy at night, and it was guarded by multiple Alsatians, no covert entry was ever attempted.[18]

★ ★ ★

Albert's swamp foray was the last time the Thai team concerned itself with Nong Douang. By 1968, the team was spending virtually all their time against the Pathet Lao residences. As a result, the External Branch recognized the need to create a second surveillance team that could be dedicated solely against the North Vietnamese.

This time, the station decided it would use a different recruiting approach. Whereas the Thai team was fully unilateral—indeed, it was not even composed of Lao nationals—the North Vietnamese team would have help from a Lao counterpart.

Truth be told, the station still did not really have a clear local counterpart in Laos. Until 1960, there had been a civilian intelligence agency (albeit with strong military involvement), but it had been absorbed—along with military intelligence, the police, and customs—into Siho's DNC in early 1961. The CIA had maintained a liaison relationship with the DNC, though the embrace was less than full given Siho's increasingly ruthless reputation and preoccupation with vice. Siho tried to soften foreign criticism by rebranding the DNC in 1964, though he remained much the pariah.

After Siho fled to Thailand following a 1965 coup, his police-cum-intelligence empire had been summarily disbanded. This had allowed the National Police to be properly resurrected that December under the Ministry of Interior. Its Special Branch was part of that resurrection, and Vattha Phankham—now a colonel—resumed command.

As before, the CIA assigned one officer to the Police Special Branch for liaison as a collateral duty. Beginning in late 1965, that officer was Douglas Beed. A Berkeley graduate, Beed was part of a five-man CIA team that trained the Vietnamese Special Police under a cover contract with the University of Michigan in the late fifties.[19] Shifting to Laos, Beed found the Special Branch to be woefully undermanned.[20] In hindsight, the branch had also been penetrated by the North Vietnamese.[21]

Rated somewhat better was the FAR G-2, the military intelligence office led by Colonel Etam Singvongsa. Etam himself was no intelligence professional; he had landed the job on account of his personal loyalty to key generals in Vientiane. But his deputy, Oudom Phanthavong, was well trained and respected. Moreover, the G-2 had an interrogation section that was of special interest to the station.

The reason for this interest was because the interrogators included a large number of ethnic Tai Dam. The Tai are an upland minority group ethnically and linguistically similar to the Lao and Thai. The Tai Dam, or Black Tai, are a subset so named because of the black clothing traditionally favored by their females.

Geographically dispersed across mainland Southeast Asia, a large concentration of Tai had lived in the rugged highlands of northwestern Vietnam during the French era. As per an 1889 treaty, the Tai accepted the French as overlords; in return the French promised to respect Tai autonomy within the twelve Tai principalities. In 1948, the French went further by recognizing a Tai Federation, allowing the ethnic group its own flag, constitution, and parliament.

Among the Tai, however, the Tai Dam proved an especially fickle lot. Despite the concessions from the French, most Tai Dam allied themselves with the Viet Minh. A smaller number took up arms in support of the French but, fearing reprisals after the fall of Dien Bien Phu in 1954, fled Vietnam for northern Laos. Those Tai Dam initially settled around the PDJ, only to find the soil less fertile than in their homeland.

Packing once again, the Tai Dam refugees shifted southwest to the outskirts of Vientiane. There they found work as domestics, government employees, and soldiers. In the last category, several gravitated toward military intelligence. This was a natural fit because most Tai Dam were fluent in Vietnamese, and their linguistic talents were put to use while acting as interrogators for the growing number of North Vietnamese prisoners.

Among the Tai Dam in military intelligence, the most senior was a major named Bounnam. He had joined the French colonial army as a noncommissioned officer in 1952, working as a translator for an intelligence unit. Posted to Dien Bien Phu, he and two Tai relatives had escaped just prior to that garrison's fall. Two eventually reached French lines in Laos; the third was eaten by a tiger along the way.

After Lao independence, Bounnam joined the ANL as a civilian employee. He eventually drew close to Siho and was badged as a warrant officer in the intelligence component of the DNC. When the latter was dissolved, he transferred to the G-2 and was given the rank of captain.

His specialty was the interrogation of North Vietnamese, and by 1968 he was promoted to head of the G-2 interrogation section as a major.[22]

For the station, Bounnam was attractive on several counts. For one thing, he was fluent in Vietnamese. For another, he—and indeed most of the Tai Dam in his circle—had a visceral hatred for the North Vietnamese. Once he was approached and proved amenable to a discreet relationship with the station's External Branch, it was decided that he would helm its second surveillance team despite that he was a serving FAR officer.

With referrals from Bounnam, seven other team members were chosen. Six of them were fellow Tai Dam; one was Tai Dang—Red Tai, a subset named for the red clothing favored by their females. All were personally close to Bounnam, including his own brother and two cousins. Of the seven, three were civilians and four were active-duty FAR sergeants. Again, though this was not a truly unilateral operation, it was hoped that Bounnam could assure silence through their strong ethnic bond.

As with the Thai team, the Tai Dam team members took call signs for internal reporting. But instead of Western first names, they were given two-digit numbers. Bounnam was "03." His second-in-command was "04." This was a sly homage to James Bond. As one of the case officers noted, "If you add the two together what do you get?"

With call signs set, motorcycles procured, and a safe house rented, the team was unleashed against Nong Douang and the two dozen North Vietnamese therein.

As was the case with the Pathet Lao residences, the team found that the North Vietnamese embassy was under regular pressure from the RLG. After FAR's costly defeat at Nambac in January 1968, for instance, a grenade was thrown into the compound. Later in December, another grenade attack took place. And in March 1969, the embassy protested when the police harassed people leaving a film screening.[23]

Still, the team began making headway in identifying visitors to the embassy. In one case during August 1968, information gathered is believed to have led the RLG authorities to detain twelve foreign nationals—seven Chinese from Hong Kong and five from North Vietnam, including two Tai Dam—after a visit to Nong Douang. Media reports alleged the twelve were seeking contact with emissaries from the Communist Party of Thailand.[24]

The team also began fleshing out patterns of life for the North Vietnamese diplomats and staff. This information proved crucial during two separate attempts at recruiting a member of the embassy. The first attempt came after the team followed one embassy member to the infamous White Rose nightclub. The CIA was able to photograph him in a compromising position with a hostess, which it then tried to use to shame him into a discreet relationship. However, the diplomat shrugged off the embarrassment and the attempt fell flat.

In the second instance, the team scored a windfall when it discovered that the embassy's chauffeur was a fellow ethnic Tai Dam. They also confirmed that several times a week he would drive a carload of diplomats to the Morning Market and wait alone in the car while they made their purchases. The External Branch prepared a note for the chauffeur with a monetary offer, which was pushed through the car window while he was idling at the market one morning. Again, the attempt failed, as the chauffeur apparently reported the note and was immediately recalled to Hanoi.

Monitoring this progress was Deputy Station Chief McAvoy. Growing impatient with North Vietnamese intransigence, he chose the nuclear option. "Get rid of them," he ordered, according to one case officer. "We'll start again from scratch!"[25]

The resultant plan depended heavily on cooperation from the FAR G-2, specifically its counterintelligence staff under Major Kheuap Khumpol. The staff members were willing participants because they were well aware of North Vietnam's continued attempts to extend its clandestine network around Vientiane and other Lao towns. The G-2 also knew it could seize this opportunity to force the North Vietnamese to reduce its staff without fear of diplomatic reprisals. After all, ever since 1967 the RLG had de facto written off its embassy in Hanoi after the left-leaning ambassador went rogue and ignored directives to return home.[26]

The agreed-upon means of doing this was to have a military jeep manned by a member of the counterintelligence staff ram into a

North Vietnamese vehicle, providing a pretext to search the car and conveniently find incriminating documents. The Tai Dam team had already determined that the embassy personnel circulated in town according to a predictable schedule: they would leave in the morning for the market or breakfast at a pho shop, then again in the afternoon to visit sympathizers in the Dong Palane neighborhood on the eastern outskirts of town.

In the end, the scheme went off with barely a hitch. At 1700 on Saturday, 9 August, a jeep surged out of the Signal Corps barracks on Rue Sam Sen Thai and rear-ended a sedan with North Vietnamese diplomatic plates heading back from Dong Palane. Inside the sedan were six from the embassy, including Second Secretary Nguyen Song Hai, Vietnam News Agency correspondent Tran Ngoc Duc, and four staffers.

As the occupants got out to observe the damage, military police cars swooped in, placed the six in handcuffs, and whisked them off to the Defense Ministry compound at Phone Kheng.

The next day, 10 August, the RLG issued a press release stating that the arrest came after the North Vietnamese were speeding and acting suspicious immediately after the accident. They announced that all six would be deported on the next ICC flight to Hanoi, which was scheduled for Friday, 15 August.

Two days later, on 12 August, the RLG conducted a news conference. This time it debuted a more elaborate story claiming the diplomats had been using their clandestine network to procure a map of the key government base at Long Tieng. Such a map, along with attack routes penciled in, was allegedly found in the trunk of the diplomats' vehicle. This prompted calls from the National Assembly that the six be tried for treason, as well as some harsh rhetoric from Souvanna Phouma: "I believe Hanoi is trying to make Laos into a new type of colony."[27]

Meantime, while Hai claimed diplomatic immunity and was allowed to await deportation from the embassy, the other five remained at Phone Kheng. All were encouraged to request asylum, though none took up the offer. They were also squeezed for biodata about other diplomats at the embassy, as well as about regular visitors to Nong Douang. This led to a pair of further arrests of Vietnamese on 18 August, including one who was a contractor doing repairs at the embassy and another who was alleged to be one of their local intelligence agents.[28]

In the end, after two consecutive flights were canceled due to inclement weather, the six were bundled aboard an ICC plane on 26 August and sent packing to Hanoi. As they landed at Gia Lam to a sympathetic crowd led by the deputy foreign minister, one of the ex-detainees defiantly shed the clothes given at Phone Kheng and emerged in only his underwear.[29]

Though perhaps not the most elegant solution, the plan had succeeded in reducing the number of personnel at the North Vietnamese embassy by a quarter, leaving the embassy temporarily shorthanded to conduct operations in Vientiane. And as two further ethnic Vietnamese civilians had been detained, it likely made pro-Hanoi sympathizers leery of contact with Nong Douang for the time being. Finally, it gave the External Branch a chance to reboot and start North Vietnamese recruitment efforts anew.

CHAPTER 6

The Flying Squad

One of the largest, most convoluted, and—ultimately—successful operations conducted by the External Branch took place in late 1970 against a pair of Japanese medical doctors.

The story had begun four years earlier when preeminent British philosopher and pacifist Bertrand Russell teamed up with leading French philosopher Jean-Paul Sartre to channel their opposition to US involvement in the Vietnam War into what would become known as the Russell Tribunal. Officially constituted in November 1966, it was intended as a private tribunal that would critically investigate and evaluate US foreign policy in Indochina.

Given the level of media attention generated by Russell and Sartre, leftist peace organizations eagerly jockeyed to participate. While most were from Europe, there was an especially vocal chorus emanating from Japan. In fact, a month before the tribunal was formalized, seventy-six Japanese activists, with strong backing from the Japan Communist Party (JCP), had established the Japan Committee for the Investigation of War Crimes in Vietnam (JCIWCV).

The activists in the JCIWCV had backgrounds in various leftist causes, especially opposition to US military bases in Japan. But they were not especially well versed on Indochina. To better prepare themselves, a seven-man team departed Tokyo on 16 December 1966 for a tryst with fellow anti-war hardliners in London. While transiting in Hong Kong, however, it fell from sight. A week later, *Akahata*, the JCP's daily newspaper, reported that the team was actually in North Vietnam for a three-week investigative visit.[1]

By the time the JCIWCV members returned to Tokyo on 20 January 1967, they were brimming with revolutionary fervor. While in Hanoi they had been feted by none other than North Vietnamese President Ho Chi Minh, who lauded the JCIWCV and urged that the Russell Tribunal hand out sentences that would outdo the Nuremburg trials.[2] The committee pledged to hold rallies in Japan during February and March with another JCP front, the Japan Afro-Asian Solidarity Committee.[3] It also promised to present physical evidence of Japanese collusion with the Americans, though it would later produce nothing more than a US Army helmet with a Japanese manufacturer's stamp.[4]

As it turned out, the JCIWCV's militancy was a double-edged sword. Bertrand Russell, for one, bristled at the insistence to add worldwide national liberation to the tribunal's agenda.[5] For another thing, the JCP, which maintained tight control over the JCIWCV from behind, clashed with tribunal founder Jean-Paul Sartre because it considered him too much of a Maoist.

The friction even turned inward, as was apparent during the first week of May 1967 when the tribunal held its first session in Stockholm. A JCIWCV delegation was in attendance, but one of its two nominated judges—Nobel Laureate and noted Japanese physicist Sakata Shoichi—was dropped at the eleventh hour. The reason: the JCP felt his ideological purity was wanting.

After this shaky start, the JCIWCV decided to hold its own independent session—dubbed the Tokyo Tribunal—in late August 1967. This would focus not only on alleged American transgressions against North Vietnam, but also on Japanese complicity. To gather more data for this tribunal, the committee sent its second fact-finding team to Hanoi in July.

Heading the team was Zenzaburo Funazaki, the chief of surgery at Saku Central Hospital in Nagano Prefecture. With him were four others, including a cameraman. Arriving on 3 July, they split into two groups. The first went to the southernmost provinces of North Vietnam; the second remained in the vicinity of Hanoi.

By the time they departed Hanoi for Tokyo on 31 July, Funazaki and his colleagues claimed to have gathered damning evidence against the

United States. This was somewhat of an overstatement; in fact, most of what they had amassed was North Vietnamese propaganda that did not hold up to scrutiny. For example, they trumpeted Hanoi's charge that the United States was spraying defoliants and other toxic chemicals over North Vietnam; in hindsight, this is known not to have been the case.[6]

On 28 August, the three-day Tokyo Tribunal opened at a public hall in Chiyoda district. To an audience of 500, the JCIWCV offered its testimony and, in a foregone conclusion, declared the United States guilty and the Japanese government complicit.

Three months later, on 13 November, the JCP's *Akahata* newspaper announced that a JCIWCV delegation of two judges and three witnesses—including Dr. Funazaki—were heading to Copenhagen for the Russell Tribunal's second and final session scheduled for early December. Once again, however, ideological differences rattled the tribunal. Specifically, the JCIWCV delegation clashed with the French Trotskyists that dominated the tribunal's secretariat. The Japanese threatened a walkout on the eve of the session, were eventually persuaded to stay, and then were sharply berated by the JCP when they returned to Tokyo for not standing up to the French. So great was the JCP's ire that they closed the door on future cooperation with European anti-war activists and even debated whether to disband the JCIWCV.[7]

Ultimately, the JCP's anger subsided and the JCIWCV remained on the books. In December 1968, the JCIWCV even sent a third investigating team to North Vietnam. This one consisted of four members who spent ten days touring the southern end of the country.[8]

Despite the fact that the latest fact-finding team garnered relatively little publicity, the US government was not happy with the continued provocative efforts by the JCP's front. Concern only grew in the second half of 1970 when the CIA's Tokyo Station got word that a fourth JCIWCV fact-finding team intended to visit North Vietnam. This time, the Japanese planned to gather data for the "International Meeting of Scientists on Chemical Warfare in Vietnam," scheduled to be held in Orsay, France, on 12 December.

For the CIA leadership at Langley, patience with the JCIWCV had fully run out. As it was known that the Japanese team would be transiting Laos on the way in and out of Hanoi, it was decided that Vientiane

Station—specifically, the External Branch—would get the assignment of frustrating the JCP's plans.

By that time, the branch had expanded and bifurcated. Clandestine operations against the Pathet Lao and North Vietnamese occupied one half of the RMB building; an emergent wing handling Soviet and Chinese targets occupied the other. The former was headed at the time by James Haase, a seasoned officer with a long history in Southeast Asia.[9] So busy were his case officers that he had taken to calling them the Flying Squad, a name adopted from the anti-robbery surveillance unit created by Scotland Yard at the beginning of the century.

Because he knew headquarters was watching closely, Haase assembled nearly his entire squad for the JCIWCV assignment. At its core were the case officers in the Pathet Lao section: Bernie D'Ambrosio, John LeClair, and Paul Seema (who had returned to the roster, this time as a US citizen). Joining them since mid-1970 was a fourth officer, William "Howie" McCabe. A lawyer by education, McCabe had entered the CIA in 1960 and was part of the successful covert-action program that prevented a pro-Cuban government from taking over British Guiana during the final years before that self-governing colony achieved total independence.[10]

Three other case officers rounded out the squad. The first, Alan, was a polyglot who handled the Tai Dam team against the North Vietnamese embassy. The second, George Evans, was a former Marine officer who had scored an earlier intelligence coup when a Cambodian lieutenant colonel ventured to Vientiane to provide conclusive evidence that most communist supplies were flowing through Cambodia's Sihanoukville, not down the Ho Chi Minh Trail.[11] The third, George Welyczko—alias George Velesko—was a Ukrainian émigré on his first overseas assignment.

A few days before the JCIWCV team was scheduled to depart Tokyo on 22 November, the eight case officers gathered at the safe house used by the Thai surveillance team. The Thais had moved four times since arriving in 1966. Now at their fifth safe house, they were located in Dong Palane, the neighborhood on the eastern outskirts of town known as a backpacker's paradise for its lower-end restaurants and bars. On a back street, the team had found a suitable villa ringed by high concrete walls that provided sufficient privacy.

Huddling in the villa's rear yard, the CIA officers spent the early afternoon eating, drinking, and playing liar's dice, an especially apropos game that put a premium on deceiving and detecting an opponent's deception. Then they got down to business reviewing the intelligence to date. They knew the Japanese team was to consist of only two members. The first was Zenzaburo Funazaki, 47, the same doctor who had visited North Vietnam in 1967 and attended the Copenhagen session. The second was Akinori Masuda, 33, the head of a hospital dispensary in Kyoto. The two were scheduled to fly to Bangkok on Japan Airlines, then take an overnight train to Nong Khai and cross to Vientiane on the morning of Monday, 23 November.

From Vientiane, the Japanese would have limited options to get to Hanoi. The ICC contracted with a French-crewed Stratoliner that flew from Vientiane to the North Vietnamese capital every Friday. Although the flight was not commercial, North Vietnam could reserve seats for guests. In addition, since October 1970 Aeroflot had initiated service with an Ilyushin Il-18 turboprop from Vientiane to Hanoi, also flying on Fridays. This meant that the two doctors would almost certainly be transiting in Vientiane for four days before catching an onward flight.

With this limited information, the Flying Squad decided the best course of action would be to prevent the JCIWCV members from ever reaching Hanoi. Brainstorming the means of doing this, the squad figured it could look for opportunities to steal their passports or other travel documents; because it would likely take longer than four days to get replacements, they would miss that week's flights to Hanoi.

On the date the Japanese were scheduled to arrive—Monday, 23 November—D'Ambrosio crossed the Mekong to Nong Khai to await the northbound train from Bangkok. Shortly before it pulled in, he went down the row of cycle rickshaws congregating near the station's exit. Pulling out a wad of Thai baht, he paid all of them to make themselves absent for the next hour.

On schedule, the train appeared and the passengers disembarked. With no rickshaws available, the two doctors were forced to walk with their suitcases the half kilometer to the Mekong ferry crossing. This was done to tire out and frustrate the overweight Funazaki.

On the Lao side of the Mekong, the Thai surveillance team was waiting as the ferry docked. The Thais easily picked out to the two doctors and followed them six kilometers into town before arriving at the government-owned Lane Xang Hotel. Members of the Flying Squad followed inside and watched as the pair checked in and went to their room.

Now the squad shifted its attention to the telephones. It had already recruited an employee at the Lao telecommunications ministry, allowing it to monitor calls in and out of the Lane Xang. Around noon, members listened as Funazaki contacted the ICC office to confirm reservations on that Friday's Stratoliner to Hanoi. An Indian working at that office told them to be at Wattay by 0800 hours.

An hour later, the unique services of Richard Lammon came into play. Vientiane Station's resident Technical Operations Officer since August 1969, Lammon had Hollywood in his blood—literally. He explained,

> I was one of the original kids in Viola Spolin's Young Actors Company, just north of Hollywood Boulevard. I was a red-headed, freckle-faced kid, and was cast in those sorts of roles. In 1947, Hal Roach tried to revive the Our Gang comedies. I was called to audition for one of the kids therein. "Very nice. We'll be in touch. Don't call us, we'll call you." They never called. I've recounted that story to a lot of people over the years, and some of them walked away thinking I got the part. I must admit that I never tried to disabuse them of that innocent misconception. Who wants to disavow one's fifteen minutes of fame?[12]

Lammon may never have gotten that part, but twenty-three years later he got his chance to show off his acting chops. Placing a call to the ICC office, he mimicked Funazaki's broken English and canceled the Stratoliner reservations. While the squad knew the ICC flights to Hanoi were normally empty, there was always the chance the upcoming flight would be unusually full and the doctors would be off the roster.

Sticking with the original plan, the squad was still hoping it could steal the travel documents of the two targets. The Thai surveillance team was ringing the hotel and three from the squad were inside monitoring the lobby and coffee shop, but the doctors had failed to emerge as of early evening.

Lammon placed a call to the doctors' room. This time impersonating the accent of the Lane Xang's Indian security guard, he told them that the hotel was having power trouble and that they could expect a blackout within the next hour. It was hoped this would prompt them to exit the hotel for dinner. Still, neither emerged.

The next morning, the Thai team resumed its vigil. Not until dusk did the doctors finally pass through the lobby and get into a sedan waiting in front of the hotel. With most of the Thai team following from a discreet distance, the targets were trailed to a Japanese restaurant on Rue de That Khao. A third man, possibly a Japanese diplomat, entered with them and the trio ordered dinner. The surveillants noted that Funazaki was carrying a denim bag over his shoulder.

Back at the Lane Xang, the squad had instructed Dick and Albert to surreptitiously enter the targets' room to search for travel documents. The Lane Xang used old-style locks, and the CIA's Technical Services had already crafted a skeleton key that could defeat them. With Albert keeping vigil at the door, Dick went inside. The luggage was not secured, enabling a quick check of the contents. Finding an envelope with documents in Japanese tucked into a side compartment, Dick took them and was back out the door within five minutes. These documents were later determined to be medical certificates listing the vaccination shots the two had taken prior to travel to Hanoi.

On Wednesday, 25 November, the Thai began their third day of surveillance. As during the previous day, the doctors only left the Lane Xang at dusk to have dinner at the Japanese restaurant on Rue de That Khao. And like the previous day, Funazaki had the denim bag over his shoulder; as no passports were found in the hotel room, the squad theorized that these and other important items were in this bag.

Thinking outside the box, the squad conjured a backup plan to torpedo the JCIWCV's Hanoi trip. To that time, the RLG had been painfully slow in outlawing heroin and opium within the kingdom. However, if the doctors were to be caught with heroin in their luggage while boarding at Wattay, the ICC would almost certainly blacklist them from the flight. Using this line of reasoning, the squad had obtained an envelope full of heroin and passed it off to Dick and Albert, who then made their second surreptitious hotel entry in as many days. As instructed, they hid the envelope deep inside one of the compartments in the luggage.

By Thursday morning, the squad had two plans—the seat cancellations and the heroin—in play. But still not sure this would prevent the pair from getting to Hanoi, it decided to try one more option. If the doctors again went to the Japanese restaurant for dinner, and if Funazaki was again carrying the denim shoulder bag, Albert would try to snatch the bag on the street and speed away on a motorcycle. While not the most elegant solution, it would get the job done.

Albert, as always, was up to the challenge. Bob, the team leader, was to be idling nearby in his motorcycle to provide a getaway. "I told Bob not to turn off the motorcycle," said Albert; "whatever you do, do not turn it off."

That evening, the doctors were met by a sedan at the hotel and driven to their usual restaurant on Rue de That Khao. Accompanied by two younger Japanese—most probably from the embassy—the sedan parked in front and the four went inside to eat.

With D'Ambrosio watching over the scene in his Volkswagen at the end of the block, Bob waited on his motorcycle and Albert loitered near the restaurant entrance.

After ninety minutes, the two doctors emerged. When Funazaki paused near the rear door of the sedan, Albert confidently strode forward and opened the door for him. Assuming Albert was the restaurant's valet, Funazaki offered a smile and bent forward to get in the car. Albert then let his hand slide over the strap to the shoulder bag and yanked with all his might. The doctor lost his footing and let the bag fall into Albert's hands.

That night, the stars were not aligned in Albert's favor. As he took off down the block in a sprint, the two younger Japanese emerged from the restaurant and—seeing what they thought was a mugging—set off in hot pursuit.

At the end of the block, Bob saw Albert approaching at full speed. But failing to heed the advice he had been given, he had turned off the motorcycle. Now racing to restart the engine, it would not turn over. Albert reached him, cursed Bob for not idling as instructed, and looked over his shoulder at the fast-closing Japanese pursuers. Figuring he was better off on foot, Albert left Bob behind and continued his sprint down the block. The two Japanese, meantime, reached Bob and grabbed his shirt. The motorcycle engine finally kicked in; lunging forward, Bob made a narrow escape with his shirt in shreds.

Albert still could not catch a break. Though he had put a good distance between himself and the Japanese, an off-duty FAR captain at the end of the block had watched the incident unfold. Thinking he had witnessed a mugging, he lunged forward and tackled Albert to the ground. Albert covered his head as the captain laid in with some sharp kicks. The Japanese pursuers caught up and landed a few kicks of their own. Albert was then put in a head lock and manhandled to a police station a block away.

From the Volkswagen, D'Ambrosio watched the comedy of errors transpire. Shaking his head, he drove away slowly from the scene of the crime.

At the police station, Funazaki briefly showed up to recover his denim bag. Albert was left behind to languish in a cell for a few hours until the Flying Squad could get the station's liaison with the Special Branch to arrange his quiet release. "There was more than $1,000 in the bag," said the senior police officer on duty. "You should have gotten away."

As Albert licked his wounds and his pride, D'Ambrosio caught up and told him to take a week's rest at the southern Thai town of Hua Hin.

The next morning, the two doctors headed to Wattay. According to their later testimony, they remained under the impression that the previous night's incident was nothing more than a case of simple street crime. That was the only bit of good news for the squad. The ICC flight was empty, and the doctors were apparently not even aware their seats were cancelled. Worse, although the Lao police at Wattay had been tipped off to make a thorough search of the luggage to find the heroin, the timid officer at the customs desk waved the doctors through without so much as a cursory inspection.

Later that afternoon, the doctors arrived in Hanoi. As luck would have it, they benefited from a windfall of sorts. A week before their arrival during the early morning hours of 21 November, the US military had staged a daring heliborne rescue operation at the Son Tay prison, 37 kilometers west of Hanoi. The prison was a dry hole—no American prisoners of war were to be found—and there were no casualties among the rescue force. Because there had been some diversionary airstrikes and napalm ground markers dropped to help with navigation, there was a fresh trove of ordnance fragments for the doctors to peruse.

Over the next eight days, the two Japanese spent considerable time in the vicinity of the Son Tay operation. There they viewed what they termed an unexploded "orange bomb" and a "spider bomb."[13] Still parroting Hanoi's claim that the US was spraying defoliants and other toxic sprays on North Vietnam, they also met with alleged victims of chemical warfare.[14]

While in Hanoi, the doctors made some odd discoveries. First, their vaccination cards were missing. Second, an envelope with mysterious white powder had materialized in their luggage. They immediately flushed the latter down the toilet.[15]

Meantime, back in Vientiane the Flying Squad was under mounting pressure to show results. Their window of opportunity was fast narrowing, as the two doctors were scheduled to depart Hanoi on the 5 December ICC flight to Vientiane, then take a plane the next morning to Bangkok and immediately return to Tokyo.

In desperation, Lammon called the Thai Airways office and, again mimicking a Japanese accent, canceled their reservations from Vientiane to Bangkok on the morning of 6 December. The squad then made reservations for every extra available seat to Bangkok for the entire following week. This all but guaranteed that the pair would not be flying out from Laos before the Orsay meeting.

As scheduled, the Japanese left Hanoi on the early morning of 5 December. At Wattay, the Lao police had again been encouraged by the squad to conduct a thorough search of the two Japanese arrivals. This time the police showed a bit more interest; however, as nothing suspicious was found—the heroin was gone—the doctors were allowed to leave the airport and go directly back to the Lane Xang. Perhaps spooked because of the recent string of unlucky happenings—the attempted mugging, the missing vaccination cards, the white powder in the envelope—the two remained sequestered in their room the entire day.

At dawn the next morning, 6 December, the pair headed to Wattay. To their surprise and chagrin, their reservations were canceled and all flights were fully booked courtesy of the Flying Squad. Desperate for an alternative, they contacted the Japanese embassy. If they could get to Nong Khai, the doctors were told, they could catch a train to Bangkok and still make their late-night Japan Airlines connection to Tokyo.

Piling their luggage into a taxi, the pair raced through town. The Thai team was tailing them, feeding updates to its case officers as it arrived at the ferry landing. As the doctors were obviously headed for Nong Khai, the squad made a fast set of phone calls to Bangkok Station. Seeking to make use of tight connections with Thai law enforcement, the squad asked that Thai customs officials scrutinize the luggage of the doctors at the Nong Khai river landing and find a reason to detain them.

As added insurance, D'Ambrosio beckoned Albert, who was back from his sabbatical in Hua Hin. "Bernie told us that if the Japanese got on the train at Nong Khai, we were to go on the train, too," he recalled. "On the way to Bangkok we were told to steal their denim bag and throw it out the window of the moving train."[16]

It never came to that. After passing immigration at Nong Khai without incident, the Japanese went up to the customs desk. There the officer on duty asked them to open their luggage. Spotting a Ho Chi Minh medallion—which the doctors had purchased in Hanoi—the officer declared they had "items unfavorable to Thailand." He told them the luggage was being kept for secondary inspection and the pair—minus passports and tickets—would need to wait at a local hotel room.

The doctors were furious but could not talk their way out. Sent to the hotel, they placed a call to the Japanese embassy in Bangkok and demanded assistance. By the time a consulate official arrived that night, a story had already been leaked to the local press that the doctors possessed code books for contacting clandestine agents in Vientiane, Bangkok, and Kuala Lumpur.[17]

This, it turns out, was the *coup de grace* from the Flying Squad. Members of the squad had tailed the doctors to Nong Khai and, as soon as the Japanese were bundled off to the hotel, got a close look at their luggage. Inside squad members found tape recordings and sixteen rolls of movie and still images. They also found an address book and three meticulous diaries. These books were rushed across the Mekong to Vientiane, followed by a message sent to Okinawa—where the CIA's Technical Services had a sizable regional base—for the urgent services of a skilled forger.

Getting the assignment was Tony Mendez, who had already been to Laos for several prior short deployments. Helping him was Reiko, the Japanese wife of CIA officer "Don Eric," who was posted to Vientiane on nonofficial cover with a travel agency.[18] Mendez and Reiko were tasked with altering Funazaki's books with incriminating entries to make it look as though the doctor was engaged in clandestine activities across the region.[19]

Working out of Don Eric's house, the pair looked over the material at hand. Besides an address book from a 1967 trip to Hanoi, Funazaki had two diaries: one for his 1967 trip, the other for his current visit.

Ironically, as Reiko quickly read over the existing entries, there were already plenty that raised eyebrows. At the beginning of the diary for the latest trip, Funazaki wrote that JCP officials had seen him off at the airport in Tokyo. And on his arrival in Hanoi, he was met by Doki Tsuyoshi, a member of the JCP Central Committee and the top JCP representative in North Vietnam.[20] This only served to further confirm that the JCIWCV was a front for the JCP.

Other entries indicated inner thoughts troubling the doctor. For example, Funazaki wrote that much of the material he gathered in 1967 was secondhand or hearsay, and he hoped that his current trip would result in "real" evidence of nerve gas—implying that even he was not convinced by the evidence to date. Then there was a 28 November diary entry about a conversation with Colonel Mai Lam, the North Vietnamese liaison officer with the ICC. Funazaki wrote that he made arrangements with Mai Lam for Japanese newsmen to visit communist-held areas of Laos and Cambodia, but they agreed to keep word from the JCP. This suggested that the internecine squabbles in the JCP had the doctor on guard.

As Mendez and Reiko had less than a day with the documents, they set to work crafting some damning fictitious entries. Although the doctors had gone back through Nong Khai because the airlines were booked, it was decided to make that travel look intentional. Reiko wrote a line in Japanese reading, "Colonel Mai Lam gave instructions for meeting North

Vietnamese agent in Nong Khai." After that, she wrote the words, "Red Gladiolus," a reference to the flowing plant that could be interpreted as code words for the agent.

Mendez then painstakingly copied these words on a few blank lines after Funazaki's 1 December diary entry. Reiko coached him on proper stroke order for the Japanese characters to make it look like they were done by a native writer.

For the address book, Reiko composed an entry that read, "Meet agent on left side of Nong Khai railroad station at 1630 hours; carry Japanese magazine and wear glasses for recognition." Finally, Mendez wrote some coded contact instructions on water-soluble paper and hid these in the spine of the diary.

Done by mid-afternoon, the Flying Squad rushed the altered documents back to the customs office in Nong Khai.

As this was transpiring, the JCIWCV in Tokyo on 7 December issued a public statement demanding that its two members be released.[21] Dragging heels, the Thai authorities gave the doctors back a few of their possessions—dictionaries, blank hotel stationary—that day. It was not until late on 8 December that the doctors got back their passports and were told they could proceed by train to Bangkok with an escort from the Japanese embassy. However, all the material they had collected in North Vietnam—sixteen rolls of film and movies, tape recordings, address book, and diaries—were retained by the Thai police.

Boarding a Japan Airlines flight at Don Muang International Airport late on 9 December, the doctors reached Haneda airport in Tokyo by the morning of 10 December. Fuming, they gave an impromptu press conference at the airport during which they recounted their travel woes.

★ ★ ★

Although they had relied on a backup plan to a backup plan to a backup plan, the Flying Squad had ultimately got the job accomplished. Funazaki did manage to cobble together a weak paper and send it to the Orsay conference, but whatever tape recordings, films, and photos he had collected were lost.[22]

In a postscript to the operation, the *Bangkok Post* ran an exposé in late March 1971 entitled "Diary of a Secret Agent." It described how the Royal Thai Police Special Branch and the Royal Thai Army's powerful Communist Suppression Operations Command, in cooperation with US intelligence officials, were still combing through Funazaki's diary for clues about his alleged clandestine network.[23]

And in a postscript to the postscript, the JCIWCV sent another two-man fact-finding team to Hanoi in early June 1972; this one came and went with virtually no media attention. Funazaki was not among them, having apparently learned his lesson. Later that same month, activists from the Russell Tribunal floated the idea of holding a third session in Tokyo, only to be shot down by the JCP because it could not get past its simmering ideological feud with Jean-Paul Sartre. On that anticlimactic note, both the tribunal and the Japanese committee were quietly disbanded.[24]

CHAPTER 7

The Holy Grail

By the fourth quarter of 1970, Larry Devlin had clocked in two years and it was time for Vientiane Station to get a new chief. Landing the job was Bernardo Hugh Tovar, 48. Born in Colombia to a wealthy coffee plantation owner and a mother from Chicago, Tovar had become a naturalized US citizen at four. At twenty, he entered the US Army during World War II and, after squeezing in time to complete a degree from Harvard, was assigned to the OSS in the Asian theater.

After the war, Tovar would continue with studies at both Northwestern and Georgetown. He then joined the CIA in 1952 and, following a stint at headquarters, was deployed to Manila. Two years later, he made a lateral transfer to Malaya and was promoted to head of Kuala Lumpur Station.

In May 1964, Tovar returned to Southeast Asia as station chief in Jakarta. Indonesia was a powder keg at the time, with the increasingly authoritarian President Sukarno overseeing a moribund economy and taking great delight in baiting the West. Also, the Indonesian Communist Party, at 3 million members the third largest in the world after the PRC and the Soviet Union, was consolidating its influence over the bureaucracy and most branches of the armed forces.

It was in this stifling atmosphere that communist members within the Indonesian military attempted a power grab by assassinating the top tier of army leadership during the early hours of 1 October 1965. Six generals were killed, but many others remained. Among them, Suharto emerged as the catalyst for a decisive army countercoup. Unleashing grassroots religious organizations—who had bristled as the competition offered by the leftists—there was a months-long orgy of violence that utterly vanquished the communist party.

None in the US embassy, including Jakarta Station, had foreseen this momentous turn of events. "We knew the Javanese led the army, all those generals with 'Su' in front of their names," Tovar would later recount. "But we barely knew who Suharto was before then."

Ironically, Tovar was picking up some intelligence on Laos from his perch in Jakarta. This dated back to April 1965 when Kong Le—who had promoted himself to major general as head of the FAN—spent a month in Indonesia as a guest of the army. At the end of that period, he agreed to send nearly a battalion of FAN students for both airborne and commando training in August. For the Indonesian army trainers, the Lao proved to be a constant disciplinary challenge. Said Tovar, "We got word that the Indonesians were complaining the Lao were contracting a lot of venereal diseases."

In August 1966, Tovar departed Indonesia. Another headquarters posting ensued, after which he arrived in Vientiane in October 1970. In fact, this was not the first time he had been to that town. As an OSS first lieutenant, he had been assigned to what was termed a "Raven mission." This had a dual mandate: part diplomatic (they were to accept the surrender of Imperial Japanese garrisons) and part humanitarian (they were to provide medical relief at Allied prisoner-of-war camps).

In September 1945, the C-47 with Tovar's nine-man Raven team had approached Vientiane. Below they could see the drop zone at Phone Kheng, later the site of the gendarmerie camp from which Souphanouvong escaped and after that the site of the RLG's new Ministry of Defense complex. One of his colleagues would later ask him about the experience:

> Hugh told me that he had no parachute training other than being told how to handle the chute in landing. Since I had made a few jumps and it was scary, I asked him if he was concerned what to do once out of the plane. He said that he never thought about it, as he was more concerned about the thousands of armed Japanese on the ground whose surrender he was supposed to officiate. Hugh always had the right perspective.[1]

Fortunately for all those involved, there was not a Japanese soldier in sight, as they had already abandoned that part of Laos. Aside from one parachutist fracturing a leg and some of the supplies getting damaged due to a faulty chute, Tovar's Raven mission concluded without incident.

Now back in Vientiane as station chief, Tovar brought a wholly different style of leadership than his immediate predecessor. Devlin, after all, had proven to be a micromanager with sharp elbows, constantly inserting himself into tactical paramilitary decisions. In doing so, he had won few fans at Udorn, the paramilitary rear headquarters. The bad blood culminated in his attempting to have the paramilitary chief at Udorn sacked when it was found he had an unacknowledged Thai family. The chief then sent backchannel appeals to the White House, which intervened to have him stay at his post.[2]

By comparison, Tovar made clear at the outset that Udorn had his confidence in executing the paramilitary program. He was also a consummate diplomat. Fluent in French, he quickly bonded with Souvanna Phouma. And little sunlight emerged between him and G. McMurtrie "Mac" Godley, who had arrived as ambassador in July 1969.

On top of all this, Tovar knew that Washington would be scrutinizing his performance. This was because Laos had just come off a disastrous first half of 1970. With Long Tieng teetering on collapse in March, Vientiane Station had taken the unprecedented step of issuing a so-called Aardwolf cable to headquarters—usually reserved for the direst of circumstances.[3] This had fixated the attention of both President Richard Nixon and National Security Advisor Henry Kissinger; the two had traded memos and phone calls on Laos throughout that month, with both displaying a remarkable familiarity with units down to the battalion level.

By the summer of 1970, the communist onslaught against the kingdom had eased somewhat. Still, when Devlin was called to the White House in July, Brigadier General Alexander Haig, the deputy assistant to the president for National Security Aaffairs, emphasized that Nixon wanted even more paramilitary pressure to be exerted against the North Vietnamese.

It was this mandate for further paramilitary expansion that Tovar had inherited. Complying with White House demands, the paramilitary program defied gravity and continued its exponential growth. To handle the influx of CIA advisors, a subsidiary of Air America—called the Pacific Engineering Company, or Penco—was used as a means of administrating contract paramilitary officers.[4] By June 1971, there were twenty-five Penco employees assigned to Udorn, as well as ninety-six assigned to Vientiane (all but two of which were either paramilitary officers or support staff dispersed to the outer provinces). This was in addition to the full-time CIA employees already assigned to Udorn and Laos under diplomatic cover, not to mention the hundreds genuinely working for contract airlines.[5]

Together, these advisors, administrators, and airmen planned and executed the expanding and multifaceted covert paramilitary campaign in Laos. The backbone to the program was increasingly conventional in nature, with guerrilla battalions being gathered into what were de facto light infantry regiments. These regiments—termed *groupements mobiles*, or GMs—sparred with the North Vietnamese to control strategic real estate, primarily around the PDJ in the northeast and the Bolovens Plateau in the south. They occasionally even slashed at the Ho Chi Minh Trail along the eastern periphery of the panhandle. One CIA paramilitary officer was normally assigned to each GM, accompanying them on combat deployments—and often remaining with them in harm's way close to the frontline.

On the other end of the paramilitary spectrum were team operations. Some of these took on a strategic dimension, like when Udorn in 1968 conceived of the Commando Raider program. The Commando Raiders were imagined as super-guerrillas to be given exhaustive training in everything from parachuting to sabotage. The idea was that they could make incursions into North Vietnam and hit targets with strategic signif- icance. In July 1969, Nixon himself had approved an initial Commando Raider outing against a North Vietnamese military headquarters at Dien Bien Phu. This did not actually take place until February 1970; it had fairly good results. Tovar inherited this Commando Raider program, though further successes would remain elusive. By 1972, with marginal results to show after spending more than $3 million, further Commando Raider strikes into North Vietnam were shelved.[6]

By comparison, most other team operations were far less flashy than the Commando Raiders—though far more effective and efficient. The majority of these teams consisted of local recruits from the Lao panhandle who were targeted against the Ho Chi Minh Trail to collect tactical intelligence that could either be exploited by the guerrilla regiments or, more frequently, by US airpower.

In a few isolated cases, the teams were composed of prisoners who were enticed to switch sides. In late 1970, the CIA's Pakse Unit had initiated a concerted effort toward these ends by upgrading its interrogation center with two-way mirrors and bugs in every room. In addition, Saigon Station provided the center with an ethnic Vietnamese assistant. Tangible results would prove elusive, however, as recalled by resident CIA officer Malcolm Kalp:

> We managed to turn two North Vietnamese prisoners. They were brought down to Khong Island by the Vietnamese assistant, and then we inserted them deep into Cambodia by an Air America H-34. The pair only sent one message after insertion and then went silent.[7]

In June 1971, Savannakhet Unit upgraded its interrogation center with a similar eye toward turning prisoners. To help run it, Kalp moved there along with the Vietnamese assistant from Saigon Station, plus one other local Vietnamese hired for translations. Said Kalp,

> This became the CIA's dedicated proselytizing facility in mid-1972 for all defectors and prisoners from around the country, whether North Vietnamese or Pathet Lao. Once they were interrogated locally, they were sent here and targeted for recruitment. We had two cooperative defectors who posed as cellmates with the recent arrivals; they helped us identify the newcomers most likely to flip. We ended up recruiting two North Vietnamese, codenamed Silver and Gold.[8]

These two North Vietnamese were added to a four-man Lao team. "The plan was for them to dress and act like a communist patrol and operate along the Ho Chi Minh Trail," said John Conley, an advisor to the teams. When an opportunity arose, they were to snatch other North Vietnamese prisoners.

The concept proved a success. Inserted by Air America choppers, this special rallier team on two occasions managed to bring PAVN prisoners back to RLG lines, both of whom subsequently turned and were able to offer valuable order-of-battle intelligence. On a third occasion, a North Vietnamese soldier was overpowered while bathing in a bomb crater; after he put up a violent struggle, he had to be executed en route to the exfiltration point.

Once, Kalp was asked to replicate such efforts in Thailand. This came after the latest in a series of long-range PAVN commando attacks against Royal Thai airbases. These attacks dated back to May 1968, when a five-man North Vietnamese intelligence cell secretly crossed from Thakhek into Thailand and placed explosives on a row of US Air Force fighter planes at Udorn. The cell was spotted during exfiltration and two members were killed; the other three managed to escape back to North Vietnam. Three months later, two North Vietnamese sleeper agents working undercover at a farm near Bangkok were able to infiltrate Utapao airbase at night and plant explosives with time-delayed fuses; both were able to make their escape back to Bangkok before the explosives detonated.[9]

Four years on, the North Vietnamese tried again. In late 1971, two sleeper agents in Thailand—Vu Cong Dai and Bui Van Phuong—had been given ten satchel charges filled with C-4 explosives and hand grenades; these they hid at a cache site near Utapao airbase. At noon on 9 January 1972, the pair took a bus close to the base and retrieved the satchel charges by dusk. Working their way through the perimeter fence lines, they approached a pair of B-52 bombers parked on the apron. Fifty meters short of their target, however, the pair were spotted and a firefight ensured. Phuong managed to retrace his steps and escape; Dai engaged in a second firefight and, according to Hanoi's account, died a hero's death.[10]

Or so they thought. Dai had actually been caught alive, though this fact was withheld from the media. Thai and US interrogators attempted to debrief him, but he refused to divulge any biographic details, much less relevant information about his attack plan.

Looking to crack Dai by other means, Kalp was brought in from Savannakhet. Posing as a Polish ICC officer, Kalp offered to act as a go-between for messages sent from Dai back to Hanoi. Growing comfortable over several visits with the faux Polish officer, Dai revealed that he had hidden a silenced pistol in the sandy soil near the Utapao airstrip before being captured; US Air Force security police later retrieved the weapon.

Dai soon divulged other details, allowing Kalp to amass a modest dossier. At that point, the CIA officer revealed his true identity and threatened to expose the debriefing to the North Vietnamese authorities. Dai realized further resistance was futile and began to speak openly about planning for the operation and the North Vietnamese clandestine support network in Thailand. But, simmering over begin duped, he ultimately opted for a prison sentence rather than rally and actively fight against his erstwhile comrades.[11]

★ ★ ★

The overwhelming number of CIA personnel assigned to the regional units around Laos were in support of the paramilitary campaign. While this was ostensibly a covert program, CIA involvement was hardly a secret. It was also a bilateral program, as it had the quiet yet full support of the RLG and in many cases borrowed heavily on active-duty FAR officers for its paramilitary cadre.

In a far smaller number of cases, there were clandestine operations conducted by the regional units by case officers from the External Branch. These theoretically were unilateral in nature, done without the knowledge of the RLG. According to one External Branch case officer, Berkeley graduate Mike Magnani from Savannakhet Unit, it was a distinction without a difference:

> We, in fact, needed the support of the Lao government; most of our operations assistants, for instance, were borrowed from the Lao army. But since they didn't care about what we were doing, we could say to ourselves that the operations were 'unilateral' and clandestine.

The operations assistant helping the External Branch in Savannakhet was Captain Thay Korasack. Thay wielded influence far in excess of his rank because he was the adopted son of General Bounpone Makthepharak, who in turn was the commanding general of the military region headquartered in Savannakhet and later, in July 1971, promoted to commander of the entire armed forces. Thay's mother, who was ethnic Vietnamese, had earlier been Bounpone's favorite mistress.[12]

As defined by External Branch case officers in the CIA's Savannakhet Unit, Thay's writ was to seek out two types of potential recruits. First, he was to look for members of the sizable ethnic Vietnamese community in upper panhandle who either had exploitable connections extending back to North Vietnam or might have clandestine links to the North Vietnamese embassy in Vientiane. As case officer Magnani noted, this was easier said than done:

> A mechanic from the Royal Lao Air Force walked in and reported to Captain Thay that he was being approached by the communists for recruitment. He was told to request to speak to someone more senior, and shortly after a North Vietnamese came to his house. We had already staked out the house and the North Vietnamese was arrested. He turned out to be a major: a senior advisor to the Pathet Lao for southern Laos. A fantastic catch! We sent him off to the interrogation center [in Savannakhet], but they couldn't get anything from him. We shipped him down to Saigon Station, but they couldn't crack him and he was sent back to us. We gave him a medical exam and noticed there were signs of tuberculosis. We offered him treatment, but he refused. He told us that he had been on missions outside of North Vietnam for sixteen years, and had only been able to visit his family once during that entire period. He was very much used to hardship, and there was nothing we could do—carrots or sticks—to break him.

Second, Thay was on the lookout for members of the Pathet Lao's clandestine network, especially those who could shed light on that organization's leadership. In fact, a source that could report from inside the Pathet Lao's Sam Neua headquarters was something of a holy grail for the CIA. This was understandable, as that hermetically sealed bastion was located in an intricate cave complex as impervious to penetration agents as it was to airstrikes.[13]

In some respects, the Sam Neua cave complex was not unique. Other Asian communist insurgencies—Mao Tse Tung's communist party during World War II, for instance, and the Viet Minh—had spent time plotting their revolutions from caves. But the Pathet Lao had amped this up to a whole new level. Located near the village of Vieng Xai, 30 kilometers west of the Sam Neua provincial capital, its cave headquarters was first established in 1964 after the earlier Pathet Lao encampments on the PDJ proved too vulnerable to aerial attack. The jagged karst formations adjacent to Vieng Xai, leeched by rainwater into a honeycomb of chambers and shafts, offered a far more secure, albeit spartan, natural shelter.

Within a couple of years, the Pathet Lao population in the caves mushroomed to over 20,000. It came to occupy close to 500 separate chambers, painstakingly enlarging many to serve as meeting rooms, theaters, offices, guest houses, vehicle garages, armories, and schools.[14] The cave population even had its own insulated collective economy, replete with Pathet Lao printed banknotes supplied by China.[15]

And it was there, under the watchful eye of North Vietnamese advisors, that the Pathet Lao leadership indoctrinated cadre, formulated doctrine, and plotted its path to political control. For the most part, Vientiane Station remained blind to what took place inside those limestone walls. On the rare occasions when snippets of information leaked out, it was often late and indirect.[16]

As luck would have it, Savannakhet Unit identified a source that looked to be the holy grail in mid-1971. This came about when Captain Thay, canvassing a refugee resettlement area near Seno airbase, got a police tip about an elderly couple complaining bitterly that their daughter was about to be marched off to Sam Neua to join her husband. Reporting this find to Mike Magnani, Thay was told to grab the parents and their daughter quietly, then bundle them back to a hotel in downtown Savannakhet.[17]

A few hours later, Magnani was sitting in front of the trio with Thay providing translations. The story emerged that the parents lived closer to the Ho Chi Minh Trail but had been displaced by recent fighting. Sent temporarily to the camp near Seno, they were irate that their daughter was soon leaving them for the caves of Vieng Xai because her husband, a school teacher at the Pathet Lao headquarters, missed his wife and had come back to escort her north. The husband himself was temporarily residing just outside the Seno resettlement camp.

Magnani thought fast. He proposed a win-win for their entire family: he would put the parents on a stipend, but this would be contingent on the wife going back to Seno and convincing her husband to come to the hotel. With money introduced into the equation, the parents were suddenly amenable to the idea of their daughter heading north.

A few hours later, the daughter was back at the hotel with her spouse reluctantly in tow. The husband, whose real name was Thonekeo, shifted uncomfortably in front of Magnani and initially spoke little. But kept in the hotel room under guard, he began to open up over the course of three days. A native of Pakse, he had been close to graduating high school when he was recruited by the Pathet Lao. He had then been forced to leave his young wife—who was from Savannakhet—when he was sent to Vieng Xai as a school teacher for the children of senior Pathet Lao cadre within the cave complex. Thonekeo was told that he would soon be promoted to principal of that underground school, but had gotten permission to return to Savannakhet to fetch his spouse.[18]

Magnani tweaked the terms of what he had outlined to Thonekeo's wife. He was still prepared to offer monetary incentives to the in-laws, but in return he demanded that Thonekeo consent to a clandestine reporting relationship from Vieng Xai. The teacher mulled this over, though not for long. He detested the North Vietnamese and their control over the Pathet Lao, he declared, and thus agreed to Magnani's conditions.

As time was of the essence—Thonekeo was expected to head back north within a few days—they needed to agree on methods of communications. Thonekeo had already been sending letters back to his wife via the Pathet Lao's network of clandestine couriers, though there were delays of a couple of weeks and the letters were no doubt read by censors. Exploiting this system, Thonekeo was given a vial of invisible ink so he could compose secret reports for Magnani, then overwrite these with innocent letters to his in-laws using a standard ink pen. The CIA's Technical Services were constantly coming up with new invisible inks for which only they had the developing formulas; provided Thonekeo did not press too hard on the paper and leave physical clues, there was little chance the Pathet Lao would be able to expose the hidden messages.

As a second form of communication, Thonekeo was given a small VHF handheld receiver similar to the Joan-Eleanor system used by the OSS in Nazi-occupied Europe during World War II. He was also given a bag of batteries, estimated to be sufficient to last two years. To operate the system, Thonekeo could compose reports in plain speech, not requiring

Morse code. He would then need to find an excuse to leave the cave complex on a prearranged date and time to make his transmission. An Air America Beechcraft Volpar would be orbiting overhead to record the messages, although, hedging his bets so as not to put the Volpar in added danger, Magnani had misled Thonekeo by telling him the signal was being monitored all the way back in Savannakhet.

Normally with an agent operation of this sort, Muphy's Law would be proven multiple unwelcome times. In the case of Thonekeo, however, everything came together according to plan. Once back in Vieng Xai, his teaching duties took him around the cave complex and allowed him to pick up a wide range of hearsay, much of it surprisingly sensitive in nature. He relayed some of the most interesting conversations in an invisible ink message he posted to his in-laws in early September 1971.

Handed a transcript of the translated letter, Magnani read over its contents several times. Thonekeo claimed that the PAVN advisors to the Pathet Lao were talking about a massive impending military offensive to take place in South Vietnam. Although this did not conform to the prevailing conventional wisdom at the time, Magnani duly forwarded Thonekeo's insights to Vientiane for further passage to Langley.

A month later, a second letter was posted. Again, Thonekeo expounded on the rumors circulating Vieng Xai about a major offensive being planned by North Vietnam against the south. Again, the intelligence was forwarded to Langley. This time, it was met with negative feedback. "Kissinger was talking to them in Paris," said Magnani, "so he discounted any intelligence that they were planning an offensive of great magnitude."

Later in November, Magnani went aboard the Volpar on its first prescheduled orbit over Sam Neua. Like clockwork, Thonekeo turned on his set and sent a transmission. Even more than in the letters, he was able now to add detail about what North Vietnam's advisors were telling the Pathet Lao leadership regarding its impending offensive.

Four weeks later in December 1971, the Volpar was back over Vieng Xai with Magnani in the rear. Moments after Thonekeo's transmission concluded, the cockpit came alive with chatter. The reason: radar and communications intercepts detected North Vietnamese MiG-21 fighters had been scrambled and were racing toward Sam Neua. Highly vulnerable, the Volpar made a beeline for the Mekong; US Air Force fighters headed in the opposite direction in search of a dogfight. With MiG incursions growing more frequent by month's end, Vientiane Station issued a blanket prohibition against further missions with Magnani on board; in his stead, Lao operations assistants would join future Volpar overflights.[19]

Of course, Thonekeo's prophesized offensive materialized in March 1972 when the bulk of the North Vietnamese army launched its Easter Offensive against the south. Striking on three simultaneous fronts, it was unprecedented in terms of size and ferocity.

In June 1972, Magnani concluded his tour in Laos. Thonekeo was considered such an important asset that a former Marine named Mac was assigned as his dedicated case officer. Under Mac's watch further Volpar overflights continued on a monthly basis, with the school principal providing unparalleled insights into the Pathet Lao mindset in its cave fortress.

All of which continued through the first quarter of 1973. By that time, the Pathet Lao, which as a group always exhibited a finely attuned sense of paranoia, was displaying added vigilance against what it claimed was a US campaign to bribe traders, teachers, and monks into penetrating its organization.[20]

Probably tied to this, the Pathet Lao brought in direction-finding equipment to search for unauthorized transmissions around Vieng Xai. Although Thonekeo's transceiver had low power and a limited range that extended in a cone to a plane directly overhead, it was not completely undetectable. According to Boutsy Bouahom, one of the Lao operations assistants handling him,

> It was early 1973, and he had just sent us a transmission giving us details about what became the Pathet Lao 18-point program, which later became their plan for taking over the country at an accelerated pace. By then we had developed a second source in Vieng Xai, and shortly after he told us that the Pathet Lao had used direction-finders to identify a school principal as a spy.

A few weeks later, a message from the second source confirmed Thonekeo's fate. He had jumped off one of the karst peaks at Vieng Xai rather than get captured.

★ ★ ★

Pressing its technological advantage, Vientiane Station conjured one other novel approach to penetrate Sam Neua. In late January 1973, the CIA began rehearsing a mission to place a tap on a telephone line that aerial reconnaissance had identified along the north side of the main road leading into the Pathet Lao headquarters. After three aborted attempts, an eight-man Commando Raider team was inserted close to the road by an Air America S-58T Twin-Pac helicopter on 10 February. Installing the tap, the team was exfiltrated 12 days later.

Unfortunately, Murphy's Law was very much evident during this operation. Because the tap had been accidentally put on the wrong line, a commando team was re-infiltrated on the night of 12 March and successfully recovered the next day.

The following week, a Twin-Pac returned to the vicinity to deploy a solar-powered spider relay onto a tree atop Phou Nia, a mountain overlooking the tap from south of the road. Overhead, an orbiting Twin Otter plane fitted with electronics equipment tested whether the relay was functioning properly; in addition, the plane carried a rescue team of parachute-equipped commandos in the event an S-58T was downed.

When the relay was found to be improperly aligned, a Twin-Pac was dispatched on 25 March to reposition the device; when leaving the mountain, however, the chopper's rotor wash blew the relay off the tree. Three days later, a Twin-Pac crew chief lowered by a hoist attempted to replace the spider relay on the canopy—only to have it again blown off by the rotor wash. Repeatedly frustrated, further attempts to align the device were put on temporary hold.

Later that spring, Vientiane Station rekindled interest in properly positioning the spider relay. On 5 May, however, a Twin-Pac crew chief discovered that the relay was missing from the mountain where it had been left two months prior. Concluding that the site was compromised, the CIA eventually located a second hill with a clear line of sight to the tap. After extensive training at a remote site in southern Laos during November and early December 1973, a Twin-Pac successfully deployed the relay on the night of 17 December, enabling the CIA to begin recording Pathet Lao phone traffic out of Sam Neua. Using a Hail Mary pass, the station at long last had access to the holy grail.

CHAPTER 8

Hard Target

The North Vietnamese and Pathet Lao were worthy opponents of Vientiane Station's External Branch, but neither could hold a candle to the CIA's tenacious twin adversaries at the Soviet embassy. Spearheading the Soviet espionage effort was the Committee for State Security (Komitet Gosudarstvennoy Bezopasnosti, or KGB), the Soviet Union's all-inclusive security agency that blended the mandates of the CIA, Federal Bureau of Investigation, National Security Agency, and Secret Service.

Foreign intelligence operations conducted by the KGB were handled by its First Chief Directorate. This directorate closely mimicked the structure of the CIA, down to its geographic branches. Like the CIA, it fielded *rezidentura*—analogous to CIA stations—at its embassies worldwide. Compared to their CIA counterparts, *rezidentura* were afforded somewhat wider sway. For one thing, the *rezident*, or station chief, usually was head of the embassy's political section. For another, KGB counterintelligence officers were responsible for security of not just the *rezidentura*, but the entire embassy. Moreover, the embassy's *referentura*—code room—was headed by a member of the Foreign Ministry's Tenth Department, which in turn was under a KGB lieutenant general. The *rezidentura* also benefited from the fact that by 1965, an estimated half of all Soviet ambassadors had intelligence backgrounds.[1]

In Laos, the KGB *rezidentura* numbered between six and ten case officers from the late sixties onward. Arriving in 1969 as the KGB's Vientiane *rezident* was 42-year-old Victor Joukov. Holding the rank of counselor, Joukov's shaven head, penchant for white suits, and thuggish demeanor gave him the air of a Bond villain. "He was the most unpleasant of the bunch," recalled one American who met him on several occasions. "The CIA officers at the embassy said he was nicknamed 'The Butcher of Beirut' for some earlier nasty episode in his career."[2]

Also arriving in 1969 were a pair of fresh younger KGB officers. The first, Vadim Arkhipov, held the rank of second secretary and was nominally in charge of the Soviet Cultural Center in downtown Vientiane. As much as Joukov had the rough edges of one who had fought his way up from the proletariat, Arkhipov was suave and privileged, the son of a general-grade officer. The second officer was Viatcheslav Chiriaev, ranked as a third secretary and ostensibly the embassy's press attaché.[3]

The KGB's junior partner was the Soviet military's Main Intelligence Directorate (Glavnoye Razvedyvatel'noye Upravleniye, or GRU). Like the KGB, the GRU has its own *rezidentura* in Soviet missions abroad. In 1961, the GRU's commanding general had decreed that the GRU *rezident* should have civilian cover with diplomatic rank, meaning that the military attaché was no longer the *rezident* but subordinate to him. By the second half of that decade, however, this decree fell by the wayside and the military attaché and GRU *rezident* were usually one and the same; indeed, all members of the military attaché's office were from the GRU.[4]

The GRU *rezidentura* in Laos was smaller than that of the KGB, totaling just four members. The *rezident* through the end of 1969 was a loud, boorish lieutenant colonel named Vassily Federov. Replacing him in March 1970 was Vladimir Gretchanine, a graying, hard-drinking colonel who had an earlier tour at the Soviet embassy in Washington cut short due to tit-for-tat expulsions.

As of the late sixties, both the KGB and GRU *rezidentura* in Vientiane had a varied plate of targets. They aggressively sought out clandestine relationships with RLG officials; this was done with an eye toward lending them insights into the wider Indochina conflict. Due to the Sino–Soviet schism, they were also keenly interested in intelligence on China. And given the hundreds of Americans in the Lao capital, it was a target-rich recruitment environment against their main rival in the Cold War.

Confronting these efforts, and seeking its own recruitment opportunities, was what came to be nicknamed the Hard Target wing of

Vientiane Station's External Branch. The first head of this wing was Doug Bonner, a tall, bald Georgetown graduate that had joined the CIA in 1954. After a short tour at the US consulate in Hanoi during the final months before French withdrawal, he spent four years in Vienna operating against Warsaw Pact targets.

When Bonner arrived in Vientiane in July 1968, he inherited an extremely modest operation-in-progress. Aside from some low-level informants in contact with the Soviet community, the station had installed a unilateral telephone tap on its embassy.[5] In addition, through the station's liaison arrangement with the Police Special Branch they were getting copies of all letters posted to and from places like China and the Soviet Union.

Leads from these sources bore only minimal fruit. In 1969, for example, it came to the attention of the External Branch that a regular flow of letters was being sent from the Soviet Union to a Lao male in his twenties living in the southern town of Pakse. This male was among the eighty or so Lao nationals who had been given university scholarships in the Warsaw Pact during the early sixties.[6] A cursory analysis of the letters—which appeared to be sent for no apparent reason—suggested the Soviets were grooming the Lao as a potential stay-behind agent, for example in the event a more rightist government severed ties with Moscow. An attempted recruitment by the branch was for naught, however, as a cold pitch of the target was firmly rebuffed.

In another early case, the station went to a farcical extreme to keep tabs on the Soviets. This began when Sheldon Cholst, a 44-year-old ex-psychiatrist from Brooklyn who was living off a massive inheritance, decided to tune in, turn on, drop out. After dodging a drug conviction in England, he made his way to Thailand and then, in early 1968, to Laos. Renting a villa just 100 meters from the US embassy, Cholst announced his residence was the "Free US Embassy" and he was founding a "Free US Government-in-Exile," which abolished all laws against narcotics, birth control, and polygamy. He also opened a psychedelic nightclub along the Dong Palane strip named the Third Eye, which famously hired hippies to work there for $1 per day and unlimited hashish.[7]

All of this could be excused as the ramblings of a flower child with a trust fund, except for the fact that two TASS reporters came to interview Cholst, then lauded his so-called government-in-exile over Radio Moscow. This suddenly got the attention of Langley, which dispatched case officer Ed Cooke to the Lao capital. Under nonofficial cover as a hippie, Cooke spent time immersed in the Dong Palane community to monitor Cholst and his fellow travelers.

As it turned out, this was overkill. Managing to burn through his inheritance in a few short months, an increasingly paranoid Cholst took to wearing disguises and became a recluse. The Soviets, perhaps realizing they had milked the story for all it was worth, never paid him a second visit.

★ ★ ★

To ramp up efforts, the Hard Target wing began to add personnel in 1970. Arriving early that year was George Velesko, 36, an ethnic Ukrainian from a landed family whose world was thrown into disarray when its homeland—then under Polish control—was simultaneously invaded by the Soviets and Germans in 1939. Things grew more dire when the Germans surged forth into the Soviet Union, only to be thrown back on the eastern front by 1943.

As the Soviets pursued the Germans westward through ethnic Ukrainian territory, the Veleskos panicked. They were ardent Ukrainian nationalists, after all, and members of the Greek Orthodox Church to boot—making it all but certain a trip to Siberia was in the offing. Packing up their belongings and fleeing west, they were among the thousands of Ukrainians seeking shelter at the Regensburg displaced persons camp in southeast Germany by war's end.

Fortunately for the Velesko family, a sponsorship letter arrived in 1949 from an uncle who had previously settled in New York. Moving to that state, George was drafted at the start of the Korean War and served in an armored replacement training division. He then took a job at the Social Security office, but his ethnic background and linguistic ability attracted the attention of the CIA, which recruited him by the mid-sixties.[8] In

Laos, Velesko was primarily made responsible for transcribing the take from the telephone tap on the Soviet embassy.

Another member added to the Hard Target wing, Carla, was the wife of a CIA polygrapher. As the operations assistant within the wing, her job was to compile dossiers on relevant members of the Soviet and Chinese embassies. This included anything of interest emerging from Velesko's translations. In addition, the station had provided the Police Special Branch with a hidden camera system at Wattay, enabling it to surreptitiously photograph persons of interest, and their passports, during arrival and departure. Copies of these photos were added to the dossiers maintained by Carla.

Lastly, the wing was augmented in mid-1970 by Howard Freeman, a former US Army Special Forces noncommissioned officer who had spent the previous five years as a paramilitary advisor across northern and northeastern Laos.

Even with these extra personnel, the Hard Target wing remained largely reactive. In two specific cases, it closely monitored interaction between the American community and known intelligence officers at the Soviet embassy. In the first instance, GRU *rezident* Vladimir Gretchanine and his wife Elena had become social acquaintances of Phil Newell, an administrator at Air America's Flight Information Center at Wattay. Other employees of Air America joined this social circle, which focused heavily on dinners washed down with copious amounts of Russian vodka and cognac. Said Terry Wofford, a British national married to an Air America pilot who attended many of their gatherings,

> The friendship [of the Newells] with Vladimir and Elena was a genuine one as far as it could be, and both embassies, including the Soviets, would not only have known about it but would have allowed it, if not encouraged it.[9]

Wofford was correct. From the start, Howard Freeman had been alerted to the Newell case and was studying the relationship to determine whether there was a grievance revealed by the colonel that could be exploited. At least through early 1971, however, the Gretchanines appeared to be contented grandparents, albeit with a drinking problem.

The second instance involved "Rob," a young American working at the expansive Six Clicks City residential compound. After having earlier been declared unfit for military service—he had lost a kidney in college—Rob had arrived in Vientiane in early 1968. Making the rounds of the diplomatic circuit, he chanced upon KBG officer Vadim Arkhipov at a French embassy function in 1969. Explained Rob,

> We got talking about Valeriy Brumel, the Soviet high jumper who had just ended his competitive career after a motorcycle accident. Vadim said he was a boxer. So we bonded over sports.

As the relationship deepened, Arkhipov introduced Rob to KGB *rezident* Joukov. Rob also was the only American invited to an October 1970 Wattay reception for cosmonaut Pavel Popovich, who was transiting Vientiane after a visit to Hanoi. Rob returned the goodwill, buying Arkhipov stereo equipment at a PX in Thailand and later arranging for him to live out a dream by driving a borrowed Mustang around Vientiane.

It was not long before Rob's ties to the KGB officer came to the attention of the External Branch. In this case, it was Doug Bonner himself who first approached Rob and began a series of regular debriefings after every significant interaction with Arkhipov. Said Rob,

> The CIA flew in a profiler from Hong Kong to quiz me about his mannerisms, his eyes. I watched videos they made of [Arkhipov], and listened to taped conversations. They wanted to analyze every little detail, as they were hoping to recruit him.

While the Hard Target wing pieced together a plan for pitching Arkhipov, the other half of the branch—the Flying Squad—stepped forward to offer a hand. This took place in early 1971 during the final few months before case officers D'Ambrosio and LeClair finished their tours and rotated back to the United States. Specifically, they offered use of their Thai surveillance team to more aggressively document patterns of life for the known intelligence officers at the Soviet embassy.

By that time, the Thai team had undergone some personnel changes. First, team leader Bob was summarily fired after uncomfortable questions arose over his handling of finances. In his place, Albert was elevated as the new team leader.

Second, team member Jack, who had taken to drinking, fell ill and was whisked back to Bangkok. Shortly thereafter, he passed away from alcohol-related cirrhosis of the liver.

Third, team member Tim took a hostess from the Vieng Ratry (Vientiane Nights) nightclub as his second wife. Word of this got back to Bangkok, prompting his first wife to storm into Vientiane. In a fiery showdown between the two, the Bangkok wife threw acid in the face of her younger competitor, blinding her in one eye. Tim remained on the team, though for a time he was rather distracted by his marital discord.

Fourth, the team took on a second female member going by the call sign Jane. A 26-year-old art school graduate, Jane found that surveillance work ultimately did not suit her tastes. After only four months on the job, she retreated back to Bangkok.

Now five strong, the team temporarily put aside its Pathet Lao targets and reoriented itself toward the Soviets. To assist, it was given a pair of concealed cameras worked up by the station's Technical Services office. The first was a mini-camera fitted within a packet of 555 cigarettes. The second, with lowlight capability, was hidden inside a thick book.

Initially, the team was directed to the Lao Bowling Center. As the first and only venue of its kind in a town short of entertainment options, the bowling alley was trending among the Lao elite, including a number of army and police generals. Soviet intelligence officers, looking for an opportunity to engage with these figures, had also become regular fixtures at the center's ten lanes. And as luck would have it, the center was located just 300 meters away from the Soviet embassy, which in 1966 had moved from its downtown location to a new walled compound at the kilometer 3 marker along the road southeast of town leading toward Chinaimo.

Very quickly, the bowling alley grew crowded. Members of the Thai surveillance team took up the sport to keep an eye on the Soviets, who in turn were bowling to meet the Lao generals. Said Albert,

> George Velekso, who we knew from the Japan operation, also began to bowl in order to get an opportunity to bump into the Russians. One time he even went out to the parking lot to help a Russian fix a flat tire on his car.

But perhaps growing wise to the fact they were getting watched while they were watching, the Soviets suddenly put a halt to their bowling jaunts. Just as quickly, the Thai team lost interest in the bowling center.

Instead, in mid-1971 the team was ordered to being mobile surveillance on one particular Soviet officer who drove a Volkswagen. By that time, the team was brimming with confidence after years of tracking North Vietnamese and Pathet Lao. But that had been fairly standard surveillance, with targets traveling along direct paths at a measured pace.

The Soviets, by contrast, were anything but standard. They sped up and slowed down, drove in circles, and took indirect paths in what in hindsight were surveillance detection routes.

On their second day following the Volkswagen, Dick and Albert had rotated to the front of the group as they trailed the car into a maze of side streets near Dong Palane. Admitted Albert,

> We followed him down what turned out to be a dead end. When the two of us turned a corner, two Russian men were leaning back against their car hood and waving at us with a smile. It was the only time in nine years that I got burned doing surveillance in Laos.

Albert and Dick sheepishly reversed direction and sped out of the maze of back streets. As Tom and Tim idled in their motorcycles along the main road, Albert took a cigarette lighter out of his pocket and produced a flame to signal his teammates that they had been burned. It was to be the end of that team's operations against the Soviets.

Following this humbling experience, the Hard Target wing initiated a program to significantly increase its abilities. This coincided with a rotation of most of the wing's members in the summer of 1971. Taking charge from Doug Bonner was Harrison "Harry" McAlpine, a 41-year-old Ohio native who had served prior tours operating against China targets in Taiwan, Hong Kong, and Singapore. McAlpine had some angst taking on the Lao assignment. "Doug was a seasoned Soviet-targeted officer," he recalled. "But I was an East Asia officer and this was my first time against the Soviets."

As one of his first orders of business, McAlpine lobbied for permission to fast-track creation of a dedicated surveillance team for the wing. This was approved and, like the first team controlled by the Flying Squad, this one was to be composed of unilaterally recruited Thai members.

Playing the role of Paul Seema this time around was a tall, thin Thai national in his late twenties nicknamed Ralph. He came highly recommended by Bangkok Station as he was a distant in-law of William Lair, a famed paramilitary officer who had pioneered the recruitment of hill tribe guerrillas in northeastern Laos back in 1961.

Ralph quickly went about selecting candidates. He limited his choices to a younger crowd in its mid-twenties; like himself, all would have college degrees. In doing so, he sought to give the team enough intellectual horsepower so members could problem-solve on their own rather than always await guidance from a case officer. It was also felt that their greater aptitude would allow for shorter, more succinct training.

Ralph's first picks were a brother and sister who were his distant relatives. The first took the call sign Tony; his heavyset sister took the call sign Ann.

Ann, in turn, suggested an extremely sociable and attractive university classmate that would become the team's second female member. She took the nickname Pat. Pat suggested one of her college friends, who joined the team under the call sign David. Finally, Ralph brought in another of his distant cousins. Nicknamed Wally, he had a pronounced artistic streak.

It was these six—with Ralph acting as team leader—that would constitute what the External Branch codenamed the Kangaroos. In order to provide training to the Kangaroos, McAlpine turned to two young case officers who were recently added to the Hard Target roster. The first, George Kenning, had grown up in Belgium and, following his CIA induction, had been deployed in 1969 to run hill tribe teams in northwestern Laos. After two years at that post, he had shifted to Vientiane in September 1971 for reassignment to the External Branch.

The second, Brian O'Connor, was a Connecticut native who had decided in college that he would join the CIA to see the world. Figuring he would enter via the back door, he went to Laos to do humanitarian work and learn the Lao language while he prepared his application. Finally getting the nod from Langley, O'Connor returned stateside for basic training. He was then deployed in 1967 to Pakse for two years, the first running road-watch teams and the second recruiting agents. After another stateside stint to complete foreign intelligence training, he was back in Vientiane by July 1971. This time he was assigned to the Hard Target wing and took over the Newell case from the departing Howard Freeman.[10]

Once informed of the Kangaroo assignment, Kenning and O'Connor debated the choice of a training venues. "We wanted somewhere that would approximate Vientiane, and where expatriates would not stand out," said O'Connor. Settling on the seaside Thai town of Hua Hin, the recruits arrived there by October 1971.

Over the next three weeks, the Kangaroos practiced surveillance techniques on foot and motorcycle. O'Connor and Kenning drafted the accelerated training syllabus based on their own surveillance training. When it was over, the two case officers made an appeal to Station Chief Tovar. "We asked that the team be given one month to familiarize themselves with Vientiane," said Kenning. "Tovar, in his wisdom, was instrumental in granting us this support."

During December, the Kangaroos moved to the Lao capital and set about memorizing its layout. They rented a walled villa on the eastern outskirts of town, close to a cluster of expatriate residences where it would not raise eyebrows for the case officers to make frequent visits. Another Thai national was brought in by the External Branch to open a florist shop downtown; this provided cover employment to the team members in the event they were stopped by the RLG authorities. As added concealment, the station's technical staff provided them with fake identification cards listing their nationalities as Lao, not Thai.

At the start of 1972, the Kangaroos were ready to go operational. "They were exceptionally motivated," commented Kenning. "They were also very creative," added O'Connor. "Wally took the initiate of taking one of the mini-cameras provided by the Technical Services office and fashioning a mount behind his belt buckle."

When it came time to select initial targets, the wing's operations assistant, Carla, had multiple Soviet dossiers at the ready. Some of the latest information was provided by a Filipino couple, which the External Branch had hired to live in a villa-cum-observation-post across from the

Soviet embassy. With a camera directed through a peephole aimed toward the embassy's driveway, the couple's sole job was to collect photographs of persons in all vehicles entering and exiting the compound.

From Carla's dossiers, the wing elected to focus on one of the known KGB intelligence officers. Virtually all the KGB personnel lived in apartments adjacent to the embassy itself, and from photos compiled by the Filipino couple, it was known which cars these officers used. From the Filipino couple, they also knew that the intelligence officers tended to leave the compound on certain nights of the week at around the same time.

Acknowledging the Soviets would be well-versed in countersurveillance techniques, the Kangaroos realized they could not trail any one car for a long distance without easily being detected. This was especially true because there was only one road leading from the Soviet embassy into town. This is where patience came into play. By deploying themselves at the city limits on the night of the week when their target was known to be active, the team members were able to identify the initial direction their target invariably turned after entering town.

The next week on the same night, the team started from that first waypoint, then followed the target for a short distance to a second waypoint. The week after that, it followed him to a third. As the Soviets in Vientiane were creatures of habit and often sacrificed good tradecraft by not greatly varying their surveillance detection routes, the team over the course of several weeks was able to piece together the entire route the target normally took to identify a tail.

That is how the Kangaroos hit paydirt. As they trailed their target one night following completion of his surveillance detection route, they watched from a distance as he appeared to rendezvous near a second car. The encounter was brief, insufficient for the team to gather any specifics on the second vehicle.

A week later, the team was again trailing its target as he ended up on the same stretch of road. The Kangaroos, taking pains to remain at a distance so as not to be burned, again observed a suspected car rendezvous.

By the third week, the team had picked out optimal viewing locations near the suspected rendezvous site in the event their target returned to that venue. They had also been outfitted by CIA technicians with a starlight scope, though it proved to be rather awkward. Ditching the scope for a commercial camera, the team laid in wait.

On schedule, the Soviet officer arrived. After a second car pulled up, a Lao male got out, retrieved a large envelope from the trunk, and handed it over to the Soviet. The light from the trunk provided just enough illumination for the team to get a photo of the face of the Lao driver. It also was able to document his license plate.

The team passed this information back to its case officers the next day, and it was confirmed that the driver of the second car was the deputy commander of the Police Special Branch. Adding insult to injury, he had conducted a meeting with his CIA handler later that same night. This discovery meant that all the CIA's bilateral operations with the Police Special Branch were almost certainly blown to the Soviets, including the hidden camera system at Wattay.

Using the same surveillance techniques, the Kangaroos on another occasion followed a Soviet target to what appeared to be a safe house. Watching a different Lao male emerge from the house an hour later, the team followed him to a subsequent meeting—again with his CIA handler. The External Branch was able to confirm he was a senior member of the Foreign Ministry. "It meant that the Soviets had an agent stable remarkably similar to our own," noted O'Connor, "with sources working for both of us."[11]

The Kangaroos had one further success during the first half of 1972. While following a Soviet intelligence officer over the course of three weeks, they noted that he had paid a short afternoon visit to Mahosot Hospital. Built by the French, Mahosot had a large internal courtyard with several small gardens. The Soviet had been inside the expansive hospital grounds only briefly; the team had not been able to confirm where exactly he had gone.

The following week on the same day, the Soviet officer approached Mahosot. A team member had already been able to position himself in one of the hospital's toilets, which had a high window overlooking the courtyard. From that vantage spot, he was able to see the Russian load a dead drop under a slab of concrete alongside one of the gardens.

Maintaining a vigil at the garden, the team saw a Lao male unload the dead drop later that afternoon. Now focusing attention on the Lao, it followed him back to the Agence France-Presse office.

Continuing surveillance against this Lao target, the team saw him load a dead drop at dusk the next week on the same day. This time the location was in a cavity below a boulder in a field on the outskirts of town.

Thinking fast, the Kangaroos retrieved the package from the dead drop and tasked one team member with rushing it back to their case officers. Meantime, two team members—Pat and David, who had started dating in real life—sat on the boulder and convincingly acted like young lovers. For as long as the couple maintained their charade atop the dead-drop location, the Soviet intelligence officer, should he arrive, would have to delay all attempts to unload it.

Very quickly, members of the Hard Target wing assembled at the RMB office to look at the package. "It was a metal tube with different color rubber bands around it," recalled Kenning. "We theorized they must have photographed the pattern of the rubber bands as a kind of anti-tamper device."

The case officers photographed it as well so that they might be able to replicate the sequence of rubber bands after they opened the tube. When they did open it, it was an anticlimactic moment. "It was the teletype roll from Agence France-Presse," said O'Connor. "Nothing but the AFP stories being sent back to France."

This episode revealed one of the inefficiencies of the Soviet intelligence system. At its core, the KGB despised overt analysis. A weather report would not normally be of interest. However, if it could steal a report off the meteorologist's desk before it was disseminated, the report suddenly became highly coveted.[12] Similarly, the AFP teletype role contained nothing sensitive, but since it was collected in clandestine fashion it was important.

Laughing among themselves, the Hard Target members repacked the tube. It was returned to the Kangaroo member with instructions to replace it below the boulder. The amorous couple then retreated from the field to let the Soviet officer empty his dead drop.

★ ★ ★

While the KGB officers lived in apartments adjacent to their embassy building, this was not true for the GRU. In 1971, two junior officers from the Soviet military attaché's office—along with their respective families—informed the RLG that they intended to reside together in the upper floor of a shop-house across from the Settha Palace Hotel in downtown Vientiane. Word of this reached the External Branch, which was able to rush in a technician to install bugs right before the two families moved in.

After cross-checking files maintained by Carla, the branch was able to confirm the identity of the first officer as a GRU captain. Given his rank, there was a modicum of interest in him.

The second officer was identified as a 24-year-old lieutenant named Evgeni Sorokin. As he was the most junior member of the GRU *rezidentura*, the branch paid him no attention.

What they did not know was that Sorokin was a poster child for discontent. A few years earlier when he entered the GRU, he dreamed of going overseas and studying French. As being married was a pre-requisite for an overseas assignment, he had rushed into a marriage of convenience. He then had lobbied to get the Laos assignment, thinking it would provide him the opportunity to master French. When he arrived, however, Colonel Gretchanine told him he would need to study the Lao language. So, now stuck in a loveless marriage and denied French lessons, Sorokin was in a funk.

Worse, Sorokin's shop-house residence was directly across from the Settha Palace, which happened to host Le Spot, one of the most popular nightclubs in Vientiane. But given his meager lieutenant's salary, he could only watch Le Spot from afar.

On most days, Sorokin spent his time as Gretchanine's personal chauffeur. In addition, he was handed one more menial assignment. It was common GRU practice for the *rezident* to receive messages from headquarters via undeveloped film in the diplomatic pouch. When it arrived, the film would be projected on a screen. But because Gretchanine had faltering eyesight, it was Sorokin's job to read the messages to him.

It was in the course of reading the messages that Sorokin became aware of an embarrassing episode that had unfolded in June 1972 in Indonesia.

There, a 33-year-old GRU captain named Nikolay Grigoryevich Petrov, alone after his family went back to Moscow for summer holiday, had squandered his savings one afternoon at a Jakarta casino. Returning to his office to clean out the GRU safe of cash to win back his money, by early evening an inebriated Petrov had fretted away these additional funds in slot machines.

In a drunken fog, the captain then conjured a plan to recoup his losses by selling information to the US embassy. He got as far as the embassy's parking lot before getting cold feet. In a comedy of errors, he then raced off and managed to wreck his car within sight of the embassy. As he inexplicably headed back to the US mission, a group of perplexed American diplomats bandaged his wounds before he again elected to make a hasty retreat.

Finally reaching the Soviet housing compound, Petrov panicked the next morning as he sobered up. His car was a wreck, the money from the safe was lost, and his colleagues were curious where he had received his bandages. Slipping out the back, he took a pedicab to the US embassy and requested political asylum.

Not yet sure of Petrov's fate but fearing the worst, the Soviet embassy went into emergency overdrive. For the next two days, nearly all available KGB and GRU officers were in the field watching train stations, bus stops, and the airport. Still, the CIA was able to smuggle Petrov out of the country, disguising him as a Marine officer and sneaking him aboard the weekly US Navy flight to the Philippines.

Fallout from the Petrov defection reverberated in *rezidentura* around the world. While not fully aware of the details behind his flight, the GRU decreed that any officer involved in a car accident would be immediately recalled back to the Soviet Union. These orders were relayed in a message that Sorokin read aloud to Gretchanine.

Meantime, Vientiane Station had been reviewing the feed from the bugs in Sorokin's residence. After a few months, they made an interesting discovery. During certain brief periods, the two GRU officers could be heard commenting on the motorcycle traffic passing by the front of their second-floor shop-house. After cross-checking with the Kangaroos, the External Branch realized that Soviet intelligence officers, as part of their

Left OSS Lieutenant Hugh Tovar in Laos, 1945. Tovar would become the CIA station chief in Laos in 1970. (photo courtesy Christopher Tovar)

Below The CIA's first paramilitary officer in Laos, Jack Mathews, with Major Vang Pao at Nong Het in Military Region 2, July 1960. (photo courtesy Jack Mathews)

Left Anti-American banners on the streets of Vientiane during the days immediately after the August 1960 coup d'état. The lower banner demands that the PEO staff depart Laos. (photo courtesy Frank Tatu)

Vientiane Station Chief Charles Whitehurst visits Hmong guerrilla forces at Long Tieng, early 1964. Brigadier General Vang Pao is on the right, Major Youa Vang Ly on the left. (author's collection)

General Siho Lamphoutacoul (left), commander of the Directorate of National Coordination. (author's collection)

Royalist Armed Forces Commander Ouane Rathikoun and Prime Minister Souvanna Phouma review Neutralist troops at Moung Soui, 1964. (author's collection)

US Ambassador William Sullivan and Royal Lao Air Force commander Thao Ma, 1965. The latter staged abortive coups in both 1966 and 1973. (photo courtesy William Keeler)

The CIA's Far East Division chief, William Colby, visits the agency's paramilitary headquarters at Udorn Royal Thai Air Force Base, 1965. From left to right: Royal Thai Army Colonel Amnuay Prapubpangsa, Vientiane Station Chief Douglas Blaufarb, Royal Thai Army Colonel Vitoon Yasawasdi (commander of Thai forces in Laos), Colby, and William Lair (chief of CIA paramilitary operations in Laos). (author's collection)

Ted Shackley greets General Vang Pao upon arrival at Long Tieng, summer 1968. Stepping off the plane is the new Vientiane Station Chief, Lawrence Devlin. (photo courtesy Jane Randall)

Vientiane Deputy Station Chief Clyde McAvoy visits Long Tieng Base, 1969. From left to right: McAvoy, Howard Freeman (Long Tieng deputy chief of unit), Pat Landry (chief of paramilitary operations in Laos), and Robert Burr Smith (Long Tieng chief of operations). (photo courtesy Susan Smith Finn)

General Bounpone Makthepharak (then Military Region 3 commander, later armed forces commander) and CIA case officer Mike Magnani (right) in Savannakhet, 1969. (photo courtesy Mike Magnani)

Thai surveillance team member Albert. (author's collection)

Thai surveillance team member Becky. (author's collection)

Thai surveillance team member Tim. (author's collection)

Thai surveillance team member Tom. (author's collection)

Thai surveillance team member Dick (left) and Paul Seema at the team's Vientiane safe house, 1970. (author's collection)

Colonel (later General) Thao Ly at Lao New Year celebrations in Savannakhet, 1970. (photo courtesy Mike Magnani)

Case officers Bernie D'Ambrosio and George Velesko, Vientiane, 1970. (photo courtesy Maya Velesko)

Planning the operation against the Japanese targets at the Vientiane safe house, November 1970. From left to right: John LeClair (back to camera), Bernie D'Ambrosio, George Evans, Thai surveillance member Albert (back to camera), Howie McCabe, James Haase. (author's collection)

みんな押収

日本人医師帰国

The 10 December 1970 edition of the *Mainichi Shimbun* carried a photo of Akinori Masuda (left) and Zenzaburo Funazaki upon arrival in Tokyo after their detention in Thailand. (author's collection)

Wattay reception for Soviet cosmonaut Pavel Popovich, October 1970. On right in the white suit is KGB *rezident* Victor Joukov. (author's collection)

KGB officer Vadim Arkhipov on a Mekong excursion with his wife, 1970.
(author's collection)

CIA case officer George Kenning (center) with Kangaroo surveillance team member
Jack (left). (photo courtesy George Kenning)

Vladimir Piguzov (spelling variant, Pigouzov), the KGB's deputy *rezident* in Vientiane. (author's collection)

Initial contact between Air America pilots and Piguzov took place at the Purple Porpoise. Monty Bank, the proprietor, stands in front of his bar. (photo © David Jenkins)

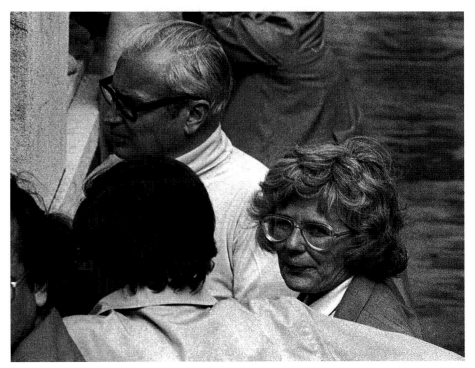

CIA officer Serge Taube—the Gray Fox—who ultimately recruited Piguzov. (photo courtesy Barry Broman)

Patch used by General Thao Ma's Revolutionary Committee during his abortive coup, August 1973. (author's collection)

Pathet Lao troops aboard a US-built truck ride through Vientiane, late 1973. (photo via Roger Warner)

US Ambassador Charles Whitehouse (left) with CIA case officer Jack Platt (center), 1974. (photo courtesy Paige Gordon)

CIA Station Chief Dan Arnold, circa 1974. (photo courtesy Dan Arnold)

Deputy Station Chief Roger McCarthy (center) with US Army attaché John Wood (left) and Soviet Colonel Vassili Soloviev during a diplomatic function in Vientiane, 1974. (photo courtesy Kevin McCarthy)

Royalist soldier and police officer (left and center) join a Pathet Lao soldier on a joint patrol in Vientiane, 1975. (photo courtesy Roland Neveu)

Evacuation boats arranged by CIA paramilitary officer Jim Sheldon arrive on the Thai side of the Mekong, 1975. (photo courtesy Jim Sheldon)

Anti-American banner hung on the USAID compound in Vientiane, May 1975. It demands that the CIA leave Laos. (author's collection)

surveillance detection routes, were circling in their cars twice around the block in front of the Settha Palace. That way, the two GRU officers could use their residence as an observation post to spot motorcycle tails.

The bugs also revealed that the GRU captain was occasionally leaving the residence at night along with Sorokin as his driver. Suspecting these were clandestine meetings, the Kangaroos were tasked with putting him under surveillance.

On the night of Sunday, 10 September 1972, the two GRU officers shared several rounds of drinks before leaving the residence with Sorokin at the wheel. As the Kangaroos followed from a distance, the Soviets drove to a patch of forest along the airport road to Wattay. At that point, the captain entered the woods and Sorokin sped off.

Deploying around the forest, the team was able to confirm that the captain linked up with a young FAR intelligence officer for a secret tryst.[13]

Meantime, Sorokin had headed back into town alone. Losing control of the wheel along the way—attributable in no small part to his drinking—he veered off the road and caused major damage to the vehicle. He immediately panicked, recalling the message he had read to Gretchanine a few short weeks earlier about the automatic recall of any officer involved in a car accident. Fearing he would be sent home in disgrace, compounded by festering disappointment over his marriage and inability to study French, he headed to the US embassy.

By chance, a CIA officer named Gene Wojciechowski was sitting in the embassy late that Sunday night. Wojciechowski was an outlier of sorts. Virtually every other member of the External Branch was assigned to the RMB building in the USAID compound. But under State Department cover as an economics officer, Wojciechowski was assigned to act as the branch's sole representative in the main embassy building. One of his roles was to handle any communist walk-ins, and he joked among his colleagues that he kept a bottle of vodka on hand for just such a contingency.

Nobody was laughing that Sunday night when Sorokin set the contingency into play. As Wojciechowski poured himself and Sorokin drinks, Harry McAlpine was called in. "Sorokin seemed impressionable and had a favorable opinion of the US lifestyle," remembers McAlpine.

"While he was in the office, he grabbed a small US flag off the desk and said, 'This is mine now!'"

Following the experience of Jakarta Station, which had faced a Soviet dragnet when Petrov went missing, Vientiane Station had recently penned a plan to get defectors quickly out of Laos. Within a couple of hours, Langley approved Sorokin's extraction by air. This involved an emergency Air America flight to Udorn, quickly followed by a second flight to Bangkok.

Once ensconced at a safe house in the Thai capital, the CIA sent out a specialist from the United States to debrief him. Brian O'Connor from the External Branch also flew to Bangkok to get any perishable information about the GRU and KGB *rezidentura* in Vientiane.

The fallout at the Soviet embassy in Vientiane was considerable. In the weeks that followed, an estimated one-quarter of the staff was quietly withdrawn.[14] Ambassador Victor Minine, who was in the Soviet Union on holiday at the time, cut short his leave and rushed back to Laos. But on 24 September, he announced he was being recalled home and requested an audience with the king to bid farewell.[15]

As for Sorokin, the CIA noted from the start that he was unlike any other defector to date. For one thing, he was the youngest GRU officer ever to seek asylum. For another, he had abandoned his wife Tatiana in Laos without any apparent angst.[16]

Bringing him back to the United States, Sorokin was kept sequestered at a safe house in the Virginia countryside. When O'Connor flew in one more time to milk him for details about the Soviet embassy in Vientiane, he noticed all was not well with the former GRU lieutenant. "He was taken shopping and saw one-hundred kinds of toothpaste," remarked O'Connor. "He was overwhelmed and confused."

A year later, word got back to Vientiane Station that a drunken Sorokin had gotten ahold of a shotgun and blew out the safe house's television. Another month after that, he opted to re-defect back to Moscow. Perhaps taking into account his youth, the Soviet legal system handed him a mere twelve-year prison sentence.

CHAPTER 9

Rock and a Hard Place

On 17 June 1971, President Richard Nixon took to the podium at the White House with a somber announcement. "America's Public Enemy Number One is drug abuse," he intoned, and it was it was "necessary to wage a new all-out offensive." Prompted to action by the mushrooming use of narcotics by American servicemen in South Vietnam, Nixon said the campaign would include a worldwide effort against drug supplies.

Though left unmentioned in Nixon's speech, Laos held an unenviable spot among the top nations fingered for illicit drug production. This was not a new phenomenon. For generations, hill tribes across northern Laos had cultivated low-grade poppies alongside crops like corn, virtually all of it to satisfy the local addict population. This cultivation encompassed much of northwestern Laos—specifically the mountains area where Laos, Thailand, and Burma converged into the so-called Golden Triangle—which was populated by a rich patchwork of tribes. It also included northeastern Laos, where poppy was traditionally harvested by ethnic Hmong.

In 1949, things began to change. Much of it was prompted by a harsh crackdown on poppy growth in China following establishment of the People's Republic. China-based hill tribes that had been dependent on poppies as a cash crop shifted south to the less governed parts of the Golden Triangle. The Golden Triangle also became home to defeated remnants of the National Chinese army, which resettled in the tri-border area to keep alive the Koumintang pipe dream of retaking mainland China.

All of which combined for a perfect storm. In a lawless part of Southeast Asia, with the right climate and altitude to grow high-grade poppies, hill tribes saw opportunity to make up for the lost harvests in China, and the Koumintang was more than happy to act as hired guns to protect mule caravans hauling out the drugs.

On the receiving end of the opium caravans were criminal syndicates. In the Golden Triangle through the late fifties, there was a network of ethnic Chinese Thai that took receipt of the contraband. In northern Laos, meantime, representatives from the European underworld, almost exclusively French Corsicans, trafficked the narcotics using a small number of private planes from both the PDJ and Wattay.

By the early sixties, significant changes took place. First, the PDJ became a highly contested warzone, depriving the Corsicans of its runways. Second, the Hmong became the hill tribe most closely associated with guerrilla warfare against the communists, internally displacing entire villages to lower altitudes less suited for poppies and turning a generation of slash-and-burn farmers into soldiers. This displacement caused domestic opium production in northern Laos to fall from 100 tons per annum to about 30, the bulk of it consumed by local addicts.[1]

While domestic cultivation plummeted, Laos took on added significance as a conduit for producers on the Burmese and Thai sides of the border. These producers now included a wide array of Burmese insurgent groups—both communist and tribal—as well as the aforementioned Koumintang remnants, all of which saw opium cultivation as a means of earning cash for weapons and supplies.

The Laos conduit was abetted by two key factors. First, the RLG had never gotten around to making opium illegal; rather, they adhered to French-era laws that pragmatically sidestepped the issue.

Second, producers in the Golden Triangle had a highly placed ally in the form of General Ouane Rathikoun. As a young officer Ouane had managed to secure assignments with battalions in the Luang Prabang vicinity, in the process ingratiating himself with the royal family. When it came time to select military region commanders in the second half of 1954, he landed control of the region encompassing the kingdom's expansive north and northwest quadrant, including the royal capital.

Shortly thereafter, in 1955, Ouane has his first encounter with the opium trade. By his own telling, troops under his command seized a plane operated by Thai traffickers that had landed at a tobacco plantation on the extreme western edge of the kingdom. In an ensuing firefight, three Thai were taken prisoner and 950 kilos of opium seized.[2]

During this period, Ouane had also displayed a good grasp of paramilitary operations when he pioneered the AD militia concept in his military region. This had been lauded by the CIA station chief at the time, as well as the Pentagon.

Dabbling in politics, Ouane showed considerable political tact when he godfathered the CDNI Young Turks in 1958 and was chosen as the group's president. Not by coincidence, as that organization flexed its muscle over the course of 1959, Ouane earned his first star and was promoted to chief of staff of the armed forces.

A few months later, Ouane flashed an opportunistic streak. Immediately following the 1960 Kong Le coup, the majority of senior army officers filed down to Savannakhet to declare allegiance to Phoumi Nosavan. Ouane, however, remained on the fence in Vientiane, no doubt because Souvanna Phouma dangled the promise to elevate him to the top slot as armed forces commander. Not until mid-November, when momentum clearly favored Phoumi, did Ouane belatedly abandon Souvanna and make his way down to the Savannakhet countercoup crowd.

Phoumi did not forget this slight. After he secured control around Vientiane during the opening days of 1961, he quickly set about conjuring new and inflated posts for his sycophants. Though Ouane was retained as chief of staff, a staunch Phoumi loyalist bypassed him to become overall military commander. It was only after incessant lobbying with the royal family that Ouane was finally able to squeeze out a promotion to major general the following year.

By 1963, the two generals appeared to reach an understanding. Taking Ouane into his confidence, that October Phoumi gave him a sensitive assignment. Ostensibly to make up for cuts in US military aid, Ouane was ordered to negotiate the sale and trafficking of opium as a government monopoly to guarantee a share for the army. Ouane was a good choice to manage this because he was intimately familiar with northwestern

Laos from his time as military region commander. And his close ties to the royal family—and, by extension, Souvanna Phouma—could secure their approval, or at least their indifference.

Specifically, Phoumi told Ouane to use a company called Sacda as the sole coordinating agent. Sacda was managed by a Thai national of Chinese ethnicity named Ts'ai Kuang-Jung (alias Savang Chaman, alias Sakda). Around thirty-eight at the time, Sakda had spent a year in the PRC before shifting to Laos in 1959. Significantly, he owned a single C-47 plane at Wattay, which he flew under the corporate title Air Vientiane.[3]

With the drug trade coordinated by Sacda, Ouane opened an opium refinery in Luang Prabang. After only half a year, however, Phoumi inexplicably ordered him in May 1964 to cease operations. Ouane would later claim this was due to mounting foreign criticism.

Trouble was, one month prior to Phoumi's countermanding order, a stalled coup had irrevocably altered the power dynamic within FAR. Whereas Phoumi had his powers significantly curtailed, Ouane had pragmatically backed the winners—and was immediately rewarded by getting his long-awaited promotion to overall armed forces commander.

As he now sat atop the FAR, Ouane was less than inclined to heed Phoumi's call to forgo the lucrative drug trade. Rather, the spent the next three years bringing it further under his thumb. This had several facets. First, he closed the refinery in Luang Prabang and consolidated operations away from prying eyes near the western border town of Ban Houei Sai. Protection was provided there by local FAR troops and government-backed guerrillas.[4]

Second, Ouane came to rely heavily on the Royal Lao Air Force to fly the drugs to Saigon, or at least to the Lao panhandle where they were reloaded on planes bound for South Vietnam. This egregious misuse of Lao military transports was one of the precipitating factors in a 1966 coup attempt by the disgruntled head of the Royal Lao Air Force, General Thao Ma.

Following that coup attempt, which resulted in the elevation of a more pliable general in charge of air assets, Ouane's misappropriation of military transports became more blatant. In addition to opium, the planes also began smuggling gold.[5] This culminated in an embarrassing international incident in March 1970 when a Lao C-47, with the Vientiane base commander and the deputy Savannakhet base commander on board, was impounded in Saigon with a cabin full of opium and precious metal.[6]

Third, Ouane ditched Sacda and forged an unholy alliance with a different network of Guangdong Chinese that dominated the regional drug trade.[7] Guangdong Chinese—that is, those who had their ancestral homeland in the Guangdong region on the southern coast of China adjacent to Hong Kong--constituted the majority of Chinese living in Southeast Asia. They had come to be disproportionately represented in banking across the region, as well in gold and narcotics smuggling.[8]

In particular, Ouane forged a partnership with Guangdong drug kingpin Hu T'ien Hsing. On face, Hsing tried to project the image of a legitimate overseas Chinese businessman. Originally based in of Hong Kong, he had obtained the Esso franchise for Laos, which consisted of a single gasoline station in Vientiane. He also became silent partner for a Pepsi bottling plant in the capital, which began construction along the banks of the Mekong in 1965 with USAID financial support.[9]

But Hsing's real job was narcotics, and in this he was a visionary. Whereas Ouane had earlier dabbled in refining poppy into opium, Hsing took it the next step by importing Hong Kong chemists to upgrade two refineries in northwestern Laos—one at Houei Phee Lork, and an even bigger facility at Houei Tap—to produce 96 percent pure white heroin. Snorted, smoked, or injected, this pure heroin was targeted toward American troops in South Vietnam.[10]

This all put the US embassy between a rock and a hard place. The embassy was acutely aware that the head of the Lao military was openly complicit in narcotics trafficking and that his intended end users were American troops. But it did not behoove them to alienate the top FAR commander, especially one that was a favorite of the king and on close terms with the prime minister. Moreover, they had no legal recourse in the kingdom, as narcotics production and trafficking were still not illegal.[11]

What steps the embassy could and did take were of questionable efficacy. To deter air force pilots from smuggling, for instance, the United States earmarked an extra 12,100 kip per month—just over $24—for each transport pilot beginning in 1969. But this paltry amount paled to the reported $12,000 per trip that pilots could make flying contraband to South Vietnam.[12] And when sanctions were demanded against the aircrew whose plane was impounded in Saigon in March 1970, the rest of the Lao air force threatened to stage a strike claiming the crew was being scapegoated by the top brass who ordered the flight.[13]

Then came Nixon's June 1971 proclamation and the embassy had no choice but to elevate the issue. Its immediate step was to pen a Narcotics Control Action Plan that sought to make drug production and trafficking illegal, and to win RLG support for anti-narcotics efforts.

As luck would have it, two days before Nixon's speech a Royal decree announced Ouane's promotion to lieutenant general. This was a going-away present of sorts, as he was set to retire on 1 July.[14]

Replacing Ouane was Major General Bounpone Makthepharak. Nicknamed "Jubilation T. Bounpone" by an earlier US ambassador in reference to the Li'l Abner cartoon's Confederate General Jubilation T. Cornpone, Bounpone brought with him his own set of shortcomings. For one thing, his performance to date could only generously be described as adequate.[15] For another, the CIA strongly suspected he—or, more probably, his wife—was engaging in commercial activity with the Pathet Lao.[16] But as he was closely linked to the southern power structure, especially Prince Boun Oum, he served the important purpose of cementing the panhandle's support within the RLG.

On a positive note, Bounpone was not seriously tainted by narcotics as his predecessor was.[17] Probably not by coincidence, one month after he was inaugurated as FAR commander, the government at long last issued a law prohibiting opium and its byproducts. This was formally promulgated in a royal decree dated 23 September.[18]

Already, in fact, at around the exact time Ouane retired from the military, Hu T'ien Hsing pragmatically closed his two heroin refineries on Lao soil. This was no doubt prompted by the loss of his main FAR patron, though the CIA speculated Hsing probably realized he had stockpiled enough heroin at a time when the future US serviceman market in South Vietnam was growing uncertain.[19]

It was also during this timeframe that the CIA, as a member of Nixon's Cabinet Committee on International Narcotics Control, had Vientiane

Station add anti-narcotics responsibilities to its agenda.[20] Early evidence of this had come in July 1971 when two paramilitary officers based in northwestern Laos did a helicopter flyover of Houei Phee Lork. Located 20 kilometers northwest of Ban Hoeui Sai near a left hook in the Mekong, Houei Phee Lork hosted one of Hsing's two heroin plants. From above, the officers were indeed able to see a fenced compound carved out of the jungle. There were also white stains visible on the ground, a hint of the slake lime used in the heroin refining process.[21] One week later, a second flyover revealed what appeared to be rushed attempts at concealing the buildings in the jungle clearing.

After getting approval from the CIA paramilitary headquarters at Udorn for a ground reconnaissance, the same two officers took to the sky during the afternoon of 2 August. They had also browbeat tribal leader Chao La and his nephew to accompany them; as Chao La held forth among the Mien tribesmen that dominated the vicinity around Houei Phee Lork, the officers shrewdly calculated that his presence would shield them from any armed resistance.[22]

Their calculation was spot on. Landing in a clearing 100 meters from the compound, the four cautiously approached. They found the site was empty of occupants, though there were still barrels of precursor chemicals strewn about. Taking just long enough to photograph their findings, they took to the chopper and departed.

Later that same afternoon, the four returned with a contingent of CIA-sponsored guerrillas. In the short interval since the first reconnaissance, persons unknown had managed to make off with all the chemicals. Confiscating a few remaining pieces of distilling equipment, the CIA officers once more departed.

At the same time, a separate sweep was conducted at the larger facility of Houei Tap. Located just 8 kilometers northwest of Ban Houei Sai, this site was also confirmed to be abandoned.[23]

Other parts of Vientiane Station soon got into the act. In August 1971, External Branch case officer Bernie D'Ambrosio, in one of his last acts before concluding his Laos tour, took along Thai team leader Albert for a reconnaissance of the stillborn Pepsi bottling plant along the bank of the Mekong. Recalled Albert,

We went there at night because it was suspected that there was acetic anhydride, a chemical used to make heroin, being stored there. We tried to climb on top of Bernie's car to look over the wall, but it was too tall. We went back on the second night with a higher vehicle, but we couldn't see any chemicals being kept there. The place was empty.

Down in Savannakhet, branch officer Mike Magnani generated his own leads. One of his sources, a Eurasian male, happened to have a sister who was married to the former FAR military attaché in Saigon. This source claimed his sister was intimately familiar with the drug flights from Laos, being on the receiving end of the shipments. With an introduction from her brother, Magnani met the sister and, after learning she was estranged from her husband, found her to be a willing font of knowledge. Said Magnani,

> She knew all about [Hsing], the Hong Kong drug kingpin in Vientiane. She also claimed to have heard that [Hsing] was paying the King $1 million per year for the drug concession.[24]

Armed with these sorts of details, Magnani was called to the embassy in Vientiane for discussions. A range of harsh measures against Hsing were discussed, but in the end nothing was approved. "Vientiane was a family posting," offered Magnani. "The risk was too high that if action was taken in Vientiane, the American community was too open to reprisals."

★ ★ ★

The second part of the US embassy's Narcotics Control Action Plan—getting the RLG to proactively support anti-narcotics efforts—took a little longer to enact. After some lobbying of Prime Minister Souvanna Phouma, Phouma handed the task to one of his more loyal officers, Brigadier General Khamhou Boussarath. Born in Hanoi to Lao parents, Khamhou had studied history in high school under Vo Nguyen Giap—years before the latter led the Viet Minh to victory at Dien Bien Phu. Entering the Lao military at its inception, Khamhou had landed intelligence roles through the rank of major. After that, he had led a paratrooper regiment and—for a very brief period in late 1968—was tapped to lead an airborne division that never came to fruition.

Ingratiating himself with the prime minister along the way, Colonel Khamhou was selected by Souvanna Phouma in mid-1969 to head a new intelligence agency called the National Documentation Center (Centre National de Documentation, or CND).[25] Its mission was to coordinate the collection, evaluation, and dissemination of intelligence from both the FAR and National Police.

Trouble was, the CND had a miniscule budget, few personnel, and virtually no clout. Vientiane Station, for its part, barely acknowledged the CND's existence. As a shill for the prime minister, Khamhou—who got a promotion to brigadier general in February 1970—seemed to spend most of his time keeping his patron apprised of political rumors circulating the capital.

When the US embassy let Souvanna Phouma know in late 1971 that it was keen to sponsor creation of a counter-narcotics unit, Khamhou had the inside track to volunteer for the job. Putting this on as a second hat, he was named commander of a new formation called the Special Investigation Group (Groupe Spécial d'Investigation, or GSI). Given space within the prime minister's office, the GSI was to coordinate narcotics control efforts across the kingdom. It was slated to total around sixty members drawn from the FAR military police, National Police, and customs.

In the GSI role, Khamhou proved to be an aggressive administrator and racked up some early wins. In March 1972, GSI officers seized almost 11 kilos of opium from a civilian passenger on a Royal Lao Air Force plane. Later that same month, GSI members revisited the two abandoned heroin refineries in northwestern Laos and unearthed some remaining chemicals and equipment hidden in the nearby jungle. And in June, they raided the Vientiane home of a Hmong member of the National Assembly, confiscating almost 10 kilos of heroin and 26 kilos of opium.[26]

The GSI also crossed paths with Vientiane Station on one occasion, albeit in a tangential manner. This came about after the group raised its own surveillance team in the capital. Recounted CIA officer Jim Sheldon,

Years later in 1976, I was based in Udorn interviewing persons who had worked with us in Laos and were applying to come to the US. One man, Paisone Bannavong, came in and recounted how he was on a surveillance team. They were assigned with watching the head of the Royal Lao Air Force because it was suspected he was in contact with drug smugglers. It turns out that his mistress was from a good Lao family, and she also happened to be dating me at the time. After the team watched her leave from a discreet rendezvous with the air force general, they followed her when she went to meet me.[27]

To GSI's credit, Sheldon never knew he was under surveillance.

★ ★ ★

In the end, the urgency surrounding the narcotics issue in Laos largely wafted away. It was not because of any silver bullet from the GSI or clandestine effort on the part of the CIA. Rather, the massive drawdown of US servicemen from South Vietnam in 1973 all but eliminated the primary consumer base from the regional equation. That, plus the continued internal displacement of hill tribe farmers and the sidelining of General Ouane combined to remove Laos—at least for the time being—as a significant link in the international drug trade.[28]

CHAPTER 10

The Art of Seduction

In the aftermath of the September 1972 Sorokin defection, the Hard Target section upped its pace. Joining the wing that same month was 36-year-old Jack "Cowboy" Platt. A Texas native and former Marine officer, Platt had entered the CIA in 1963 and shortly thereafter began a five-year tour in Austria against Soviet targets. As his mode in Vienna was as an economics officer, he maintained this same cover in Vientiane—despite that he physically sat at the RMB office in the USAID compound.

Once Platt settled in, fellow Hard Target officers Kenning and O'Connor passed to him control of the Kangaroos. By that time, the team had undergone some personnel changes. After doing the heavy lifting during recruitment and initial deployment, team leader Ralph took leave of Laos. Wally, the artistic member, returned to Thailand. Replacing them were two new Thai members: one call-signed Victor and a second nicknamed Jack. Meantime, Tony was promoted to team leader in Ralph's place.[1]

Now in charge, Platt maintained the breakneck pace of the Kangaroos. The KGB *rezidentura* remained their primary target; this included new *rezident* Gueorgui "George" Vorobiev, who arrived in April 1972 to replace the departing Victor Joukov.[2] Unlike the gruff Joukov, Vorobiev reeked of privilege and spoke American-accented English with native fluency. He was a regional expert, having served in Bangkok for several years during the early sixties.

Also on the Kangaroo target list was the deputy KGB *rezident*, 34-year-old Vladimir Mikhaylovich Piguzov. A Southeast Asia specialist, Piguzov had his first overseas posting as assistant press attaché to Cambodia in September 1969. He was there only for the final tumultuous months of the Sihanouk regime, returning to Moscow in May 1970. In February 1971, he arrived in Vientiane with his wife and two-year-old son for his second overseas tour.

The Kangaroos were also on the lookout for any Soviets appearing in Laos who were among the 105 suspected intelligence officers expelled from the United Kingdom in September 1971. This bunch was soon reappearing in embassies around the globe, sometimes under new names. One became a first secretary in Sri Lanka in February 1972. Another surfaced as a third secretary at the Soviet embassy in Bangkok in May.[3] As best the Kangaroos could tell, however, none of the new arrivals in Vientiane matched those sent packing from London.[4]

George Kenning and Brian O'Connor were, for their part, looking to score a Soviet recruitment. "I don't think we ever generated a single intelligence report," noted O'Connor; "We were so focused on trying to hook a Soviet."[5]

This was far easier said than done. In the case of Colonel Gretchanine, the GRU *rezident* had maintained his robust social schedule with the Air America crowd but concluded his tour in 1973 without presenting a good opportunity to be subverted.

In the case of Vadim Arkhipov, the prospects had appeared brighter. As his close friendship with American instructor Rob extended into a third year, Arkhipov announced his tour was set to conclude before the end of 1972. Realizing time was running out, the External Branch appealed to Rob to dangle an offer on their behalf. As Rob remembers it,

> Up on the rooftop of the Soviet Cultural Center, I made the pitch. Our relationship cooled after that point. I had given him a special air pistol that he coveted, but he then returned it to me several weeks later. I always felt guilty that I misrepresented myself since I really liked Vadim and considered him a good friend.

There was even thought given to approaching the KGB *rezident*, George Vorobiev. He was an ardent tennis player, and there was ample opportunity to bump into him on the courts.[6] Moreover, the telephone taps on the embassy had revealed a possibly exploitable weakness: he was sleeping with the wife of one of his officers. But ever the crafty professional, Vorobiev proved impenetrable.[7]

Somewhat better luck was had with the Poles, who had retained their presence in the ICC despite that that body was largely dormant. Commensurate with their truncated mandate, the Polish contingent had atrophied by the late sixties to just a commissioner and a couple of assistants.[8] Commissioners were getting rotated roughly every other year, and as of the opening of 1973 the incumbent was counting down the weeks before his tour ended. On several occasions during diplomatic events, he had gone out of his way to greet US diplomats and, by his flirtatious manner, made it fairly evident he was game for a closer relationship.

When this promising lead was handed over to the External Branch, the Hard Target wing knew that the clock was ticking and that it needed to move fast. Unfortunately, the Polish commissioner normally stayed within the ICC compound near Wattay, and it would draw an inordinate amount of attention for an American diplomat to go knocking there.

A better option was the upcoming Lao New Year celebrations, which fell over a three-day period every April. It was customary for the king to invite the foreign diplomatic corps to Luang Prabang for this event, where they were feted with a military parade and an audience with the royal family. Several from the US embassy were invariably in attendance, and it was normal for the ICC delegates to also be present.

Assuming their Polish target would be heading to Luang Prabang for the April 1973 festivities, Kenning, O'Connor, and Platt joined the US contingent. To their relief, they were able to bump into the commissioner almost as soon as they arrived and agreed on meeting him at his room at the down-market Phousi Guesthouse. When Kenning and Platt knocked on his door, they were taken back. Said Kenning,

> We came in his room, and he was already drinking heavily. A couple of bottles of good vodka in his suitcase. Yes, he was very much agreeable to a clandestine relationship, but he was almost incoherent with all the booze. What was even funnier was that his price for being recruited was that he wanted us to give him an American luxury car in a gaudy color. Basically, he wanted a pink Cadillac.

When the CIA officers returned to the RMB office in Vientiane, they reported on their trip. "We recommended against any recruitment," said Kenning, "because [the Pole] just seemed like a bad drunk."

Despite this negative assessment, Vientiane Station decided to press ahead. The station "ended up sealing the deal," commented Kenning, "and arranged for the pink Cadillac to be delivered in Europe."

★ ★ ★

By several orders of magnitude, the External Branch's biggest potential score was with the deputy KGB *rezident*, Vladimir Piguzov. As the American targets officer within the *rezidentura*, Piguzov's mandate was spotting and recruiting people from among the vast US community in Vientiane. In such a target-rich environment, he had decided to focus on Air America personnel. This was no doubt influenced by two factors. First, it was an open secret that Air America was a CIA proprietary, so it would be a major feather in his cap if he could recruit a person connected—albeit somewhat indirectly—to the Soviets' primary adversary. Second, many Air America pilots—as the GRU's Colonel Gretchanine could attest—were prominent on Vientiane's social scene and thus rather easily approachable.

Perhaps no nightspot was more associated with Air America than the Purple Porpoise bar. Featuring a circular front door framed, appropriately, by a pair of concrete porpoises in bas-relief, the establishment was run by a jovial British expatriate called Monty Banks. This name, of course, was a play on the word *mountebank*, meaning a charlatan who swindles people out of their money. Indeed, Banks was a Cockney cardsharp without peer in Vientiane.[9]

The inside of the Purple Porpoise was a small, simple affair. A bar ran lengthwise down the right side of the building. There were a couple of high bar stools, but most of the furniture ran low to the ground with clusters of chairs and sofas around tables fashioned from tree trunks.

As for clientele, Banks catered his venue to foreigners who shunned the media. Air America made up much of that group, but it also included diplomats from a wide range of countries. Thus, it was not entirely out of the ordinary for Piguzov to start visiting at nights, initially keeping to himself at the bar and getting recognized as a familiar, benign face.

Over time, the Russian gravitated toward the dart board for what was a popular pastime in those days. And it was over friendly games of darts that the KGB officer eventually achieved his goal of befriending several American pilots.

To the credit of the Air America aviators, once they realized they were socializing with a Soviet diplomat, they reported their encounters to their company's designated security officer. That officer was, in fact, a fulltime CIA employee detached from the Directorate of Support in Langley. He, in turn, relayed details of the trysts to Gene Wojciechowski, the Hard Target representative seated at the embassy.

Under normal circumstances, word would have been sent back to the Air America pilots to give Piguzov the cold shoulder and break off contact. But in this case, something unusual was taking place. Over the course of the dart games, Piguzov began pouring out his soul. This could have been a clever ploy to bond with the Americans, but it did not seem to be the case. Rather, the KGB officer appeared to be genuinely seeking friendship and reaching out.

Eventually, Brian O'Connor managed to bump into Piguzov at a French diplomatic function. As he recalled,

> I had never met him but knew him from the photos we had. I chatted with him a bit. He seemed relaxed and confident. Very pleasant, good English.

Strategy sessions at the RMB office ensued, and it was decided to let the current arrangement play out. One particular Air America pilot was to act as an intermediary, and he was encouraged to maintain regular interactions at the Purple Porpoise. The findings from those sessions would be relayed via the Air America security officer to Wojciechowski at the embassy.

Over the course of several months, intriguing details started to emerge. Piguzov appeared to be demoralized by the 1968 Soviet invasion of Czechoslovakia. He also hinted that his grandparents, who had been relatively well-off landowners, had suffered greatly during the Soviet collectivization of farms. Both of these points were filed away as potential topics to exploit.

Just as promising, Piguzov fancied himself an inventor. Specifically, because of the high cost of ammunition in the Soviet Union, he had created a device that he claimed could test pistol marksmanship without using bullets. In fact, he told his Air America friend that he had crafted a prototype and brought it with him to Vientiane. Piguzov was convinced that his device had the potential to be a commercial success.

When word of Piguzov's invention was relayed back to the RMB office, it sparked another round of discussions. The CIA officers eventually settled on a plan for the Air America pilot to tell Piguzov that he had friends who were avid shooters. If Piguzov could lend him his prototype, it could show it to his friends to see what they thought of the invention.

This plan was put into effect, and a few days later the Hard Target officers were gathered around a table examining Piguzov's crude device. Explained O'Connor,

> It was a tin metal tray, about one-and-a-half inches in diameter. It had metal around the edges sticking up about a quarter of an inch. The tray had a dimple in the very center where a BB would be placed, and a small bar on the bottom of the tray that was attached to a simple clamp that could fasten to the barrel of the pistol. When the pistol was dry-fired with no bullets, the force of the hammer would jar the BB out of the dimple. If it ran straight ahead toward the target, a real shot would also hit the target. If the BB rolled to the right or left, the shot was not on target. At least that was Piguzov's theory. In practice, it was hard to aim at the target and see which way the BB ran because it only went a very short distance from the dimple in the center to the edge of the tray.

The quick conclusion at the RMB office was that the aiming device was clearly not viable. Still, it obviously meant a lot to Piguzov. That led the Hard Target officers to come up with a new plan of having the Air America pilot tell Piguzov that his friends all thought it was a great idea and that one friend in the United States had a company who might be interested in marketing it. In reality, the CIA officers would send it back to headquarters, where technicians could fashion a good commercial copy that looked better than his crude tin prototype. This improved version could then be sent back to Piguzov with a promise that it would be marketed and he would get a share of the profits.

If all went according to plan, money from the supposed profits could be handed over to Piguzov on a regular basis. This would get him accustomed to receiving discreet payments, hopefully opening the door to an eventual recruitment.

Before that transpired, O'Connor concluded his Laos tour in the summer of 1973 and rotated back to Langley. By coincidence, he was called into a meeting at headquarters with a dozen technicians who had just taken receipt of the aiming device. As they passed the invention around the table, it quickly became apparent that the requirements from Vientiane Station had not been properly communicated. The technicians were fixated on improving the design so that it had a chance of working as advertised, but said it would take many months of research and development. "I told them it wasn't important for the device to work," O'Connor interjected. "All they had to do was make it look cleaner, more professional, and get it back to Vientiane as soon as possible."

In the end, the indirect contact via the Purple Porpoise dragged on and Piguzov departed Laos in April 1974. The relationship had been developed to a significant extent, and the External Branch was frustratingly close to making a pitch—but the marriage was not yet consummated.

★ ★ ★

While the Soviet Union took up the preponderance of attention, the Hard Target wing's mandate also included the People's Republic of China. For several reasons, the Chinese posed a challenge vastly different from that posed by the Soviets. For one thing, there was a sizable ethnic Chinese population in Laos, some of which was recent migrants who had left the PRC via Macao and Hong Kong. From there, many illegally entered Laos through Phnom Penh with false identity papers claiming birth in Cambodia. These migrants, with extended family still in the PRC, remained generally sympathetic toward Beijing.[10]

For another thing, the Chinese diplomatic presence in Laos was far smaller and, for many years, less publicly visible than that of the Soviets. This was a direct reflection of the frenetic events taking place within the PRC. When Beijing first established its embassy in Vientiane in October 1962, China was still towing a line of peaceful coexistence with its Southeast Asian neighbor.

By 1966, however, the Cultural Revolution engulfed China and ushered in a chaotic period as communist radicals sought to purge their society of residual capitalist and traditional elements. Tied to this, the PRC adopted a hard-line, isolationist foreign policy that not only pushed confrontation with the United States and the Soviet Union, but even began to grate against North Vietnam because of the latter's apparent willingness to start peace negotiations with Washington.[11]

In line with this inflexibility, China's diplomatic presence in Vientiane waned. In January 1967, the Chinese abruptly recalled both their ambassador and chargé. Diplomatic ties were not fully cut, but the embassy functioned with only a skeleton staff that largely shunned contact.

While the Cultural Revolution still raged, Beijing had a slight change of heart in February 1969 and pragmatically decided to dispatch Counselor Yueh Tai-Heng back to Vientiane. Another year after that, a military attaché was assigned there, as well as a correspondent from the New China News Agency.[12]

By the opening of 1971, China's foreign policy had come full circle. With the arrival of Kuo-Ying as the new chargé in Vientiane, Chinese diplomats aggressively began to explore unilateral initiatives to expand Sino-Lao ties at a time when the US was seeking to decrease its role in Southeast Asia.[13] This included a charm offensive focused toward Prime Minister Souvanna Phouma.

The efforts soon began to bear fruit. In May 1971, Souvanna Phouma gave a *New York Times* interview in which he downplayed the threat posed by a major Chinese road-building effort in northern and northwestern Laos. In early July, he gave another interview in which he underscored the need for Chinese participation in an Indochinese settlement. Later that month, he instructed his cabinet to increase contact with Chinese diplomats. As a result, Acting Foreign Minister Khamphan Panya hosted a dinner for the Chinese that was attended by numerous senior RLG officials. During that occasion, Panya leaned on the Chinese to build a pavilion at the annual That Luang festival in the capital.[14]

Finally, toward the end of that year a CIA clandestine source revealed that Chargé Kuo-Ying had gone out of his way to assure the head of the RLG National Assembly that China was doing all that was possible to persuade the Pathet Lao to arrive at a negotiated settlement.[15]

Operating against this more assertive Chinese diplomatic presence, the CIA's External Branch had a willing partner in the Police Special Branch. Since 1966, the Special Branch had been opening and copying all letters coming from and going to the PRC. Most of these, they found, were appeals from family members in China asking for money and goods. The Special Branch also appears to have tipped off its Thai counterparts in December 1970 when two Chinese intelligence officers allegedly crossed from Vientiane to Nong Khai district; both fled back to Laos before Thai investigators could question them.[16]

The CIA augmented the Special Branch's take with its own unilateral efforts. These were initially spearheaded by a single officer of the External Branch who was posted to Luang Prabang in 1970. As one member of the royal court explained, this town was a good pick on several counts:

> Half of Luang Prabang had Chinese blood. It was the only town that had an official Lao mayor and an unofficial Chinese mayor. It also had a Chinese consulate, the only foreign consulate in town.[17]

Still, the output from this officer was not especially impressive. According to a senior member of Vientiane Station,

> These were amateurish pursuits that produced intelligence of pocket litter value: match boxes, ticket stubs, some market data. Miniscule value at best.[18]

In mid-1971, the Hard Target wing looked to increase its China coverage with the arrival of a 50-year-old Chinese American officer named Ben. Born and raised in China, Ben had previously been assigned to Indonesia under USAID cover in early 1964 to monitor the meteoric rise of that country's Chinese-backed communist party. He was still in Jakarta during the deadly October 1965 upheaval that resulted in the decimation of Indonesia's communist ranks, as well as the severance of ties between Indonesia and the PRC.

Despite Ben's best efforts once he arrived in Vientiane, progress against the Chinese target remained frustratingly slow. For reasons not readily apparent, he sat in the RMB office but was not afforded USAID cover like the rest of the Hard Target case officers; rather, he was given a cover assignment under Air America's construction subsidiary Penco. This would have left him off invitations to most diplomatic functions.[19]

Severely limited in his ability to bump into Chinese officials on the diplomatic circuit, Ben instead had to network primarily among local Chinese businessmen.[20] This, plus the fact that he never had a dedicated surveillance team on tap, meant that seduction of the Chinese target would be relegated to something of an afterthought by the Hard Target wing.

CHAPTER 11

Suspicious Minds

For every CIA station that fields an External Branch, it stands to reason there is an Internal Branch. In the case of Laos, the latter had the RLG in its sights. In particular, a large part of its efforts involved shielding Prime Minister Souvanna Phouma from domestic political pressure.[1]

Doing so was understandable. With every passing year, Souvanna had grown increasingly indispensable in Washington's eyes because he personified the RLG's brand of pro-Western neutrality. Also, he was seen as the linchpin in having the RLG positively contribute to an overarching peace agreement that would allow for the United States to end its involvement in Indochina.

At the same time, Souvanna could be a hard sell domestically. At times gruff and patronizing, he had gotten off to an especially bad start with the new National Assembly that took office in 1965. This followed limited elections in which only civil servants and other members of the government had voted. The fresh batch of legislators were rather young and assertive—and Souvanna had wasted no time speaking down to the lot.

If anything, relations between the two worsened in 1966. By midyear, the assemblymen had reached their collective breaking point. Refusing to submit to the prime minister's inflexibility and arrogance, they rejected in September the national budget he submitted. Souvanna interpreted this as a vote of no confidence, so he appealed to the king to dissolve the National Assembly and call for general elections.

All of this put the king in a bind. Realizing the prime minister was just as much to blame for the impasse, the king refused to take sides. The

King's Council, however, approved the dissolution by a razor margin and opened the path for new polls in January 1967.[2]

Enter the Internal Branch. "Since the US government was sinking valuable resources into Laos, we wanted to know with more certainty where the inchoate Lao political process was going," explained Deputy Station Chief Jim Lilley. "We wanted to limit the surprises."[3]

Playing the role of Souvanna's Guardian Angel, the station spent generously behind the scenes to winnow the electoral slate to favor the prime minister's allies. Their efforts worked, at least for the short term, with Souvanna's candidates winning forty of the fifty-nine assembly seats in 1967.[4]

As it turned out, the prime minister's parliamentary allies were fickle. Most of the legislators soon began to show primary loyalty to the military commanders from their respective regions. Moreover, within three years an emergent opposition bloc had coalesced around the Sananikones. Aptly described as the Rockefellers of Laos, the entrepreneurial Sananikone clan had risen to prominence in and around Vientiane after a local royal family suffered a humiliating defeat to the Thai in the early 19th century. As of late 1970, its ranks included senior FAR officers, a minister, and president of the National Assembly. In addition, Kouprasith Abhay, the ironfisted commander of the Vientiane military region, had a mother and wife from that extended family.[5]

Enter the Internal Branch once more. Distributing stipends to cool tempers, the CIA in early 1971 helped mute criticism by the Sananikone legislative bloc. Publicly, it was alleged that the Sanaikones had a change of heart because they saw Souvanna as slightly more palatable than a government dominated by southern rightists.[6]

In fact, the Internal Branch's machinations were an open secret. According to Richard Howland, a Foreign Service officer who arrived at the US embassy in 1971 as political counselor,

> What did the [US embassy's] political section do? Well, it was difficult for me to figure out what the political section did. Key figures in the parliament were "influenced" by the CIA, so that they wouldn't try to overthrow Souvanna with a motion of no confidence. No point reporting on that—the CIA had the real story.[7]

In January 1972, another parliamentary election was held with the Internal Branch, yet again, working the back room to ensure a slate favorable to the prime minister.[8]

But by mid-1972, even the CIA's best efforts in the National Assembly seemed to be coming up short. As before, the Sananikone bloc was rattling sabers and threating a no confidence vote. This time, however, there was a personal dimension impervious to payouts. Specifically, the Sananikones were livid with Souvanna's choice of finance minister, Sisouk na Champassak. A southerner closely allied with Prince Boun Oum, Sisouk displayed a level of arrogance on par with Souvanna. He had also repeatedly clashed with the Sananikones over the years, becoming the closest thing the clan had to an archnemesis.[9]

The political infighting in Laos came at a monumentally bad time for Washington. By the opening of the second quarter of 1972, PAVN's Easter Offensive was in full swing in South Vietnam and the RLG's own security situation was increasingly precarious. Livid with the turn of events, President Nixon was venting toward his foreign policy team and demanded that it craft new recommendations to chasten the North Vietnamese regime and force Hanoi to reach a negotiated settlement.

One of those feeling the heat from Nixon was the CIA's Dan Arnold. Born in Illinois, Arnold had moved to Pennsylvania as a child and at the tender age of 16 enrolled in the University of Pittsburgh. One year later, during a fit of patriotic fervor, he had implored his father for permission to volunteer for the Marines. To this his father understandably refused. As consolation, he then asked his father if he could join the university's ROTC program. This time his father acceded—not realizing that an ROTC member could go on active duty without need for a parental waiver.

The headstrong Arnold lost no time in pursuing his wish to join the Marines. In January 1943, the corps readily obliged. By the following year, he was in the Pacific. Arnold landed in the second assault wave at Eniwetok, then in the first wave at Guam. He took away shrapnel in his left hip and a bullet scar in his upper left arm as souvenirs.

Later in 1944, Arnold's regimental commander picked him as one of three to return to Quantico to be commissioned. That fortuitous decision no doubt saved his life, as his battalion was nearly wiped out in brutal combat on Okinawa in early 1945.[10]

Not yet finished with the military, Arnold volunteered again, in 1947. Rather than the Marines, this time he entered the army's 82nd Airborne Division and served as a special agent in the division's Counter-Intelligence Corps Detachment.

His appetite whetted for intelligence matters, Arnold joined the CIA in 1952. Two years later, he began a four-year tour in Manila. In 1962, he began another four years as deputy station chief in Bangkok. Then, starting in 1968, he served two years as station chief on Taiwan.

Immediately after the Taiwan tour, Arnold returned to Langley and was appointed chief of Vietnam Operations. At the time, this was the largest office in the CIA's clandestine services, with worldwide responsibility for operations tied to North Vietnam, South Vietnam, Laos, and Cambodia. Still in this position in late April 1972, he was attending a Saturday night dinner party in northern Virginia when he received a telephone call from CIA Director Richard Helms:

> Dick informed me that he had just received a call from Henry Kissinger, who ordered that a wide-ranging disinformation program be devised to create havoc in Hanoi. The program had to be done immediately, which meant that I left the dinner and went to the office and for the next 36 hours or so we crafted a very elaborate program which was promptly approved and immediately implemented.

The program Arnold's office submitted was designed to make it appear like American intelligence officers were in secret contact with a dissident faction among North Vietnam's top communists. The intent was to stoke tensions and suspicions within the already paranoid DRV Politburo, potentially weakening the unity of its leadership.

As per the CIA plan, many stations around the world would be involved in conveying the campaign's underlying themes, which would then be reinforced by assets controlled by other stations. Precise scripts were prepared, all of which were designed to be reported to Hanoi to persuade that its regime was penetrated and that the United States was going to significantly raise the ante.

To lend credibility to the rumors, select assets were to convey advance word that the United states was taking airdropped mines out of storage and that planes capable of delivering them were moving from Japan to the Philippines. The ultimate US intent, they were to reveal, was to mine Haiphong harbor.

In fact, the mining operation was real and went into effect a few short days later on 9 May.

Then, on 17 May, Nixon telephoned Major General Alexander Haig, the deputy assistant for National Security Affairs, and demanded a widened and rejuvenated psychological warfare campaign against North Vietnam. The following day, CIA officials were present during a top-secret brainstorming session at the National Security Council. The results from that session, which were presented to Nixon, included calls for a massive dissemination of leaflets and a variety of gray and black radio-station transmissions into the DRV.[11]

Also part of the program would be the CIA's disinformation campaign that had already been set in motion. In fact the next salvo in that campaign was to be fired on 22 May from Vientiane Station, where an agent with ties to the DRV embassy had been doubled. As this agent had earlier passed on advance word about the Haiphong mining, his bona fides were burnished. He was now to convey to an intelligence officer at the DRV embassy that his American sources were apparently in touch with Politburo dissidents who wanted to "end this stupid war." He was also to hint that the dissident DRV faction had wanted the Haiphong mining as the only tangible way to break the power of the hardliners in Hanoi.

On 22 May, the meeting with the DRV intelligence officer took place. There was a snag, however, when the double agent strayed from his script and the DRV officer appeared to miss the intended nuances.[12]

Although a second meeting in Vientiane was planned within the week, the disinformation campaign had gone global by then. Similar messages were being conveyed not just to North Vietnamese sources, but also to Soviets and, to a lesser extent, Chinese for further conveyance to Hanoi. Many of these mental bullets were being fed to sources based in France and India.[13]

A few weeks later, Vientiane Station again factored into the heightened psychological warfare program against the DRV. As the RLG already had radio transmission facilities that were broadcasting anti-communist programming to minority groups in northern Laos and across the border in the DRV, the CIA intended to piggyback on those broadcasts with bogus coded messages supposedly intended for hill tribe guerrillas operating inside North Vietnam. In fact, this was a revival of a semi-notional hill tribe resistance movement the CIA had raised years earlier in the DRV called the Committee for the Liberation of Oppressed Minorities. That movement had been abandoned in August 1971 when its Lao-based Tai Dam leadership demanded that an actual resistance be funded—but polygraphs revealed that half of the leadership had been, or was still, in touch with the Pathet Lao or PAVN.[14]

As with all psychological warfare operations, it was difficult to gauge the success of the CIA's disinformation program. The United States did not have any well-placed sources in Hanoi that could report on resultant schisms within the Politburo. Moreover, the DRV media was too circumspect to openly discuss internal dissent. Still, most communist regimes are susceptible to cannibalistic introspection, and it was hard to believe Hanoi was immune from these destructive tendencies.

★ ★ ★

Vientiane Station's Internal Branch had one other critical mandate besides shielding the prime minister from his own legislature. Although the United States financially underwrote the RLG, Souvanna Phouma was nobody's puppet. There was always a fear, albeit small, that he might go his own way and try to negotiate a side settlement with the communists, similar to what he had attempted in 1956–58. Were he to do that again without closely coordinating efforts with Washington, there was a chance he could derail the delicate dance Kissinger was trying to perform with his DRV counterparts at the Paris peace talks.

To be sure, Souvanna had resumed attempts to engage his half brother via letters that were being shuttled back and forth to Sam Neua. During 1970, in fact, the two nearly agreed on a limited ceasefire around the PDJ. The following summer, another round of letters discussed possible negotiation venues in Vientiane and the PDJ.

In all these cases, the complicating factor was the Pathet Lao's insistence on a bombing halt as a prerequisite for a ceasefire. This greatly concerned Washington, as the United States wanted to continue with a concerted bombing campaign along the Ho Chi Minh Trail to keep pressure on the DRV. Souvanna was well aware of Washington's perspective on this matter and to date had deftly sidestepped this Pathet Lao demand.[15]

In July 1972, the issue again came to the fore. In yet another exchange of letters, Souphanouvong was once more dangling the possibility of a ceasefire. Reviewing the proposal in a closed-door Special Actions Group session in Washington, Kissinger asked whether the Pathet Lao proposal again required a bombing halt as a prerequisite. Yes, came the response, the United States would have to first stop attacks along the Ho Chi Minh Trail.[16]

One week later during a further Special Actions Group tryst, the topic was revisited. This time, the group agreed that it needed to get more clarity about Souvanna's intentions regarding his separate negotiations with Souphanouvong. Reading between the lines, there was apparently some concern that the prime minister might be veering from a coordinated script.[17]

Charged with getting clarity was the Internal Branch. Assuming Souvanna would have candidly discussed the bombing halt and ceasefire proposals in cabinet meetings, the branch turned toward one of its best placed agents—the acting foreign minister.[18]

Handling this particular source was case officer Adger Emerson Player. A graduate student from the University of Colorado, Player had entered the CIA in 1960 and got his first overseas posting to Ghana two years later.

While in Ghana, Player had garnered worldwide attention. This came about during an especially vitriolic anti-American rally in Accra during 1964, culminating in a 200-man mob entering the US embassy grounds and pulling down the flag. With barely a pause, Player stared down the protesters and ran the flag back up the pole. Two Congressmen proposed awarding him the Medal of Freedom for his heroics, but the matter was not further pursued, probably because the added publicity would have been detrimental to his CIA career.

From Ghana, Player shifted to the Congo. Over the two years of his tour, which coincided with Devlin's second tenure as station chief, CIA operations helped beat back and decisively defeat Cuban-backed communist rebels.

Taking a break from Africa, Player next surfaced on Taiwan in 1968 for Chinese language training. In September 1969, he arrived in Vientiane and was given cover in the Economics Section. In reality, he was posted to the Internal Branch and took over a stable of sources in the RLG legislative wing and Foreign Ministry.

Fast forward to August 1972, and Player was counting down the weeks before his Laos tour concluded. To address Washington's urgent requirement for information about Souvanna's ceasefire overtures, one of his last assignments was to conduct a series of meetings with the acting foreign minister to keep apprised of cabinet discussions. It was also decided that these meetings would be held in Player's car at night while he drove in circles around Vientiane.

At this point it should be noted that Player happened to be one of the rarest of species: a Black case officer in the CIA. To that time, the Agency was thoroughly dominated by white, mostly Anglo-Saxon, middle-class liberal arts college graduates. As of 1967, there were reportedly less than twenty African Americans out of 12,000 non-clerical CIA employees.[19]

While posted to Ghana and the Congo, skin tone could have very much worked in Player's favor. But in Laos, he would have stood out and been memorable—especially a Black man driving around with a Lao passenger in the evening and especially while the FAR had started enforcing a late-night curfew with checkpoints around the city.[20]

The solution, the two men decided, was to use disguises that would hide both of their ethnicities.

Of course, the CIA had a large body of experience using disguises in clandestine operations. In one of the more elaborate examples, an Agency makeup expert had been rushed to Burundi in May 1964 to help exfiltrate a 24-year-old PRC diplomat that had defected to the US embassy. Disguising the defector as a Caucasian female, he was able to successfully walk out past a gauntlet of Chinese and Burundi police lying in wait.[21]

More often than not, the CIA's disguises—at least those used in Southeast Asia—were on the simpler end of the spectrum. For example, while vetting a Lao source in a Bangkok safe house in 1971, Brian O'Connor had been told to simply brush some gray streaks in his moustache and wear eyeglasses to pass himself off as older than his real age.

But then in 1972, the CIA had benefited from a revolutionary advancement. Secretly partnering with a Hollywood special effects artist who had earned an Academy Award for the simian prosthetics in *Planet of the Apes*, the Agency had prepared prototypes for masks that slipped over the entire head. From a moderate distance, say while behind the wheel driving, these were convincing enough to change ethnicities. For example, a Black man could become a Caucasian, or a Caucasian could become an East Asian.

For use by Player and the acting foreign minister, two of the Caucasian mask prototypes were sent to Vientiane along with two CIA disguise experts. All four men rendezvoused one night in a safe house, where the masks were individually fitted to the two subjects. In addition, Player was given thin latex gloves that extended up to the elbow, transforming his arms into a light beige tone.[22]

With a modicum of practice, Player and the Lao were able to don and remove their masks in a few short seconds. Although the masks were extremely hot and uncomfortable in the Vientiane weather, the strong air conditioning in Player's car made them tolerable enough. Both men—Caucasians from a distance—were able to breeze through checkpoints without question over the next several days, with the acting foreign minister offering detailed insights into Souvanna's most recent cabinet musings on negotiations with the Pathet Lao.[23]

★ ★ ★

In the end, movement toward a ceasefire became a race to the finish. On 17 October, senior Pathet Lao member Phoumi Vongvichit ventured to Vientiane as a stand-in for Souphanouvong to begin face-to-face talks with Pheng Phongsavan, representing Souvanna Phouma. As the pair made some initial progress, Kissinger and his DRV counterparts inked the Paris Peace Accords on 27 January 1973. Just under a month later, on 21 February, the two Lao negotiators finalized and signed their own peace deal.

According to this new Vientiane agreement, a ceasefire went into effect the following day. Each side would be frozen in place, with the RLG allocated control of the territory it held as of 22 February. Similar, the Pathet Lao zone was deemed to be all territory in communist hands as of the same day. Neither side would be permitted to cross ceasefire lines and encroach into the other's zone.

The ceasefire, it turned out, was one of the only concrete details in the entire document. For example, within thirty days both the RLG and Pathet Lao were to set up a provisional coalition government with even representation. They were also to set up a national political coalition council with even representation. But complicating matters, the national political coalition council was equal in stature to, but independent of, the provisional coalition government. How exactly the two equivalent bodies would interact was not readily apparent.

Within sixty days after the provisional coalition government was formed, the document demanded that all foreign troops withdraw. How this would be verified and enforced was not spelled out. The ICC was theoretically to continue to perform its duties, but now it was subordinate to a new joint commission to implement the agreement, which was to be staffed by lower-ranking officials who had to act unanimously. Thus, the ICC, which had long been hobbled by the need for unanimity, was now to answer to a new commission that also had to act unanimously.

There would be free and fair elections to select a permanent coalition government, but no timetable was given.

Both Vientiane and Luang Prabang were to be "neutralized," but no timeframe was given.

While all these critical details were lacking, thus requiring a new round of negotiations to spell out protocols, it was readily apparent that Laos would no longer be the same. And it was while facing these monumental uncertainties that Vientiane Station headed into the uncharted waters of 1973.

CHAPTER 12

Writing on the Wall

Assuming the best but planning for the worst, Vientiane Station in 1972 had already started preparing in the event Laos became diplomatically hostile. Some of its schemes had fallen short. Recalled Brian O'Connor,

> Those of us in the External Branch were given an assignment to go around town and start selecting dead drop locations in the event Laos fell. [One of the officers] picked a hole next to a distinctive-looking old tree on the bank of the Mekong. He said that the tree had been there for hundreds of years, and it would be there for a couple of hundred more. Within a couple of months, it had been chopped down.

The paramilitary headquarters in Udorn had had even less success. In early December 1972, it had initiated a program whereby fifty Thai college graduates without any prior military experience would be given advanced stay-behind agent training. Accordingly, the fifty soon started arriving at a Thai training camp for this short-notice metamorphosis. As with the other Thai-based training programs being orchestrated by Udorn, the instructors were provided by the US Army Special Forces. But as the Green Berets were not themselves fluent in such traditional spy craft, the program concluded with poor results and none of the intended agents ever crossed the Mekong.

By the following year, contingency planning was handed off to a new cast heading Vientiane Station. In as station chief was Dan Arnold, the former chief of Vietnam Operations who had arrived in mid-1972 as deputy station chief in Laos. When Hugh Tovar made the lateral shift to station chief in Bangkok in May 1973, Arnold was promoted to take his place.

Arriving as the new deputy station chief was Roger McCarthy. A gregarious New Yorker, he had been a young Morse code operator in World War II and was hired by the CIA as a communicator. Sent to Taiwan with Western Enterprises in 1953, he began his tour with a bang, literally. That July, he was on the CIA team supporting a major Nationalist raid on the island of Tungshan, just off the Fukien coast. It proved to be a major fiasco, with Nationalist paratroopers jumping into a murderous crossfire and dozens drowning off the beach. The airborne element lost nearly half its number when a withdrawal was ordered forty-four hours into a planned three-day operation.[1]

Despite these horrific losses, McCarthy had turned in a strong performance and earned a berth stateside to complete intelligence officer training. He was subsequently posted as an instructor at the Saipan training base and was on hand in 1956 when six Lao from SIDASP were sent for a tradecraft course. McCarthy came away less than impressed, noting that the Lao would get easily spooked and hold each other's hands during nighttime drills.

In stark contrast, McCarthy was still on Saipan during the arrival of an initial cadre of Khampa tribesmen from Tibet. He deeply connected with the stoic Khampa, and later seized the opportunity to assume command of the Agency's Tibet Task Force through the end of 1961.[2]

Following further tours in Taiwan and Peru, McCarthy next went to Southeast Asia in 1969 as the ranking officer in Danang, South Vietnam.[3] In 1971, he returned to headquarters as deputy head of the Indochina desk, then deployed in June 1973 as deputy station chief in Vientiane.

For the other arrivals at Vientiane Station during 1973, cover assignments were now something that needed to be addressed more seriously. Prior to that year, Laos was considered—from a counter-intelligence perspective—to be extremely friendly territory. "The US very much controlled the turf," summed up one station officer. After all, hundreds of CIA officers had filed through the kingdom without the RLG quibbling about who was declared and who was not. This had led to covers that were ludicrously thin—Penco, for instance. It had also given rise to occasional lapses in counterintelligence judgement. For example, one of the case officers handling a unilateral surveillance team thought nothing of hosting outdoor movie showings for them at his residence on multiple occasions.[4]

Given the welcoming embrace of the RLG and limited size of hostile foreign intelligence services in Vientiane, such shortfalls could be overlooked.

After the signing of the February 1973 ceasefire agreement, however, all bets were off. Pathet Lao officials would be taking over an unprecedented number of cabinet posts in the near future, and their security forces would also be entering Vientiane in large numbers. As a corollary, the North Vietnamese, Soviet, and Chinese embassies would likely grow emboldened. All of this meant far more scrutiny of Vientiane Station.

To adjust to the new paradigm, there appear to have been proactive attempts to better conceal some incoming members to the station. For example, Frank Sommers, a Soviet target officer who had completed earlier tours in Frankfurt and Vienna, arrived in mid-1973 and was afforded Political Section cover while posted to the External Branch at the RMB building. Similarly, two more new arrivals, both young and with prior experience in South Vietnam, were named as commercial officers at the main embassy.

But old habits die hard. John Cothorn, an African American officer who had served one prior tour in South Vietnam under an alias, arrived at the External Branch in March 1973 under his real name. Moreover, he was still given USAID cover, albeit with the administration analysis staff rather than the usual RMB.

★ ★ ★

Besides endeavoring to do a better job at concealing its members, Vientiane Station had more immediate concerns. On 16 February, five days before the Vientiane agreement was signed, the Soviet embassy handed over to the Pathet Lao an An-2 biplane with Aeroflot crew. Based at Wattay, it was to be used for regular shuttles between the capital and Sam Neua.[5] Two months later, Aeroflot assigned another plane—this one an An-12 four-engine turboprop—to fly twice weekly between Vientiane and Hanoi.

All of this was in support of ongoing negotiations between the RLG and Pathet Lao to produce protocols that would flesh out the skeletal ceasefire agreement. After little movement through midyear, Souphanouvong's representative, Phoumi Vongvichit, ventured to Vientiane during the first week of July and there appeared—for a brief moment—to be an uptick in progress.[6]

This optimism would not last. One week later, citing the glacial pace of talks, Souvanna Phouma stepped into the fray and declared he take a direct role in negotiations with the Pathet Lao.[7] Meetings were set to resume on 19 July.

At that point, Vientiane Station conjured a major clandestine technical operation. Its focus was on the Somboun Inthavong Hotel, a Lao-managed establishment one block south of the That Dam black stupa. The hotel had just two floors. The popular Lido nightclub occupied most of the ground floor, while rooms on the upper level were to be taken over as meeting venues for the peace talks. The station wanted to wire the rooms designated for the Pathet Lao delegation to glean insights into their negotiating stance and strategies.

As a matter of urgency, the station brought in a team of technicians. The technicians were to install bugs over the course of a night, though there might be the need to reposition the microphones over the ensuing days or weeks. To do so without being exposed, the station wanted additional eyes that could keep the exterior of the hotel under watch while the specialists were at work.

As this was a highly compartmentalized unilateral operation, it was decided not to use any of the surveillance teams operated by the External Branch. Instead, the call went out to an unusual source. During the CIA's paramilitary campaign that raged in the Lao countryside, there had been a major project—code-named Unity—to introduce more than two dozen battalions of Thai volunteers. To coordinate air support for these battalions, the CIA hired forward air guides, or FAGs, that were embedded with the troops. These FAGs were Thai civilians who were fluent in English; they used their linguistic skills to vector in tactical airstrikes from orbiting US Air Force planes. Understandably, they amassed considerable trust from both the air force and their CIA paramilitary advisors.

Following the February 1973 agreement, the Thai volunteer battalions, like all other combatants, had to abide by a ceasefire in place. This armistice was holding through midyear, making it less important for the FAGs to remain deployed at the front. Reasoning that two FAGs could be spared for use in Vientiane, a pair of them—who had gone by the radio call signs Hawkeye and Ringo—were flown in an Air America light plane to the capital on 18 July. Once there they were introduced to Tom, a Chinese American paramilitary officer who had earlier advised a Hmong guerrilla regiment in northeastern Laos. Like the FAGs, Tom was underutilized after the ceasefire and available for supplemental tasking. Recalled Hawkeye,

> We were told to watch outside the hotel beginning that night from midnight until dawn. We had to report to Mister Tom every fifteen minutes, and tell him if there was any unusual activity, any unusual arrivals at the hotel. We were told that five technicians were inside installing bugs in the meeting rooms. We kept this up for three nights, then rested.[8]

The technical mission was a success, with talks progressing through the second half of the month without the Pathet Lao delegates wise to the bugs. On 1 August, tentative agreement was reached on the neutralization of Vientiane and Luang Prabang. To accomplish this, each side would be allowed to station one infantry battalion and one thousand police in Vientiane, and two infantry companies and five hundred police in the royal capital.

All of this had put the FAR generals and rightist politicians in a funk. Irate at what they saw as capitulation to the Pathet Lao, their discontent was approaching critical mass. It must be kept in mind that Laos had not had a proper coup in years. There had been a few ludicrous attempts in the interim, usually traced back to a pair of former army officers exiled to Thailand. The first was Phoumi Nosavan, the erstwhile strongman through 1965. The second was Colonel Bounleut Saycocie, a former military attaché in Washington, graduate of the US Army's Command and General Staff College at Fort Leavenworth, and head of FAR logistics. Bounleut had instigated the short-lived January 1965 coup (but pragmatically switched sides and temporarily avoided repercussions), then had been forced to flee the kingdom after backing Thao Ma's failed 1966 power grab. A 1968 military tribunal had belatedly tried him in absentia for the former transgression and gave him twenty years.[9]

From the Thai side of the Mekong, the unrepentant Bounleut had continued to talk up threats. In October 1970, he allegedly tried to hire Thai nationals to fight on his behalf in Laos. Two months later, a dozen members of his wife's family were arrested in Savannakhet, allegedly because the renegade colonel was looking to incorporate them into his Quixotic plans.[10]

In early 1971, the conspiring grew even more bizarre. On 9 April, eight more people were arrested in Vientiane, including the editor of the Information Ministry's news bulletin. The mastermind behind this coup attempt was Amphorn Suvannabol, a colorful Thai politician who had twice served as a legislator from Nong Khai before taking a distinctly leftist turn and railing against the United States at a 1964 Beijing symposium.[11]

Decades earlier Amphorn had attended high school in Vientiane and briefly fought with the Lao Issara. His association with Laos since that time, however, had been nil. While this made him a most unlikely candidate for prime minister, he claimed that unnamed FAR officers—Phoumi Nosavan's name was suggested—had wanted him to swoop into Laos and take over from Souvanna.[12] Needless to say, the plot earned eye rolls and little more.

During the first half of August 1973, the coup rumors took a new turn. During the second week of the month, several FAR officers secretly traveled to Bangkok as tourists; there they huddled to vent about the direction of the peace talks. During the trip, the name of Thao Ma—the former air force chief exiled in Thailand since 1966—was mentioned more than once. The following week, Thao Ma's name again surfaced when General Sourith don Sasorith, the air force chief, let slip at a diplomatic function that the rebel general might return to Laos in the near future.[13]

Despite such forewarning, Thao Ma, crossing the Mekong by boat at 0500 on 20 August, achieved total surprise. Accompanied by sixty followers—including six loyal T-28 pilots, Colonel Bounleut Saycocie, and former DNC Lieutenant Colonel Pany Phongthibsavat—the renegade aviator easily consolidated control over Wattay.[14]

Carrying satchels of blue-and-while rebel armbands and shoulder patches for their so-called Revolutionary Committee of the Coup d'état, the coup force was soon joined by an estimated 200 FAR sympathizers. There were also rumors that General Vang Pao, the Hmong chieftain and commander of the military region in northeastern Laos, hinted his support and two days earlier had quietly moved a contingent of Hmong troops closer to the capital.[15]

It did not take long for word of the odd happenings at Wattay to filter into town. Jim Sheldon, a CIA officer stationed at the embassy to coordinate the downsizing of paramilitary operations, was alerted by an American pilot that had been heading to Wattay:

> I got an early morning wake-up call that 'Thao Ma was coming.' I contacted others in the Station and we quickly converged at the embassy. Dan [Arnold] told me to head over the Defense Ministry, and Roger [McCarthy] was to go to Chinaimo. We were carrying HT radios so we could stay in touch with each other.

As the two CIA officers departed for those destinations, Bounleut and Pany boarded separate M706 scout cars at Wattay and headed into town. Pany drove past the front of the Defense Ministry compound at Phone Kheng; driven off by automatic-weapons fire, he steered back into town and joined Bounleut at the government radio station. Commandeering the facility, they issued a communique at 0700 hours calling for the replacement of Souvanna Phouma by Prince Boun Oum.

Concurrently, a third rebel group took over the national bank, while a fourth drove to Souvanna's residence, only to find the prime minister gone. This was because the US *chargé d'affaires*, John Dean, had moments earlier convinced Souvanna to leave his house and seek sanctuary at the US ambassador's residence.

Back at Wattay, Thao Ma and his six loyal pilots had boarded T-28s at 0600 and taken to the sky. Fulfilling a personnel vendetta against General Kouprasith, Thao Ma and another pilot dive-bombed Chinaimo, leveling Kouprasith's two-floor brick villa. The general was not inside; however, his nephew, Lt. Colonel Thongkham Abhay, was killed in the attack.

On hand to see the airstrike was Roger McCarthy, who had already reached Chinaimo and quickly rendezvoused with Kouprasith. Both were seeking shelter under a massive banyan when bombs obliterated the general's house. "Kouprasith was initially suspicious of CIA involvement," said McCarthy, "but as we watched the explosions from under the tree I was able to disabuse him of this sentiment."

News of the unfolding coup quickly spread across the kingdom. By 0930, FAR troops retook the radio station and began broadcasting statements from Kouprasith, Bounpone, and Souvanna.[16] Half an hour later, the deputy commander of the Vientiane military region led a column of scout cars from Chinaimo toward Wattay. There a standoff ensued, with sporadic gunfire cutting across the gates of the airbase.

The coup attempt soon began to unravel after a FAR soldier, firing a truck-mounted machine gun, hit Thao Ma's orbiting T-28. Streaming smoke, the general crash-landed at Wattay. By that time, FAR troops had pushed their way onto the tarmac. Wounded but still very much alive, Thao Ma was lifted from the cockpit, transferred to the back of a truck, and driven to Chinaimo.

Once there, the rebel general was thrown at the feet of Kouprasith. The vitriol shared between the two was apparent when Kouprasith grinded his boot across Thao Ma's cheek, the ultimate Lao insult. The coup leader was then tossed back into the truck. With McCarthy witnessing, Kouprasith ordered his bodyguard to place a bullet in Thao Ma's stomach, then his chest. The corpse was taken to a ditch and unceremoniously dumped.

With Thao Ma dead, the coup fizzled. Those rebels holding the bank disappeared. At the radio station, Pany had already taken to his scout car and tried racing toward Wattay, only to run out of gas en route. Taking to foot, he was captured by the armor commander from Chinaimo. More fortunate was Bounleut, who, having earlier fled from the radio station to the airbase, stole a chopper and flew to Thakhek; he then crossed the Mekong by boat into Thai exile once more. Another three rebels commandeered a light plane and flew to Bangkok.[17]

McCarthy was still at Chinaimo when several rebels captured at the radio station, plus Pany, were brought before Kouprasith. The FAR general gave them a stern lecture and challenged them to justify their actions. Taken away, Kouprasith turned to the CIA officer. "They will be questioned, then attempt to escape during the night," explained the general in a matter-of-fact tone. "They will not succeed."[18]

By 1100, FAR was cleaning up the last vestiges of the uprising. Except for two burning jeeps and discarded armbands at Wattay, little remained as evidence of the coup. Later that afternoon, the diplomatic corps flocked to Souvanna's house to offer congratulations.

In the end, the Thao Ma coup attempt proved the last gasp of the rightists. Without further incident, the long-awaited protocols to the ceasefire agreement were signed on 12 September. Topping the agenda was the formation of a Joint Commission to Implement the Agreement (JCIA), essentially a watchdog organization to ensure the ceasefire was not violated. As a matter of priority, the commission would select the locations where Pathet Lao military and police units would be stationed in Vientiane and Luang Prabang.

Surprisingly, the JCIA made fast progress. In Vientiane, the Somboun high school, located a block away from the DRV embassy, was renovated during September to serve as the compound for the Pathet Lao contingent in the capital.

In Luang Prabang, the chairman of the RLG delegation to the JCIA went there during the first week of October to locate suitable office space and living quarters for the Pathet Lao. For the main office, he chose a building opposite Wat Visounnaraj, the so-called Watermelon Stupa, named because of the distinctive shape of its dome. Whether by design or accident, he chose two strategic locations for the Pathet Lao troops: next to the bridge leading to the airport, and on the high ground south of town astride Route 13 heading to Vientiane.

Getting advance word of these selections, Vientiane Station once more rushed specialists from the Technical Services Division to Laos. They continued to Luang Prabang and laced the Pathet Lao's soon-to-be main office with bugs. Useful intelligence on Pathet Lao plans was later gleaned from these microphones.

On 10 October, Pathet Lao Radio stated that the first wave of Pathet Lao soldiers and police had already left Sam Neua for transit through Hanoi. Two days later, a pair of Aeroflot An-12 transports from Gia Lam airbase, North Vietnam, landed at Wattay. From them stepped cadre and soldiers from the Pathet Lao 206th Public Security Battalion. Over half of them were armed with AK-47 assault rifles; a smattering of rocket launchers was also seen. They were taken directly from Wattay to their new quarters at the Somboun high school.

On 18 October, a Chinese Il-14 twin-engine plane lifted the first load of Pathet Lao troops from Hanoi to Luang Prabang.

Further sorties took place intermittently over the next month. By the third week of November, the Soviets had carried just short of 1,000 Pathet Lao to Vientiane. Having outstripped the Somboun high school, the Pathet Lao also took over the entire Somboun Inthavong Hotel (the same venue where the negotiations had earlier taken place). Meantime, the Chinese had moved 368 men to Luang Prabang.

Facing this unprecedented number of Pathet Lao in the capital, diplomats at the US embassy tried to give it a positive spin. As of early November, the Pathet Lao were not too conspicuous around town, the Americans cabled back to Washington. Some were even attending the town's annual fair.[19]

Vientiane Station was far less optimistic. This was driven home by a report from Domenic Perriello, an officer with the Internal Branch who had experienced sharp communist elbows during a prior tour in Indonesia. He and his family were living at the time in a predominantly Lao neighborhood behind the That Luang temple. In late November, uniformed Pathet Lao—supposedly unarmed—had started making foot patrols around town to demonstrate their presence. As it happened, one of those foot patrols meandered through the side streets near That Luang. Also by chance, a guard had forgotten to close the back gate to the Perriello residence.

Without asking permission, two Pathet Lao entered the yard. This prompted Snoopy, the family's dog, to bark at the intruders. Immediately, one of the Pathet Lao pulled a handgun from under his shirt—a violation of their supposed unarmed status—and leveled it at the offending canine. Watching this transpire from inside the house, Perriello rushed outside and screamed in Lao for the man not to shoot.

As the gravity of the situation dawned on the two Pathet Lao, the pair beat a hasty retreat, and Snoopy lived to see another day.

Returning to the embassy later that afternoon, Perriello reported the incident to Chargé Dean. The diplomat reacted with astonishment: "They agreed not to carry weapons."

Perriello was less than impressed. "He actually expected them to keep their agreements," said the CIA officer. "We assumed they would not and of course they did not."

CHAPTER 13

Eye of the Hurricane

Snoopy's close call aside, Laos closed out 1973 with the ceasefire lines holding steady and a deceptive calm descending upon the capital. The FAR generals were sufficiently lulled by it all to rescind Vientiane's evening curfew, which had been expanded—but never fully enforced—following the Thao Ma coup attempt.[1]

In this proverbial eye of the hurricane, Vientiane Station faced new challenges. For the External Branch, there was some shifting of boundaries as the Pathet Lao target—traditionally part of its turf—was to be handed over to the Internal Branch following the launch of the coalition government.

Even before the Pathet Lao were removed from the External Branch's mandate, the Flying Squad had been hit with serious attrition. The majority of its officers had already departed in 1971. During the summer of 1972, three others finished their tours and left the kingdom.[2] The following year, Paul Seema returned to the United States to become a special agent in the newly created Drug Enforcement Administration.[3]

Filling this personnel void was Richard T., a former Marine enlisted man who had joined the CIA after completing graduate studies at Temple University. Born into wealth—his father was a successful property developer—Richard brought to Laos his Italian wife, a pianist of some renown. She had taken an immediate dislike to Vientiane and soon left him to write movie scores in Hollywood.

Alone in one wing of the RMB building, Richard inherited control over the Tai Dam team and the original Thai surveillance team. Of the two, the Tai Dam members were released from duty and their team disbanded.[4]

The original Thai team fared slightly better. Over the course of 1973, it had taken on two new males and one female. None of the three lasted past the training phase, however, leaving the roster with the same five members as before.[5]

Ironically, despite an exponential rise in the number of communists in Vientiane, there was little for the Thai team to do. The Pathet Lao, after all, were no longer part of the External Branch's bailiwick. Moreover, the DRV was now roundly recognized as the country to which the Pathet Lao ultimately deferred. As a result, their embassy at Nong Douang was suddenly a hive of activity as their access across the Lao government mushroomed.

For the five Thai team members, watching the North Vietnamese embassy would have simply inundated them with data points. Also, the city was fast filling with pro-communist sympathizers that would have greatly increased the chances of detection. Because of all this, Richard could only conjure the occasional project to keep his team busy. Said team member Dick,

> [Richard] once told us to find a Vietnamese woman who taught at a Vietnamese school near the Morning Market. We knew her name, so I wrote a letter in Lao and had a young boy at the school deliver it. We waited but she never came out. The mission was scrubbed. We really weren't doing much, not like the old days with Bernie and John.

For the Hard Target wing on the other side of the RMB building, personnel reductions had been less severe. Harry McAlpine and Jack Platt both departed in mid-1974. Still in place was Frank Sommers (who took the top slot from McAlpine) and John Cothorn.

The wing was also assisted by Jim Anders, a new arrival in April 1973. Anders had served a prior paramilitary tour in South Vietnam, where he was declared to the host government. But with Vientiane Station now taking greater pains to camouflage its officers in Laos, Anders sat undeclared in the main embassy building with cover as a commercial officer.

Augmenting the wing like before were the five Kangaroos. Team member Victor had left by 1974, replaced by a new member named

Charlie (who immediately became Pat's object of affection, supplanting David). With Platt gone, control over the five went to Sommers.

During the course of 1974, the wing faced a potential windfall as a range of communist nations established diplomatic relations with the Lao government. In June 1974, for example, North Korea sent a delegation headed by its vice foreign minister and declared plans to open an embassy. During the final quarter of the year, Poland—which had an ambassador accredited from Hanoi—announced its intent to open an embassy. Also, East Germany and Cuba normalized ties.

In most of these cases, however, realization of plans was taking time. Only North Korea dispatched a couple of diplomats but, true to its reputation as a Hermit Kingdom, it assiduously avoided all contact with the rest of the diplomatic corps.

The Hard Target case officers, as a result, fell back on their mainstays. Cothorn gave special attention to the Polish members of the ICC. That commission had been effectively without a serious mandate for a decade, and the February 1973 ceasefire agreement only served to underscore its irrelevance.

In April 1974, a new Polish commissioner, Mieczyslaw "Mike" Klimek, had arrived in Vientiane to shuffle papers. Cothorn went out of his way to bump into him at diplomatic events, where he discovered both had a fondness for chess. Dinner invitations for games of chess followed, though Klimek never revealed any vulnerabilities that could be pried open.

Jim Anders, for his part, untainted with any USAID affiliation, focused on the Soviet target. Within the Soviet embassy, the KGB *rezident* was still George Vorobiev.[6] He was joined by a second George—George Drojine—who was a far more reserved, often melancholy apparatchik.

On the military side, the Soviet presence was ratcheted upward. In June 1974, a new senior military attaché, Colonel N. Tsarkov, arrived in town. According to US air attaché Albert DeGroote, Tsarkov stood out for all the wrong reasons:

> Tsarkov was right out of central casting for a James Bond movie. He was rude, arrogant, a diehard communist, and completely delightful because he was also stupid. Any time we wanted to spread disinformation, Colonel Tsarkov was available to soak it up.[7]

Arriving at the same time was a second colonel, Vassili Soloviev. An artillery officer by training, Soloviev spoke little French and even less English. Somewhat of an introvert, he struck his American military counterparts as an intelligence analyst who had spent his life pouring over reports rather than meeting with sources.[8]

In addition to these attachés, the Soviets had added GRU officers under civilian cover that appeared to be targeted toward Western nationals. Heading them was a suave operative with good, accented English named Badalyan. He began frequenting the restaurants and bars popular with Americans, as well as the Lao Bowling Center. He was either exceptionally skilled or very ineffective at his job, as a dedicated counterintelligence effort could not catch him compromising any members of the US community.

One other GRU member arriving in Laos was Belyakon, a young and seemingly impressionable officer on his first tour. The Hard Target wing quickly identified him as a potential recruit and began to find opportunity to bump into him on the cocktail circuit. But perhaps sensing another Sorokin in the making, the Soviet embassy abruptly recalled Belyakon to Moscow after less than a year.

★ ★ ★

The Hard Target wing also continued with China as part of its mandate. Tracking the Chinese was Dennis Obermayer, who had arrived in late 1973 under cover as a USAID trade specialist. He found a PRC embassy that, in terms of personnel, had changed little over the preceding years. Kuo-Ying, who had been there since 1971 as counselor, was upgraded to ambassador in June 1974. On the military side, the stodgy Colonel Chen Shu-Ling, who had arrived in 1970, was now the doyen of the foreign attaché group.[9]

Activities at the PRC embassy had also not changed much. Unlike the Soviets, which dedicated part of their intelligence effort against US targets in Vientiane, the Chinese largely ignored the Americans and instead held regular social and movie events for the local Chinese community.[10] According to a senior Police Special Branch officer,

> For the most part, their propaganda was about the economic and social advances made by Beijing. They [also] used propaganda to attack the government of Taiwan and the living conditions in various countries of the Free World.... They arranged for propaganda materials to be sent from Hong Kong and distributed in various provinces of Laos. For example, they had a newspaper called "Knowledge for the Youth."[11]

The effectiveness of the embassy's hamfisted lobbying efforts was questionable. While economically significant, the ethnic Chinese segment of the Lao population was largely apolitical and not linguistically unified. Still, as with the DRV embassy, the Chinese diplomats felt compelled to cultivate support among their overseas compatriots. Added the CIA's Obermayer, "I assume they also used these [propaganda] opportunities to vet potential fellow travelers."[12]

★ ★ ★

Compared with the External Branch, Vientiane Station's Internal Branch was beset with an unprecedented sense of urgency. This was because its target—the Lao government—had been transformed in the space of a few short months into something almost unrecognizable. Whereas the branch was previously matched up against a relatively pliable, reliant RLG, it was now to face a coalition half composed of communists that were as mysterious as they were threatening. "We all tried meeting [the Pathet Lao], but it was nearly impossible," lamented John Cothorn. "They didn't mingle, except maybe some very low-level ones."

The officers of Vientiane Station were not the only ones struggling to keep pace. The Lao generals, too, were getting whipsawed by the tectonic political shifts. Heading into 1974, the FAR still had overwhelming military superiority in Vientiane. But on 27 March, the capital was neutralized as joint police and army units officially took charge of the city. Forfeiting its numerical advantage, FAR stripped most of its troops from Chinaimo; the excess soldiers were diverted to Phou Khao Khouai, a mountain redoubt 40 kilometers to the northeast.

A similar progression had taken place in Luang Prabang. There the excess FAR troops were moved north of the city, while the Pathet Lao were able to position their units at its strategic approaches.

The next day, 28 March, an An-24B transport plane made a test flight from Hanoi to Vientiane. Gifted by the Soviets, it had Pathet Lao roundels hastily painted on the fuselage. As no Pathet Lao were yet qualified as pilots, it flew with a North Vietnamese crew.[13]

Another three days after that, Prince Souphanouvong departed Sam Neua by convoy for Hanoi. Before leaving the Pathet Lao headquarters, he told reporters that he wanted to be personally present in Vientiane for the final negotiations on the coalition government.

At noon on 3 April, the An-24B landed at Wattay. The tarmac was packed with most of the diplomatic corps, monks, an honor guard, an enthusiastic crowd of thousands, and Souvanna Phouma.

As the plane taxied to a halt, the rear ramp lowered. Arya Panya, the son of senior diplomat Khamphan Panya, was among the onlookers:

> What surprised me was that before the passengers exited, armed Pathet Lao came down first. They circled around to the front and set up an arc in fighting positions, with their assault rifles pointed toward the terminal.

Behind them, Souphanouvong descended the ramp. He was followed by a pair of senior Pathet Lao military officers and his top negotiator, Phoumi Vongvichit.

A sharp-eyed CIA officer, also among the crowd, noted one other familiar face that emerged from the plane. Captain Luangpraseuth, a former officer in the Vientiane municipal police, had gone missing several months earlier. His family, mostly rightists, claimed he had fled to Thailand due to a gambling debt he owed to gangsters. His sudden appearance with the delegation from Sam Neua put the lie to that story. Moreover, as Luangpraseuth had been privy to some of the Special Branch's joint operations with the CIA, those had obviously been blown to the Pathet Lao.

As Souphanouvong approached the masses, his half brother Souvanna gave him a warm embrace. Monks then came forward to offer a blessing, followed by a line of diplomats extending handshakes. Notable was the absence of any FAR generals.

Stepping in front of a microphone, the prince admitted that obstacles to national reconciliation remained. "We have had much experience with these," he added with a smirk.

As it turned out, the number of obstacles was actually quite limited. One day after Souphanouvong's arrival, all Lao factions reached final agreement on the composition of a Provisional Government of National Union (PGNU). Approved by the king the next day, 5 April, the PGNU was theoretically headed by the existing National Assembly and had a cabinet evenly divided between the RLG and those selected by the Pathet Lao. To cement the balance, every cabinet minister had his deputy drawn from the opposite faction.

As the RLG looked over its half of the cabinet, there was some cause for cheer. Perhaps its brightest hope was the prickly, articulate Sisouk na Champassac as defense minister. The rightists could also take comfort knowing that the Pathet Lao had assigned a mostly bland, incompetent lineup to their half of the ministry seats.[14]

There was good reason for this. Established at the same time as the cabinet was the Joint National Political Council (JNPC), an independent Luang Prabang–based body equal in power to the PGNU. Not only did Souphanouvong decide to head this council himself, but the Pathet Lao stacked it with assertive personalities. By contrast, Souvanna had seen fit to assign RLG officials of relatively minor stature.

Not surprisingly, Souphanouvong and his fellow Pathet Lao were easily able to dominate their more diminutive RLG counterparts. And since the JNPC was just as powerful as the cabinet, the Pathet Lao merely sidestepped the latter and did an end run around the coalition government. This became readily apparent when the council almost immediately began consideration of the 18-Point Political Program championed by the Pathet Lao. The program not only attacked the United States and Thailand by name (and insisted that the United States pay war reparations), but also called on the coalition government to support national liberation movements in Southeast Asia and the rest of the world.

With barely a question raised, the JNPC unanimously adopted all eighteen points.

In the cabinet, the Pathet Lao began using the political equivalent of jiujitsu. As the coalition insisted on unanimity in its decisions, the Pathet Lao ministers liberally used their veto power to paralyze the cabinet's decision-making process. They also maneuvered to block the opening of the National Assembly, which had been set for 11 May.

Meantime, as soon as the coalition government was formally established the clock began ticking for all foreign military powers to leave the kingdom by 4 June. For its part, the United States managed to reduce its defense attaché office to 30 uniformed in-country personnel—all officially accredited as diplomats—plus a 56-man support staff at Udorn.

With regard to the CIA, it had already spent 1973 dismantling its vast paramilitary network and merging guerrilla units into the FAR. It also spent the first two quarters of 1974 withdrawing the Thai volunteer battalions that had added crucial backbone to its war effort. On 22 May, the final three Thai battalions were flown out of northeastern Laos.

With the merger of its guerrilla forces and departure of the Thai, the CIA had little need for its up-country presence. By the 4 June deadline, it summarily closed Long Tieng Unit, Luang Prabang Unit, Savannakhet Unit, and Pakse Unit. From a massive paramilitary network that once numbered in the hundreds, the Agency now maintained just a single paramilitary officer in the kingdom.[15]

Back in Vientiane, the noncommunist elements within the coalition government could not have missed the precipitous drawdown by the United States.[16] Also adversely impacting morale was the shifting attitude of Souvanna Phouma. Whereas he once colored his neutrality with a pro-American bias, the prime minister was now pragmatically skewing left. "He was ambivalent, lazy, and inconsistent," sniffed the CIA's Roger McCarthy.[17]

Souvanna's lack of backbone was on full display during the opening of July. Acquiescing to Pathet Lao calls for the National Assembly to be dissolved, he claimed that the cabinet was unanimous in this decision—even though it clearly was not. One day later on 11 July, he oversaw a special session of the cabinet when it approved the Pathet Lao 18-point program with only cosmetic changes.

All of this apparently took a toll on the prime minister. On the afternoon of 12 July, Souvanna, who had a history of heart trouble and diabetes, suffered a massive seizure. As one French and four Lao doctors attended to the ailing 72-year-old, there was a run on the Lao currency. Rumors began to swirl as to who would be selected as the new premier should he die, with no lead candidate readily apparent.

In the end Souvanna held on, just. While he convalesced at home from what was identified as a heart attack, the next step in the coalition agreement—the exchange of prisoners—took place on 19 September on the PDJ. A total of 173 PAVN and 7 Pathet Lao were released by the rightists, while 150 Thai and 20 RLG prisoners were set free by the communists.

While this was a positive step, one could not help but notice the increasingly shrill propaganda campaign being waged by the Pathet Lao. They began seeing spies everywhere, including three American novice monks who were ordained at a Vientiane temple in June.[18] They even began spreading ludicrous stories about the United States releasing a deadly species of leech in the Mekong and developing a new strain of rat that could instantly devour a rice paddy.[19]

On a far more serious note, the Pathet Lao began to probe across the ceasefire line in the western extremes of the kingdom. At the end of September, after Souvanna departed for France to recuperate from his heart attack, Pathet Lao patrols attacked the town of Xieng Lom. To the surprise of the communists, who expected that no counterattack would be mounted while the prime minister was absent, a flight of T-28s pounded them back into the jungle.

During the same month, two former CIA-sponsored guerrilla companies revolted at Ban Poung, 23 kilometers northeast of Ban Houei Sai, after not receiving wages or a food per diem for three months. Marching into Ban Houei Sai, the companies confronted the town's resident FAR commander. After receiving their back pay and getting agreement that the FAR commander would be replaced, they quietly returned to the field. Subsequent investigation showed that Pathet Lao forces near Ban Poung had offered encouragement to the rebels.

Three months later, the same two companies—around 100 men in total—again were contemplating mutiny. Their stated grievances were several: withheld pay, underrepresentation of Lao Theung tribesmen in the FAR, and the fact that the Ban Houei Sai commander had not yet been replaced. Unstated—and even more important—was the fact that the rebel leader, Captain Chanh Souk, was disgruntled after being demoted to company commander following the guerrilla integration into the FAR.

This time around, Chanh Souk was closely coordinating his efforts with the Pathet Lao 408th Battalion, elements of which were roaming the vicinity of Ban Houei Sai. Indeed, it was Pathet Lao troops that, at 0200 hours on Christmas Eve, launched a mortar attack on the FAR garrison at Ban Houei Sai, sending the local FAR battalion fleeing down the Mekong toward Xieng Lom. The FAR commander, fearing for his life, scurried across the Mekong into Thailand. The garrison left behind two artillery pieces and half a dozen recoilless rifles, all of which were seized by the Pathet Lao.

In Ban Houei Sai at the time was an expatriate population of several dozen, including nineteen Americans, nine Filipino doctors and nurses operating a medical clinic, one Briton, and an Italian priest. Most of the Americans were aid workers, plus a pair of agricultural specialists and a Protestant missionary with his family. Jack Huxtable, the USAID provincial coordinator at Ban Houei Sai, already knew their days in town were numbered:

> Even though no one wanted to talk about it, there was a realization that USAID would soon be leaving Laos when the provisional government began operations. USAID/Ban Houei Sai was already programmed to close operations and the RLG governor was getting ready to leave.[20]

By sunrise on 24 December, Pathet Lao soldiers fast-tracked the closure when they positioned themselves in front of the town's USAID compound and at the USAID boat dock, preventing departure of the expatriates. Chanh Souk, belatedly moving into town with his two companies, admitted to the US detainees that he had lost control over the insurrection.

In Vientiane, USAID personnel monitoring their radio net heard the rebels contemplating use of the Americans as hostages. Informed of this, Station Chief Dan Arnold looked to establish a secure communications capability at Chiang Khong—the Thai town directly across the Mekong from Ban Houei Sai—to provide the embassy with up-to-date information from a close source.

Getting the assignment was Jim Sheldon, the lone paramilitary officer still assigned to the embassy. Sheldon was a good choice, as he had spent time at both Chiang Khong and Ban Houei Sai during an earlier paramilitary tour in 1965.

By late on 26 December, Sheldon, along with one of the station's telecommunications officers, arrived at Chiang Khong and was given permission to set up shop at a vacant Thai police compound. As the first order of business, the pair coaxed a Thai contact to smuggle a small radio over to Jack Huxtable. Sheldon also attempted to get in radio contact with the various guerrilla leaders still in the Ban Houei Sai vicinity. It was a fairly eclectic bunch, including Lao Theung and Mien guerrilla leaders that Sheldon knew from years past. All appeared to now be deferring to the Pathet Lao.[21]

As it turned out, the USAID hostages were already on cordial terms with the rebellious Chanh Souk. At their suggestion, the captain wrote a letter to Brigadier General Tiao Vannaseng, a well-regarded FAR officer who had recently been named deputy commander of the FAR military region headquartered in Luang Prabang. The letter was rather hyperbolic, with Chanh Souk demanding that the "rightists be punished." But it served the purpose of getting Vannaseng to initiate negotiations.[22]

Soon after, on 29 December, the coalition government dispatched two ministers—one from the RLG faction, one Pathet Lao—to finalize a solution. This tipped the balance, and on Monday morning, 30 December, the expatriates were allowed down to the boat dock to cross the Mekong. In return, the rebels were once again promised that the local FAR commander would be changed.

While the hostage situation was amicably resolved, US Ambassador Charles Whitehouse was far from satisfied. In Laos for just over a year, Whitehouse had seen his fair share of crises. A decorated Marine dive bomber and Yale graduate, he had joined the nascent CIA in 1947 and packed in four overseas tours—to Belgium, the Belgian Congo, Cambodia, and Turkey—in just over nine years. Whitehouse had then switched to the Foreign Service and spend most the next decade in Africa, including a 1966 episode when he himself was taken hostage in Guinea.[23] He had most recently been deputy chief of mission in Saigon before landing the top slot in Laos.

Once the evacuees were safe in Vientiane, Whitehouse had an audience with Interior Minister Pheng Phongsavan, one of the two negotiators returning from Ban Houei Sai. When Pheng pledged that the officials whose performances led to the problem would be replaced, the ambassador was unmoved. He pressed Pheng on whether plans were being made to remove incompetent officials in other cities so similar issues would not arise. Yes, said the minister, immediate changes were coming in Pakse and Thakhek.

In fact, the coalition government enacted almost no remedial action. For weeks, General Vannaseng remained at Ban Houei Sai in a vain attempt to recover weapons stolen by the Pathet Lao, lure back the FAR garrison, and restore the civilian administration.

Worse, the incident would prove to be a template for anti-Royalist forces across the kingdom.

CHAPTER 14

Surreptitious Entries

Keeping with both the letter and spirit of the April 1974 protocols, the CIA had fully eliminated its up-country paramilitary presence by that year's June deadline. In fact, only two case officers were retained outside of Vientiane. Jerry Daniels, owing to an excellent rapport with the Hmong built over the previous decade, stayed at Long Tieng to focus on stay-behind and stability operations.[1] Kenwood F., undercover with USAID's Office of Refugee and Rural Affairs, remained at Luang Prabang to keep tabs on the neutralization of that town and, later, the machinations of Souphanouvong's JNPC.

Very quickly, however, Vientiane Station realized its course correction had been too severe. In particular, Station Chief Arnold wanted eyes to monitor developments in the panhandle. Accordingly, two young case officers were brought into the kingdom in September 1974. The first, Daniel Ster, was a 28-year-old on his first Agency deployment. The second, 31-year-old Rex Wilson, had a prior tour in South Vietnam's Mekong Delta under his belt.

Once in Laos, both officers spent a month in the capital getting acclimated. After that, Ster headed to Savannakhet, Wilson to Pakse. Although the USAID mission in Laos looked set for imminent dissolution, there was little choice but to give the two men cover as aid workers. Both would be the lone Agency officers in their respective towns—without any cypher clerks or secretaries—meaning they would be coding their own reports and handing the encrypted teletype tape to uncleared USAID radio operators for passage to Vientiane.

Wilson was especially excited about his prospects. Having just completed eleven months of intensive Lao language training in Washington, Station Chief Arnold's marching orders were to spend the first few months blending into Pakse's tiny USAID community and living his cover. He recalled,

> My wife and I were welcomed into the small American AID contingent in Pakse where there were six AID officers, three with wives and families. I was anticipating at least 3–4 years in southern Laos. We moved in with most of our belongings for the long stay.

As it turned out, ominous storm clouds were building almost from the moment Wilson arrived. In October 1974, there was a small anti-rightist protest in Pakse. Then, in January 1975, students took to the street in Thakhek, the town at the top of the panhandle. There the students employed a variation of a tactic first seen in Ban Houei Sai: a small number would launch a demonstration against corruption or some other genuine grievance. As they were on the royalist side of the ceasefire line, the noncommunists would try to take steps to control the rallies. The students, however, would demand to negotiate with the coalition government, including the Pathet Lao, and then demand intervention of the joint police. This tactic would overtly introduce Pathet Lao influence into the rightists' zone for the first time.

The noncommunists were flummoxed by all this, and at a complete loss to devise an effective counterstrategy. "The Pathet Lao were pretty sophisticated in their overt behavior while systematically moving to assume full command and control," the CIA's Arnold would later comment. "Pretty smooth operators actually."

★ ★ ★

While the situation in Thakhek festered, there was an unusual détente in Vientiane. In particular, there had been a series of benign, almost cordial, interactions between the US embassy and Soviet intelligence operatives. The first of these took place during the early morning hours of 16 January 1975, when KGB officer George Drojine woke the US air attaché, Colonel Al DeGroote, with an emergency phone call. The

An-2 biplane that Aeroflot was operating for the Pathet Lao had gone missing, he told the American attaché. It had been on the way to Sam Neua with a crew of four Soviets and eight Pathet Lao dignitaries.

Drojine knew that DeGroote flew the US embassy's C-47 and appealed to the colonel to help search for the missing aircraft. DeGroote promised to ask for the ambassador's permission, though the search ultimately proved unnecessary once the An-2 wreckage was soon located in the karst east of the Sam Neua provincial capital.[2]

Two months later, Station Chief Arnold held a dinner at his residence to honor the outgoing MI-6 station chief and his replacement, Mark Scrase-Dickins. What was remarkable were the other guests: KGB *rezident* George Vorobiev and his wife Ludmilla, as well as the GRU *rezident*. Arnold and Vorobiev had crossed swords for a decade, first in Thailand in the early sixties and then in Laos. That night, however, there was nothing but toasts and smiles. "I suspect the Soviets and the British were very pleased and burnt up the airwaves in reporting on the dinner party," surmised Arnold.

The following month, Vorobiev again had reason to contact his CIA counterpart, when Phnom Penh fell to the Khmer Rouge on 17 April. Not showing any favoritism toward the Soviet bloc, the victorious Khmer revolutionaries had demanded that the seven-man Soviet embassy vacate with a convoy of expatriates headed for the Thai border. When the Soviet embassy in Vientiane lost contact with its compatriots, officials panicked.

As the CIA had the means of tracking the convoy's progress, Arnold twice invited Vorobiev to the US embassy to brief him on its status. "I assured him that all personnel including the Soviets were alright," remarked Arnold. "He was most appreciative."[3]

Events in Phnom Penh, of course, were not happening in a vacuum. On 30 April, Saigon was overrun and communist morale across Indochina began to skyrocket. On 1 May, a small rally was held outside the US embassy in Vientiane. A week later on 9 May, protesters again massed in front of the embassy. This time they threw rocks and tore down the US flag.

Meantime, on the road between Vientiane and Luang, Prabang communist forces—boosted by tanks—moved against the Sala Phou Khoun junction on 5 May. Hmong troops holding the crossroads quickly began to fold. Defense Minister Sisouk attempted to mobilize two battalions for a counterattack; both refused to budge.

Without opposition, the tank-led communist troops pushed through Sala Phou Khoun and edged south toward Vientiane along Route 13.

Inside the capital, the FAR leadership started throwing in the towel. On 10 May, Sisouk quit. The same day, Souvanna Phouma recalled Vang Pao and announced that the Hmong general would be replaced by Brigadier General Monivong Kindavong, the prime minister's nephew. Hearing this, Vang Pao ripped off his general's stars in disgust and threw them on Souvanna's desk.

The next day, 11 May, Constitution Day ceremonies were held in Vientiane. The king arrived in a black Russian limousine; Souvanna came in an American Ford. Both passed in front of a joint honor guard. Both contingents bowed to the king—signifying, said the media, ongoing respect for the monarchy by the Pathet Lao.[4]

During his address, Souvanna acknowledged a "new situation" had abruptly occurred in Indochina. "It is necessary to yield to the evidence," he conceded, "and prepare for the future in accordance with the march of history."[5]

Later that day, Souvanna appointed Khamouane Boupha as acting defense minister to replace Sisouk. This set a new precedent, as the 1973 accords dictated that each side would replace its own ministers.[6] General Bounpone, the FAR commander, pledged to cooperate with the feisty Boupha, though by 13 May he was confiding to accomplices that he was seriously considering fleeing the kingdom.

Up at Long Tieng, meantime, Vang Pao heard Souvanna's concession speech and began preparing for life in exile. In a three-day airlift, thousands of Hmong—including the general and six of his wives—were flown to Thailand. Jerry Daniels, the last CIA officer in northeastern Laos, was at Vang Pao's side during the flight. At 1100 hours on 14 May, the last evacuation plane departed the Long Tieng runway, leaving behind some 14,000 refugees.

In other provinces, angry mobs surged forward. On the morning of 12 May, local USAID employees reported that students were marching across the Nam Khan Bridge into Luang Prabang. Remaining Americans, including the CIA's Kenwood F., congregated at a hotel just outside town to monitor events.[7] By 1500 hours, when it was evident that the situation was untenable, they all drove jeeps 10 kilometers south to Xieng Ngeun village and boarded waiting planes to Vientiane. The town's USAID compound was subsequently vandalized and pilfered.[8]

Two days later, it was the turn of protesters in Savannakhet. That morning an angry mob—led by teenagers wielding assault rifles—broke into the USAID compound and bundled three Americans off to the governor's office. Two of the three were bona fide USAID: Sanford "Sandy" Stone, the area coordinator, and Charles Pearcy, a logistics officer. The third was the CIA's Dan Ster. All three, along with the governor, were subjected to a mock trial and declared guilty of crimes against the state.

Unaware of what had transpired with his colleagues, Peter Flynn, the deputy head of the USAID office, was returning from the airport with the monthly payroll when a crowd of unruly teens accosted him. Eventually allowed to proceed to his residence, Flynn and his Thai wife could see armed youths blocking the front. "Our greatest fear was that they would get trigger happy and accidentally fire off a round or two," he recalled.[9]

The following day, after loud complaints from the US embassy, the coalition government promised to send negotiators to Savannakhet to secure the release of Stone, Pearcy, and Ster. By that time, the three hostages had been allowed to leave the governor's office and return to their residences.[10] Armed students enforced their house arrest. Although there was a sizable FAR presence in Savannakhet, the regional commander, Brigadier General Nouphet Dauheuang, was notable for his reluctance to intervene.

For Dan Ster, the situation was especially tense. The protesters, intent on exposing CIA activities in Savannakhet, were working their way through the American community with suspicions and accusations. To the credit of that community, and to Ster's tradecraft, his true employer remained hidden.

In fact, Ster was able to convince the armed students guarding his residence to let him go on nightly bicycle rides for exercise. The captors would attempt to follow on bikes, but Ster was easily able to outdistance them before circling back into town and making his way to the rear walls where other families were detained. Whispering in the dark, he would discreetly exchange information before reappearing back at his house.[11]

Not until a week later did two negotiators from the Ministry of the Interior belatedly reach Savannakhet. Their talks bore fruit, and on the late afternoon of 22 May a pair of US embassy planes were given permission to stage an evacuation. Sandy Stone called members of the community and told them to prepare one suitcase apiece; vehicles would come to fetch them in an hour. Other expatriates in town were also offered seats.

As planned, the C-47 transports landed in Savannakhet at 1800 hours. Eighteen Americans piled into the first plane; Japanese and British aid workers, as well as some European missionaries, loaded into the second. Two hours later, both aircraft were safely at Udorn.

★ ★ ★

Further down the panhandle, the security situation in Pakse was following a similar pattern. Beginning in March, there were rumblings in the town's only high school. On 5 May, thousands of students and workers began to mass in front of the provincial buildings to complain about price hikes. Three governors—from Sedone, Attopeu, and Saravane—were made virtual prisoners and the radio station was occupied. A day later a delegation from Vientiane flew in to talk down the protesters, but the rightist members were loudly heckled.

Following another five days of rallies, power was handed over to the regional military commander, Brigadier General Soutchay Vongsavanh. When Soutchay had been first promoted to that position in July 1971, he represented a new kind of FAR general. A longtime paratrooper who physically towered over his military peers, he had received US training on numerous occasions and was lauded by Washington for his aggressiveness in combat. But now facing a military region on the cusp of revolt, Soutchay had to rely on his diplomatic tact to keep the protesters in check.

The US embassy was not taking any chances. On 12 May, they flew out thirteen dependents and nonessential personnel to Udorn and Vientiane. That left just four Americans—all accredited to USAID—in town. Of the four, one was the CIA's Rex Wilson. Much like Ster in Savannakhet, Wilson had been taking pains to keep a low profile:

> I spent my early months in Pakse establishing my cover identity as an AID worker focused on building schools, bridges, and other community projects. I was also actively spotting for potential agents with access to the Pathet Lao. In fact, I was able to recruit one key agent—a Lao businessman who traveled throughout southern Laos and had access to many sources in Pathet Lao–controlled areas— and was given several others by Vientiane Station.[12]

By the second week of May, Wilson could not help but feel his days were numbered. Thousands of students were blocking commerce in and out of Pakse. Worse, he received word that Ster had been detained in Savannakhet.

On 15 May, he made his way to the airport and was able to catch a helicopter flight to Khong Island. The province chief on the island, as head of the only bastion of rightist control on the Cambodian frontier, was still eager to discuss AID initiatives even at that late hour. Before heading back to Pakse, Wilson was beckoned to see the local FAR commander. His men were woefully under-armed, said the Lao officer, and he implored Wilson for a shipment of rifles.

Wilson was taken aback. "I remained steadfast in my USAID cover," he said, "but told him I would pass on the request to the military attaché in Vientiane."

Early that evening in Pakse, Wilson's most trusted agent—the Lao businessman—called for an emergency meeting. When he arrived, he reported that Pathet Lao on Khong Island had seen Wilson speak with the FAR officer and were preparing to arrest him the following morning. Wilson thanked him, then finalized preparations for him to serve in a stay-behind capacity.

As USAID personnel had already been taken hostage in Savannakhet, Wilson took the Pathet Lao threat seriously. Following quick discussions with other members of the American community, it was decided that he would evacuate to Vientiane the next day. Accordingly, he spent the night preparing a report for Vientiane Station outlining the agent's information and requesting an aircraft to fetch him.

After finalizing the report and encrypting the tape, Wilson realized he needed to destroy all his files and crypto equipment before departure. Once that was done, he headed for his house in the town's southern suburbs. There he packed his camera, jewelry, and survival items in a gym bag, then returned to the USAID compound. It was already morning.

At that point, delays ensued. The USAID radio operator tried sending Wilson's message several times, only to find too much interference on the radio to get any traffic out.

As luck would have it, word reached the compound that a US Air Force plane was inbound for Pakse. Rushing to the airport, Wilson asked the pilot for a ride out. Without hesitation, he was flown to Udorn.

Three days later, hundreds of Pathet Lao, supported by three tanks and artillery, paraded through downtown Pakse. The Ministry of Interior sent word down to General Soutchay not to offer any resistance.

Another four days after that, following an established reporting protocol, Wilson ventured to Ubon, Thailand, to meet his stay-behind agent. The Lao businessman reported that the CIA officer's residence had been occupied by an armed communist mob the day he left. The agent also offered a detailed assessment of Pathet Lao inroads across southernmost Laos, only for Wilson to inform him that the US government was no longer interested in that intelligence. Rather, Wilson suggested that he might want to consider escaping with his family.

By the third quarter of 1975, the agent, his wife, and children were newly resettled refugees in the US.

★ ★ ★

Luang Prabang, Savannakhet, and Pakse were just appetizers. The ultimate prize, of course, was Vientiane.[13] Not failing to disappoint, dozens of protesters began storming the main USAID compound in the capital during the early morning hours of 21 May. Two US Marines barricaded

184 • SPIES ON THE MEKONG

themselves inside—one in the main USAID building, the other in an office used by the defense attaché—as the mob looted the commissary and vandalized vehicles. They hung hundreds of banners across the complex, many reading "American CIA Go Home."[14]

By the late afternoon, most of the student-led mob, some armed with machetes, had dispersed during a torrential downpour. An estimated 250 protesters were still inside the compound.

Of even greater concern, that same afternoon the joint police force had taken up positions outside Six Clicks City, the sprawling American residential complex at Kilometer 6. As the Pathet Lao half of the joint force browbeat the rightist half, they prevented anyone from entering or exiting the vicinity. In effect, hundreds of American dependents were now under house arrest.

Within the embassy, Christian Chapman was the ranking diplomat, since Ambassador Whitehouse had been transferred to Bangkok the previous month. Trouble was, Chapman was at a complete loss while negotiating with either the protesters or police. The coalition government, after all, was in tatters, but the Pathet Lao had yet to formally seize control. That left a vacuum with rightists fleeing by the day and no Pathet Lao with sufficient stature present to make critical decisions.

After a couple of tense days, the embassy received tentative approval to evacuate its population from Kilometer 6. Late on the afternoon of 23 May, buses pulled out of the residential compound en route to Wattay, where Royal Air Laos planes were chartered to make shuttles to Udorn. The CIA's Jim Anders, who was handling a student asset, received word that protesters were also headed for the airport:

> We had intelligence that the students were on the way. We got the passengers on the plane quickly and I suggested to save time they go ahead and taxi; they could strap in luggage on the way rather than sit on the tarmac. Shortly after the plane left the tarmac the students showed up. They demanded the plane return but they were ready for take-off and were not called back.

Further evacuation flights continued though week's end. By that time, Vientiane Station had been reduced to Station Chief Arnold, Deputy Station Chief McCarthy, paramilitary officer Jim Sheldon, three undeclared case officers in the main embassy, and three case officers who had been seated—prior to 21 May—at the RMB building.

The RMB building, of course, was still inaccessible due to the ongoing occupation of the USAID compound. Dozens of protesters were still roaming the grounds, with members of the joint police blocking the entrances. The two Marines—along with a Federal Electric subcontractor and several Lao telephone operators—remained holed up inside, forced to rummage through desks for candy bars and crackers.

Not until 27 May was Chargé Chapman able to corner Pathet Lao officials with sufficient authority to reach an accommodation on the USAID compound. According to their deal, USAID would permanently close its doors by 30 June. In exchange, American officials were allowed to reenter the compound the following afternoon. This allowed the two Marine guards finally to emerge from behind their barricades. It also allowed USAID paymasters to temporarily open their offices and belatedly distribute salaries to local staff. All the while, a few dozen protesters patrolled among the buildings, and armed police were scrutinizing all who entered and exited.

For Vientiane Station, the occupation of the USAID compound had been cause for considerable angst. After all, the RMB building was brimming with files detailing the External Branch's efforts against communist targets. Were the Pathet Lao to force their way in, they would no doubt share this intelligence windfall with their Soviet, North Vietnamese, Polish, and Chinese comrades. The station also maintained a separate smaller office for the Technical Services Division in the rear of the compound; this was packed with espionage gear such as miniature cameras and bugs, as well as a range of silenced weapons.

Once the occupation had been somewhat lifted on 28 May, both USAID and the defense attaché's office came to a monetary arrangement with a senior Pathet Lao negotiator to move their files out of the compound. The process worked well, with the protesters looking the other way as documents and other materials were secured and removed.

The CIA operated by a different set of rules. "We didn't want any Pathet Lao officials seeing what we were removing," said Jim Anders. "Payoffs didn't fit our pattern of activity so it had to be done unilaterally."

Sanitizing the RMB building, the station determined, would be a multistep process. For an initial entry, Richard T., the External Branch officer, beckoned Thai surveillance team members Albert and Dick. "We were told to go quietly inside and destroy documents with the shredder," explained Albert. "[Richard] promised us a bonus of $6,000 for the mission."

As instructed, the two Thai walked to the USAID compound shortly before noon. Since Dick spoke perfect Lao, they agreed to act like Pathet Lao sympathizers if challenged. The police guards, however, barely gave them any notice on the way in.

Their orders had been to wait in front of the RMB building, where a case officer named Art would open the door for them. An ethnic Korean, Art was the son of a medical doctor who had practiced medicine in Shanghai before World War II. His family moved to the United States, where Art later served in the army during the Korean War and—given his fluency in Chinese—helped interrogate Chinese prisoners.

After a few tense minutes, the two surveillance members saw Art approaching from the opposite direction. Huddled around the cypher lock, Art keyed in numbers. Albert noticed his hands were shaking. As the reinforced door cracked open, the two Thai slipped inside. Art bid them goodbye and immediately departed.

Richard's directive was simple. They were to remain on the ground floor and pass whatever documents they could find through the shredder. After half an hour of this, they had destroyed whatever was lying in the open. Albert also noticed three Pentax cameras, one of which he wrapped in his jacket upon departure.

As the two left the building, they stopped in their tracks. A trio of protesters was rounding the corner, seemingly looking for a fight. Dick barely skipped a beat, shaking his fist in the air and yelling words of revolutionary encouragement at them. The protesters returned the sentiment and kept walking.

Upon exiting the compound, the two took a circuitous route to Richard's house to report the results to their case officer. They also reminded him about their bonus, to which Richard mumbled a promise about paying them at their next meeting.

Almost immediately, a second entry took place. This time, paramilitary officer Jim Sheldon and two members of the station's support staff bluffed their way past the police guards by claiming they were part of a USAID payroll team. The three then locked themselves in the RMB building overnight to gather all remaining personal belongings, photos, and documents from the ground floor. These were shredded, placed in plastic bags, and drenched with water (and urine) to make them all but impossible to reconstruct.

After this, Sheldon and the same two support officers made a discreet entry into the Technical Services office by again pretending to be a payroll team. There they spent four hours destroying one-time pads and other gear. The silenced weapons were hidden in the office's air vents.

One last visit to the RMB office was deemed necessary. For this, the remaining case officers got in their cars and approached the compound during lunch when most of the police were away from their posts. As the convoy drove past the RMB building, Jim Anders jumped out of Roger McCarthy's car and keyed the cypher lock. He then spent the next twenty minutes packing compromising materials from the upper floor into two diplomatic pouches.

Like clockwork, Anders exited the building as McCarthy pulled in front. The bags were thrown into the rear seat and they joined the convoy of station cars heading for the back gate. As the police were slow in searching the vehicles, the drivers all started honking their horns in unison. Flustered, the police opened the gate. The convoy was home free.

CHAPTER 15

Dénouement

On the same day the USAID compound was seized, Brigadier General Soutchay was ordered to fly from Pakse to Vientiane for a two-week indoctrination session. Along with all other remaining FAR generals, Soutchay ventured to Chinaimo to join the seminar.

While the session sounded benign, Vientiane Station was pessimistic about the prospects for FAR officers and former RLG officials. To assist in the discreet departure of key indigenous personnel, Station Chief Arnold instructed Jim Sheldon at the opening of June to establish ratlines out of the kingdom. The station's lone paramilitary officer tackled the assignment with ingenuity:

> There were still about fifty crew and support personnel who worked for Continental Air Services. We hid all fifty in a mail tug that had been used by the embassy at Wattay. While the Pathet Lao guards were distracted, the tug was towed to the far side of a Royal Air Laos C-46. They jumped inside and immediately took off for Udorn.

Sheldon arranged for hundreds of others to be taken across the Mekong at night in a secret effort coordinated with the Royal Thai Navy. For this, he had speedboats arrive at specific times at remote places along the riverbank. Guided in with flashlight signals, the boats would take on their passengers and race to the Thai side before Pathet Lao patrols could react. In this manner, several members of the royal family were carried into exile. Among them, Sheldon rescued Princess Marina Rangsi, the young wife of former Defense Minister Sisouk:

We told Marina to bring a small bag. But she insisted on bringing a nanny, plus two enormous trunks carried by a muscular coolie. We diverted to the river, lugging the trunks down a long set of stairs to the bank. When the speedboat came, the luggage made it sink to the gunwales. I can almost guarantee they were filled with gold.

On 7 June, the Chinaimo seminar concluded. Soutchay returned to Pakse and held a conference with his headquarters staff and battalion commanders. Agreeing the situation was untenable, he flew back to Vientiane to ponder his fate.[1]

Six days later, Deputy Station Chief Roger McCarthy headed to his new house in the late afternoon. After his family was flown out to Thailand the previous month, dozens of Pathet Lao squatters invaded his prior, spacious dwelling.[2] Without recourse, McCarthy had moved to a tiny one-bedroom cottage away from prying eyes. As he stepped inside, his heart skipped a beat: Soutchay was sitting in the dark living room. The general explained that he had been instructed to begin yet another seminar the following day. This time, he had a bad feeling about his prospects. In fact, he had already sent his family into Thailand from Pakse.[3]

McCarthy was prepared to help. Telephoning Sheldon, he used coded language to arrange an emergency shuttle across the Mekong that night. Fifteen minutes ahead of the scheduled river rendezvous, the general was loaded into the trunk of the CIA officer's car and they headed south. McCarthy intentionally timed the trip for when Thai kickboxing started; the Pathet Lao at the Tha Deua checkpoint invariably left up the boom as they watched the televised matches at a nearby bar.

En route, Sheldon pulled alongside in a motorcycle. As the hulking Soutchay switched to ride pillion for the final stretch, he looked like a Russian circus bear on a tricycle. Exactly as planned, a speedboat materialized at the bank and the general was soon speeding toward Thailand.[4]

Other members of the FAR top brass were in continued denial as to the dangers that lie ahead. Shortly after Soutchay's flight, Jim Sheldon implored Brigadier General Chao Sinh Saysana to flee. The son of royals from the Luang Prabang and Xieng Khouang houses, Chao Sinh was a combat engineer by training. Beginning in 1965 he had been put in charge of CIA-sponsored guerrilla forces in the northwestern sector, at which time he had first met Sheldon.

Over the ensuing years Chao Sinh was rated among the best combat leaders Laos ever produced, which no doubt placed him high on the list of generals set for Pathet Lao reprisals. Yet he dismissed Sheldon's pleas, unconvincingly claiming he would be safe because he had an aunt in the Pathet Lao.[5]

Sheldon had also begged Brigadier General Thao Ly to leave. A dashing paratrooper, Thao Ly had started in Siho's DNC before leading a FAR airborne regiment. He had then been commander of CIA-sponsored guerilla troops in Savannakhet and head of an infantry division before being named FAR chief of intelligence in September 1973.[6] Like Soutchay and Chao Sinh, he was a highly regarded combat officer and thus despised by the communists. But also like Chao Sinh, he shrugged off the threat by reasoning that the Pathet Lao would respect his general's stars.

For his part, Roger McCarthy met General Bounpone and his wife at a diplomatic function. The CIA officer urged them to escape, but the wife insisted she wanted to sell their house first.

In mid-June, during one of his last acts before departing Laos, Dan Arnold made his own appeal to Bounpone:

> It was the night before I was to leave Laos. We met very secretly in a safehouse close to the river. It was about ninety minutes, largely with me trying to persuade a man to leave his country to save his life. He was resolute, his position being that as commander he had a responsibility to stay and try to do whatever he could for his officers and men. I left the meeting convinced he was a dead man walking but one could not help but respect him for what was unmistakable courage.

As it turned out, Bounpone got a brief lease on life when he departed on 22 August for medical treatment in China. While he was there, the Pathet Lao started baring their fangs. On 4 September, they publicized a trial in absentia for a dozen RLG dignitaries who had fled.[7] Six of them—including Vang Pao, Kouprasith, and Oudone Sananikone—were given the death penalty. Sisouk and General Etam got life in prison. Three others—including Soutchay and former intelligence chief Khamhou Boussarath—were to serve twenty years in jail.[8]

On top of this, all remaining FAR officers—including 23 generals—were directed to a special reeducation seminar in Sam Neua. By that late hour, Thao Ly was resigned to his fate. On the day before he was to be taken away, he met with Arya Panya:

> I saw the general at his house very early in the morning. He handed me a case and asked me to give it to the King. In it were the names of 12,000 men from Savannakhet who had fought in the CIA guerrilla forces. He said they could be a secret army to fight the communists.

Even in the highly unlikely event such a thing was possible, Thao Ly would not live to see it. Once the seminar started, it proved to be a Pathet Lao euphemism for prolonged communist indoctrination, torture, and hard labor. The harshest treatment was meted out to the generals, sixteen of whom were killed. Among the fatalities were Bounpone (who was repatriated from China to Sam Neua), Chao Sinh, and Thao Ly.

With the FAR leadership thus interned, the king was forced to abdicate on 2 December.[9] In place of the coalition, the Pathet Lao formally established the People's Democratic Republic of Laos later that same month. The last domino of Indochina had fallen.

★ ★ ★

For Vientiane Station, the second half of 1975 saw further downsizing. With Arnold gone by June, McCarthy was elevated to station chief. Only five others remained with him: two undeclared case officers, two communications officers, and a secretary.

One of the case officers, Jim Anders, had paid out a final bonus to the Kangaroos in July and instructed them to vacate the kingdom. The original surveillance team led by Albert was also told to cross the Mekong. With dwindling assets, Anders did his best in an increasingly hostile environment:

> We had less and less former RLG sources, one of them in the Ministry of Foreign Affairs. I did a few brush passes with them through the end of 1975. We also tried to develop third country nationals who might have Pathet Lao access, but we found that the Russians dominated.

Oddly enough, the CIA officers had common cause with their Russian counterparts. This came near year's end, when Pathet Lao paranoia led to more roadblocks around town manned by teens with guns. In the diplomatic community as a whole, foreign nationals were getting physically removed from their vehicles; some physical altercations and overnight detentions ensued.

In the case of Anders, he had encountered a checkpoint on 31 October but refused to exit his car. Ratcheting up the confrontation exponentially, a heavily armed Pathet Lao platoon followed him to his residence to enact a house arrest.[10] In desperation, the new deputy chief of mission, Tom Corcoran, told the Foreign Ministry it could either declare him persona non grata or let him go; it opted for the latter. Anders later explained,

> The only think that worked in our favor was the fact that many of those occupying the checkpoints couldn't read or tell the difference between an American, Australian, Czech, or Russian. As a result, there was a united front from the diplomatic community in making representation to the Foreign Ministry to get this stopped. To the Ministry's credit, it was done within a reasonable amount of time.

As for Roger McCarthy, he closed out his tour in June 1976 with the station earmarked for even further reductions. During his final months, he noticed the Russians had erected a garish statue of Souvanna Phouma near their embassy. The casting had been faulty, however, with stains streaming from the eyes like tears.[11]

McCarthy looked at the statue and saw it as a perfect metaphor. That Souvanna was crying over the fate of his country was almost a given. The Russians apparently took notice and removed the statue for repairs; it was never returned.[12]

★ ★ ★

Many alumni of Vientiane Station were immediately redirected to the ongoing Cold War skirmishes in Thailand. There, Dan Arnold had taken over as station chief in 1976 after a brief interlude in South Korea.

Under Arnold, Mike Magnani and Richard T., both previously with the External Branch in Laos, took control of the original Thai surveillance team. Of the five that reassembled in Bangkok, Becky resigned almost immediately. The remaining four—Albert, Dick, Tim, and Tom—were used by Magnani as singletons to infiltrate leftist Thai labor unions and college campuses. This proved to be dangerous work when Thammasat University exploded in an orgy of violence in October 1976. Said Albert,

> Tim, Dick, and I were ordered to go inside the Thammasat campus. We were given pocket vibrators, which were the only 'hi-tech' gear we ever received. We were inside the campus for thirty hours straight, and I saw leftist student leaders being beaten nearly to death by rightist paramilitaries. Finally, our vibrators went off. It was considered too dangerous and we were allowed to withdraw.

In the wake of this incident, Albert and Dick were redirected toward foreign communist targets.[13] Dick went to work as a carpenter at the Vietnamese embassy; in renovating the roof over five months, he used crossbeams laced with microphones. Albert, meantime, was assigned with watching visitors to the Lao embassy.

In December 1980, during the first anniversary of the Soviet invasion of Afghanistan, case officer Richard T. gave the team a special assignment. Albert made hundreds of T-shirts lauding the occasion, and they were handed out at Thai college campuses along with faux vouchers promising more shirts and cocktails at the Soviet embassy the next day. Nearly 1,000 people showed up, then threw rocks when the Soviets failed to make good on the promised party.[14]

For the Kangaroos, life after Laos was more tranquil. David used his bonus to open a sporting goods store in Udorn. Charlie and Pat split up, with the former investing in a Bangkok supermarket catering to the expatriate community.

For Ann, the lure of surveillance work continued to beckon. In 1983, she was hired by Bangkok Station to talent-scout a new unilateral team. Eight years later, she was back on the payroll to mentor yet another team.

Jack went to work for a time at an electronic company in Udorn. In 1982, when George Kenning took over the CIA base in that town, Jack was enticed to work for the Agency as a local staff. Shuttling back and forth to Bangkok on weekends to see his wife, his car ran headlong into a truck. Jack died instantly.

CHAPTER 16

Cloak and Keris

This is the story of a seed sown in Laos, to be reaped 2,700 kilometers to the south in the steamy urban jungles of Jakarta. Its intersecting narratives begin with Serge Taube, the CIA officer who served in Vientiane through 1965. Within the Agency he was an Asia hand, posted to Indonesia before Laos, then Burma immediately afterward.

But Taube, a Volga German and native Russian speaker, managed to land a place on the shortlist of candidates for the position of station chief in Moscow in 1969. That October he got the job, which on paper was a promotion.

There was a catch, a big catch, actually. Due to the smothering KGB presence on its home turf, CIA officers in the Soviet Union had little breathing room and could hardly be expected to score any real successes.

Driving home the point, just days after Taube arrived in the Soviet capital, and well before he had been able to start socializing around town, a cluster of older women materialized at the embassy and asked to speak to the station chief. Taube greeted the ladies and was told they were childhood friends of his mother. They did not say how they knew Taube had arrived. They did not need to. The message was unmistakable: the KGB knew exactly who he was and had him in its sights.

Taube was thus humbled from the start. He knew there were narrow boundaries set for his behavior in the Soviet capital, and he was to abide by them.

Except when he didn't.

Taube, after all, had a most persuasive personality. Combined with his linguistic skills and cultural sensitivity, this was a highly potent combination. It was only a matter of time before he found the narrowest of cracks in KGB coverage. While details are understandably sparse, he eventually did the impossible: he allegedly became the first CIA case officer to recruit a Russian from inside the Soviet Union.

In late 1971, Taube came back to Langley and returned to the East Asia Division. There he was handed the Cambodia desk under Dan Arnold's Office of Vietnam Operations. It was to be a study in frustration, as news from the Khmer Republic was uniformly negative. PAVN had crushed some of the best Khmer military units early on, allowing the Khmer Rouge to spread largely unfettered across the countryside.

Two years later in 1973, the deputy station chief position in the Khmer Republic opened up. Taube grabbed the slot and was soon winging his way to Southeast Asia. Phnom Penh Station, he found, was unique in one aspect. For stations worldwide, Soviet targets were invariably part of their operating directive. But Cambodia was one of those very rare exceptions, no doubt because Langley felt the urgency of the war required the station's full attention.

That barely fazed Taube. Once on the Phnom Penh diplomatic circuit, he ran across a Soviet diplomat and his wife. Very quickly, Taube assessed the Russian as a closeted gay man who had brought along a wife solely as camouflage. Homosexuality was still very much taboo in the conservative Soviet bureaucracy, forcing the diplomat to live a lie and creating a potential vulnerability. When Taube asked headquarters for permission to work the Soviet for possible recruitment, he got its consent.

Taube's weapon of choice was the 1969 buddy drama *Midnight Cowboy*. Having the reels rushed out to Phnom Penh, he arranged for a private showing at his residence. For the Russian diplomat, the film's seedy depictions of prostitution and homosexuality were too enticing to turn down. Shortly thereafter, Taube made arrangements for a gay access agent to travel to Phnom Penh. Even as the Khmer Rouge noose tightened around the capital, a successful dalliance took place between the agent and the target. Hooking the Russian in this most unorthodox manner, Taube would later hand off control to another officer elsewhere in Southeast Asia.

In the CIA's Clandestine Service, a case officer has really made it when his colleagues assign him a moniker. For his guile and appearance, Taube was known among his peers as the Gray Fox by the time he returned from Phnom Penh. "With his slicked back hair," said fellow Cambodia alum Barry Broman, "he looked the part."

To that time, the Gray Fox had scored two Russian recruitments under extremely trying conditions. Now he was on the prowl for a third.

★ ★ ★

When KGB deputy *rezident* Vladimir Mikhaylovich Piguzov departed Vientiane in April 1974, frustration in the station's External Branch was running high. His relationship with the Air America pilot at the Purple Porpoise was exceedingly close, leading branch officers to believe they were on the cusp of a recruitment. But the stars had not aligned in time, and they were left deflated over an opportunity lost.

In many such cases, there are no second chances. Piguzov, however, was not one of them.

In the third quarter of 1976, the Soviet embassy in Jakarta informed the Indonesian Foreign Ministry that Piguzov would be arriving in December to fill the position of first secretary in its political section.

At the time, the CIA had an extremely close relationship with a special task force under Indonesia's State Intelligence Coordination Agency (Badan Koordinasi Intelijen Negara, or BAKIN). The task force, in fact, was trained, equipped, and paid for by the Agency. Its sole purpose was to monitor communist diplomats stationed in Indonesia, primarily to ensure that they were not attempting to subvert Indonesian nationals.

As was custom, the Foreign Ministry passed on details of pending Soviet diplomatic arrivals to BAKIN, which in turn handed them off to the special task force. The CIA would then crosscheck the names with its database to determine whether they had known intelligence connections; if so, the task force would single them out for surveillance.

In the case of Piguzov, the fact that he was resurfacing in Indonesia set off a wave of excitement in Langley. Not wanting to blow its second chance, the Agency looked for the right case officer who could reestablish contact and bring the recruitment to fruition.

Not by coincidence, Serge Taube was soon packing his bags to be in Jakarta as deputy station chief by year's end.

Since any pitch to Piguzov would be highly sensitive, the approach would be unilateral. Furthermore, the Agency did not want to risk spooking its prospect with surveillance by the task force. Accordingly, the database results for Piguzov that the CIA handed over to BAKIN were unusually thin, noting only that he had previously been in Cambodia and Laos and that he spoke very good English and French. No mention was made of his known KGB ties.[1]

On 10 December 1976, Piguzov landed in the Indonesian capital. He was accompanied by his wife, seven-year-old son, and a daughter that had been born two years prior. Now on his third overseas tour, he ranked high in the *rezidentura*. And, as with Vientiane, he was targeted against Western nationals, primarily Americans.

As luck would have it, just a couple of months before Piguzov's arrival, the Jakarta *rezidentura* had just scored a major coup with an American walk-in.

That American, David Henry Barnett, 43, had long nurtured dreams beyond his simple upbringing. Raised in a rural corner of Pennsylvania, his high school was so small he had only a single classmate.[2] Struggling to escape such a remote setting, he attended the University of Michigan and then entered the army.

Assigned to the Counter Intelligence Corps, the intrigue appealed to Barnett. Continuing with an intelligence career after military service, he got an eighteen-month CIA contract as an instructor at their Camp Peary training site in late 1958. Following a brief teaching stint at an all-boys school back in Pennsylvania, he returned to the CIA for another eighteen-month contract.

In March 1963, with two contracts under his belt, Barnett was accepted into the CIA as a full-time staff officer. It was during a headquarters assignment on the Indonesia desk in 1965 that he was exposed to a top-secret and highly successful project codenamed HABRINK. The background to this was as follows. Beginning in the early sixties, when

Jakarta was planning a massive military operation to seize control of West New Guinea from the Dutch, Indonesia appealed to the Soviet Union and became the recipient of one of Moscow's largest and most diversified arms aid programs. Most of this was directed toward the Indonesian navy, with a smaller amount extended to the air force.

Fast forward to October 1965 and the Indonesian Communist Party was subject to bloody reprisals as General Suharto replaced the West-baiting Sukarno. In the chaos during regime change, the CIA quietly began plotting how it could get its hands on some of the Soviet hardware or, failing that, the classified technical manuals.

Very quickly, Jakarta Station identified a senior Indonesian naval officer who agreed to enter into a clandestine arrangement. Under him were twenty-nine subagents, many of them also from the navy. The officer was paid per manual, eventually earning the princely sum of $400,000.

For the CIA, the information gleaned under HABRINK was priceless. For example, they were able to get the technical details on the SA-2 surface-to-air missile system, which had been used very effectively by PAVN to shoot down American planes over North Vietnam. Once HABRINK obtained the SA-2's guidance system, the United States determined the radio frequencies used to direct the missile and jammed them, thus saving untold lives of American pilots.

HABRINK also got details on the Whiskey-class diesel electric attack submarine, fourteen of which had been supplied to the Indonesians. This included how long the subs could stay submerged without recharging their batteries. As this was longer than the United States had previously estimated, the new intelligence was used to shape American naval strategy.

It did not stop there. HABRINK for the first time provided information on the Styx anti-ship missile. Also, intelligence was gathered on the Komar missile patrol boat, the Riga frigate, the Sverdlov cruiser, the Tu-16 Badger bomber, and the associated Kennel air-to-surface missile.

After two years of dealing with HABRINK from headquarters, Barnett got the nod in August 1967 to be deployed to Indonesia. There, under cover as a political officer, he was assigned as head of the CIA base at the US consulate in Surabaya, Indonesia's second-largest city, on the eastern end of Java island. As head of the base, his primary focus was the Soviet consulate in the same city, assessing the Soviets therein for possible recruitment.

After just over two years at this post, Barnett's CIA career showed signs of flatlining. For one thing, his colleagues found his personality grating. "He was an arrogant unfriendly loner," said Domenic Perriello, a case officer in Indonesia before shifting to Laos. "Many of us wondered how he passed the psych tests with that kind of nature."

Barnett also expressed frustrated over his Agency salary. For a family of three—he and his wife had had a son—he wanted more.

In January 1970, Barnett resigned from the Agency and returned to his native Pennsylvania. Years earlier, when he taught at the all-boys school between CIA contracts, they had told him then that there was always a job awaiting him. Now he wanted to take them up on the offer. What's more, with his résumé burnished by government service during the interim, he had allusions that the headmaster job could be his.

Unfortunately for Barnett, the best he could eke out were slots teaching English and wrestling. The former CIA officer did this for just over two school years before realizing that opportunities were not to be had in Pennsylvania.

By now scrambling to come up with a better alternative, Barnett recalled the economic prospects around Surabaya. To be sure, after Suharto unleashed market forces in 1965, the Indonesian economy started to show quick gains from its former moribund status. But as a foreign national, Barnett would have been subject to severe limitations on investment and ownership.

Forging ahead anyway, Barnett returned to Surabaya with his family in tow in the fall of 1972. There he opened a small business—CV Kemiri Gading—seeking to export rattan furniture overseas.

The business struggled, forcing Barnett to take a salaried job as a manager at a nearby shrimp farm. Growing desperate, he siphoned off funds from the farm to help keep his rattan business afloat.

After four years of such juggling, Barnett at long last realized that his Indonesian company was not going to succeed. Worse, he owed $100,000 to the shrimp farm.

Desperate, Barnett conjured a plan to pay off his debt. While he was head of Surabaya Base, he had assessed a Soviet cultural officer for possible recruitment. He had, in fact, met him on a number of occasions. That same Soviet officer was still in Indonesia, but had since shifted to the Jakarta embassy. He was not only easily accessible; Barnett knew his residential address.

One day during the last week of October 1976, Barnett strode up to the Soviet officer's house. He had penned a note saying he was willing to sell secrets from his CIA career. The price-tag: $70,000.

When the cultural officer answered the door, Barnett pressed the note in his hand. Glancing down, the Russian read it. He curtly told Barnett to return the following Sunday.

As instructed, Barnett went back at the cultural officer's house on 31 October. This time, he was sitting across from a member of the KGB *rezidentura* who introduced himself as Dmitriy. Barnett repeated his offer, whetting Dmitriy's appetite with the kinds of information he could provide. The Russian was game, but wanted to shift to a more secure setting for their next meeting.

A better venue, dictated Dmitriy, would be in the gated compound the Soviet embassy maintained in South Jakarta. Among the dozens of homes inside, one doubled as a safe house. To get there, Dmitriy told Barnett to wait along a quiet street downtown. A KGB officer would pass by in a car and pick him up, then drive in a circuitous route to ensure they were not being tailed. Once satisfied, he would bring Barnett inside the compound and directly to the safe house, away from prying eyes.

In late November 1976, Barnett had his second meeting with Dmitriy at the compound. During that meeting, he revealed the names of more than two dozen CIA colleagues in Indonesia and elsewhere in Asia. He also told the KGB about the assessments he had performed on seven Soviet diplomats at their Surabaya consulate, and which of the seven the CIA was likely to have pitched.

For this information, Dmitriy handed over an envelope stuffed with $25,000. Since both sides were amenable to an ongoing dialogue, he outlined an elaborate plan for Barnett to go to Vienna in late February

1977. Prior to that time, they would meet once more in Jakarta for Dmitriy to hand over funds to cover travel expenses.

By that time, Piguzov had arrived in Indonesia. Given his rank and mandate, he was briefed on the Barnett case. Moreover, when Barnett arranged to get his travel funds in early February 1977, it was Piguzov who was driving the car on the countersurveillance route to the Soviet compound.

On 22 February, Barnett flew to Brussels. From there, he transferred among multiple trains across Western Europe before arriving in Vienna. Taken to a KGB safe house, he was debriefed over eight hours by three KGB officers. In the course of that meeting, Barnett revealed the details of HABRINK. This included the identity of the Indonesian naval officer who sold the manuals, as well as the fact that the United States had used the intelligence to develop effective countermeasures and strategies.

On that occasion, he was given another envelope with $15,000. He was also urged to return to the United States to get a job in the intelligence community, perhaps as a staffer on one of the intelligence committees in the legislative branch.

Returning first to Jakarta, Barnett had another meeting with Dmitriy in the Soviet compound in late March. Once more, Piguzov was driving the countersurveillance route. This time Barnett was paid $30,000, thus reaching the $70,000 he had demanded in his original note.

As this transpired, Jakarta Station was working overtime to find Piguzov about town. Although Jakarta was a sprawling metropolis, the areas frequented by foreign nationals were actually quite small, and it was only a matter of weeks before the Soviet officer was located.

At that point, the case was handed over to Serge Taube. In short order—mere weeks—he was able not only to make contact, but to forge the beginnings of a strong personal bond.

Piguzov, it turned out, was waiting for a CIA pitch. Ever since the Purple Porpoise, he had prepared himself to conspire against the Soviet Union; the comradery he quickly developed with Taube sealed the deal. Commented one CIA officer privy to the case,

> [Piguzov] was not motivated by sex or drugs or money problems. He saw the Soviet empire glass as more than half-empty. He was a determined man. And

liked the money, of course. But he also liked the recognition and sincere thanks he always got from his handler.[3]

Added Harry McAlpine, who was involved with the Piguzov case in both Laos and Indonesia,

> He enjoyed the American lifestyle and freedoms, and was frustrated by the strictness of the Soviet system. That, and hard cash.

By the second quarter of 1977, Piguzov was already reporting to Taube. One of the first things he revealed was that Barnett had contact with the KGB *rezidentura*.

News of this made Langley shudder. Never before had a CIA staff officer sold out to the KGB in this manner; indeed, it was an Agency mantra that Soviet monetary incentives would not work with its officers.

Barnett's treason also created a counterintelligence migraine. If he was immediately arrested upon return to US soil, it could alert the KGB that there was a leak in their Jakarta *rezidentura*; it was imperative that Piguzov be shielded from such scrutiny. Alternately, the Agency could try to triple Barnett, using him to feed disinformation back to the Soviets. In reality, however, triple agents get unhitched from any loyalties and are exceedingly difficult to steer.

In the end, Barnett forced their hand. In June 1977 he flew from Jakarta to Washington, where he circulated around the capital and tried to get a job at either the Senate Select Committee on Intelligence or the White House. While his applications did not appear to gain much traction, the CIA made doubly sure of this by quietly spreading word a few weeks later that Barnett should be disqualified from consideration.

In early July, Barnett returned to Jakarta. That month he met two KGB officers in the compound, with Piguzov once more driving the countersurveillance route. This led to another short job-hunting trip to Washington in August, followed by another round of meetings with the Soviets in Jakarta during the fall.

As before, the KGB was pressing Barnett to get an intelligence-related job in Washington. Only then, it emphasized, would he be worthy of continued renumeration. If he could not get rehired by the CIA, it was suggested that he try the Defense Intelligence Agency or Research Bureau at the State Department.

Not until April 1978 did Barnett head back to Washington in search of employment. This time he would be in the states for eleven months before returning to Indonesia in March 1979.

Meantime, Taube and Piguzov continued to meet periodically during the course of 1978. Throughout this period, BAKIN had the Soviet embassy's telephones tapped on behalf of the CIA. On three occasions that year, the tap inadvertently recorded conversations in which the CIA was apparently trying to trigger meetings with Piguzov. On the morning of 25 September, for example, BAKIN transcribed the following short exchange with a Mr. Loren, who claimed to work at the Hilton Hotel:

> Loren: Mr. Piguzov?
> Piguzov: Yes.
> Loren: This is Loren from the Hilton Hotel.
> Piguzov: Yes.
> Loren: The cashier made a mistake on your bill when you dined at Taman Sari Grill last Wednesday.
> Piguzov (interrupting): I will come to there to discuss this privately.
> Loren: Call Extension 243 when you arrive.

When meetings did take place, part of the discussions between Taube and Piguzov focused on how the CIA would maintain contact with the latter once his Jakarta tour was over. As Piguzov already had three overseas postings, he was due for a longer stint within the Soviet Union. That would all but discount the possibility of further face-to-face meetings with a handler, instead limiting contact to dead drops.

There was also the matter of how and when the US authorities would move against Barnett without incriminating Piguzov. As he had already put in an application for renewed CIA contract work, the Agency decided in January 1979 that the best course of action would be to hire Barnett part-time on special assignments so it could keep him under watch. The task given to him was working on training material for new recruits, none of it especially sensitive.

After landing this job, Barnett flew back to Jakarta in late March. He reported his contract to his KGB contacts, but they did not appear to be particularly enthusiastic. He did two more shuttles to Washington at midyear and in the fall, with Jakarta meetings sandwiched in between.

By then, Piguzov had informed Taube that his tour was almost over. Taube, too, was overdue for rotation. His replacement, Harry McAlpine—who had headed the External Branch in Vientiane when Piguzov was first encountered—had already arrived in Jakarta in July 1979 and was overlapping with Taube for a smooth transition.

On 23 November 1979, Piguzov bid farewell to Indonesia. He had not informed Jakarta Station of the specific date, though it assumed his departure after he went silent through the New Year.

Waiting a decent interval, the CIA decided it was time to pounce on Barnett. Bringing the Federal Bureau of Investigation (FBI) into the case, special agents arrived at Barnett's office on 18 March 1980 and confronted him with their suspicions.

Barely without hesitation, Barnett confessed to his treason. He also let them know that he had plans to meet a KGB contact in Vienna on 25 April.

Though Barnett posed a flight risk, it was felt that he should be allowed to continue with the Vienna meeting to put more time between his exposure and Piguzov's departure from Indonesia.

On 12 April, Jakarta Station asked BAKIN to confirm whether Piguzov had concluded his tour. On 22 April, the Indonesians replied that the Soviet had departed on 23 November 1979, though his wife and children did not leave until 7 December.

Three days later on 25 April 1990, Barnett staged a brief meeting with a Soviet contact at a radio shop on Taberstrausse in Vienna's Second District. An FBI agent positioned across the street kept Barnett under watch and monitored the encounter.

Upon return to the United States, Barnett sat for further FBI sessions before being publicly indicted on espionage charges in late October. To these, he pleaded guilty and was ultimately handed an eighteen-year sentence.

As questions were sure to be asked how he was caught, the FBI was allowed to claim credit for allegedly detecting phone calls Barnett had received from a KGB contact while in Washington. Senator Daniel Inouye, chairman of the Senate Select Committee on Intelligence, lauded the bureau by claiming that the alleged surveillance effort was a "brilliantly executed operation which demonstrated that our counterintelligence personnel and the sophisticated technology they employ are out ahead of the KGB."[4]

This cover story fell apart almost immediately. Inouye clarified that he had first been informed of Barnett's attempted penetration in the spring of 1978. But an unnamed Senate source contradicted this, telling reporters that word of suspected KGB ties had been forwarded to him back in 1977 when Barnett first applied for a Senate staff job.

Reading these media accounts, the Soviets would have realized Barnett was exposed almost from the start, either in Jakarta or possibly on his first trip to Vienna.

Still, no suspicions appear to have been leveled against Piguzov. In fact, upon return to Moscow he was given a choice assignment at the KGB's Red Banner Institute. Nicknamed "the Forest School" because it was located among dachas in a wooded area north of the capital, the institute's main task was preparing intelligence officers from the First Directorate for overseas assignments.[5]

Within a few short years Piguzov, who by that time held the rank of KGB lieutenant colonel, was promoted to secretary of the institute's communist party branch. This ideologically powerful slot made Piguzov one of the few staff privy to the real names of the students, which numbered about 300 per annum in the mid-eighties. For the CIA, this was pure gold. Remarked case officer Jack Platt,

> Think of it, for five years the Agency benefited from knowing the names and evaluations of all the graduates of their Institute!

There the tale might have ended with Piguzov counted among the Agency's most important penetrations of the KGB. But there was one more layer of treachery yet to come.

★ ★ ★

For Aldrich "Rick" Ames, his CIA career brought a strong sense of *déjà vu*. He was a second-generation Agency employee whose father, Carleton

Ames, had been a college professor who joined the CIA in 1951 and, with non-official cover as a Fulbright scholar, was posted to Burma for three years in the middle of that decade.

While Carleton's career initially showed promise, alcoholism cut it short. Put on probation for a time, he retired at age 62 as only a mid-level analyst.

Following in his father's footsteps, Rick Ames joined the Agency in 1962. And like his father, early tours in Turkey and Mexico were marred by drinking. During both, his performances were rated as middling.

In between times overseas, Ames was assigned to the Soviet–East European Division. Part was spent in New York City handling two important assets at the United Nations. Then in September 1983 he was placed in the division's counterintelligence section, giving him access to the most sensitive plans and operations against the KGB and GRU.

Just one month later, Ames came under increased pressure on the home front. He separated from his wife, with the pending settlement promising to be expensive. Compounding matters, he was living with a high-maintenance Colombian girlfriend he had met during his Mexican tour.

Financial strains continued to gnaw at Ames through the first quarter of 1985. At that point, in an almost exact repeat of the Barnett approach, he contacted the Soviet embassy in Washington with an offer to sell secrets in exchange for a Russian bailout.

Compared to Barnett, the secrets Ames held were infinitely more marketable. Giving the KGB a taste, he passed them a list of ten moles in June. Among them was Piguzov, whose crypt in CIA files was GT/JOGGER.

Two months later, Ames's divorce was finalized. He then married his girlfriend and the following year was posted to Rome. Again, his performance was described as mediocre.

By the time Ames was in Italy, the KGB was acting on the initial list he provided. General Rem S. Krasselnikov, head of KGB counterintelligence, was a meticulous professional who built a solid case against every mole in order to make it conform to Soviet criminal statutes. Explained the CIA's Jack Platt,

He took great pride in having the Politburo sign off on arresting a suspected traitor. He couldn't afford to be wrong, especially in the case of [Piguzov] who was in an embarrassingly sensitive position.

Not until more than a year later, in late 1986, was Krasselnikov satisfied of Piguzov's guilt. Reportedly, he was recorded walking his dog in a Moscow park while servicing a dead drop.

Once arrested, Piguzov was brought before a doctor and found sane. In February 1987, he stood in front of a firing squad.[6]

Much as the CIA had fretted about not exposing Barnett's arrest for fear of leveling suspicion against Piguzov, the KGB deliberated about burning Ames. In the end, however, it decided to wrap up all the moles he exposed in relatively short order.

Back in Langley, there was a sense of disbelief at the Agency as their best Russians spies went silent in quick succession. Some felt this might have been due to a Soviet wiretap or bug. By 1990, however, the Agency was certain its crown jewels had been exposed by a mole in its own ranks. Narrowing down the list of officers who knew of the exposed assets, it had focused the investigation on Ames by March 1993.

In February 1994, the FBI had enough evidence to make an arrest. Like Barnett, Ames pleaded guilty; he received a life sentence. Of the top thirteen names he exposed, all but four were executed.

★ ★ ★

From Jakarta, Serge Taube was cross-posted to Paris as the deputy station chief in 1980. He would have one further overseas posting—New Delhi—before retiring from the Agency. Word of Piguzov's arrest reached him just as he was leaving.

A chain-smoker all his life, the Gray Fox, rumor had it, was the only officer allowed to smoke inside "the Bubble," the nickname for the superinsulated room found in some stations to protect them from eavesdropping. It finally caught up with him in February 1991, when he died at the age of 59. He never learned the identity of the mole that had led to the downfall of his prized recruit.

Maps

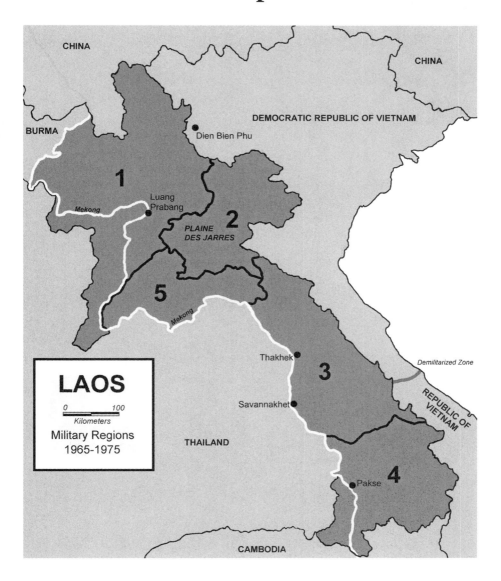

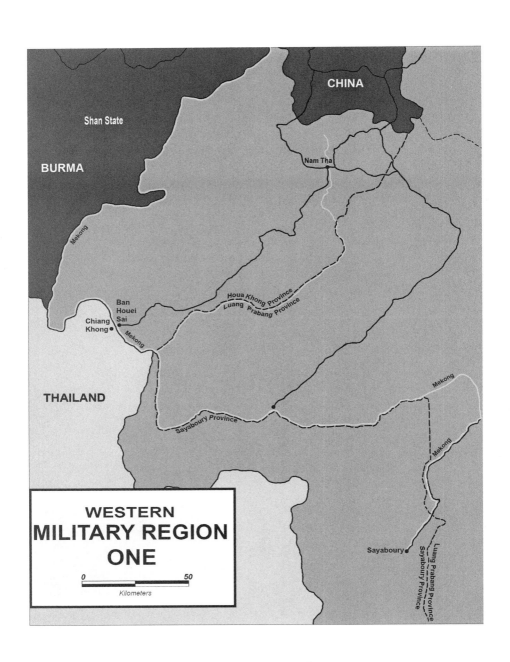

CHINA

Shan State

BURMA

Nam Tha

Mekong

Houa Khong Province

Luang Prabang Province

Ban
Houei
Sai

Chiang
Khong

Mekong

Mekong

THAILAND

Mekong

Sayaboury Province

Sayaboury

Luang Prabang Province
Sayaboury Province

WESTERN
MILITARY REGION
ONE

0   50
Kilometers

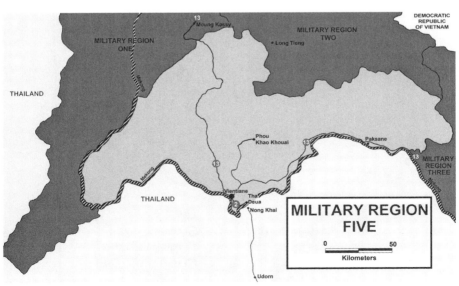

GREATER
VIENTIANE

0   4
Kilometers

THAILAND

13
Wattay
Airbase
North Vietnam
Embassy
USAID
compound
Kilometer 6
Phone
Kheng
That Luang
Mekong
Dong
Phalane
Soviet
Embassy
Chinaimo
Tha
Deua
2
Mekong

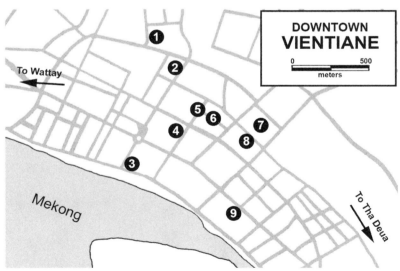

DOWNTOWN
VIENTIANE

0   500
meters

To Wattay

Mekong

To Tha Deua

1 Chinese Embassy   6 U.S. Embassy
2 Settha Palace Hotel   7 Morning Market
3 Lane Xang Hotel   8 Pathet Lao Office
4 Somboun Inthavong Hotel 9 Mahosot Hospital
5 That Dam ("Black Stupa")

Select Bibliography

Published Books

In English

Barron, John. *KGB: The Secret Work of Soviet Secret Agents*. New York: Reader's Digest Press, 1974.

Chalermnit Press Correspondent. *Battle of Vientiane 1960*. Bangkok: Niyomvithaya Printing Press, 1961.

DeGroote, Albert. *A Flight through Life*. lulu.com, 2013.

Devlin, Larry. *Chief of Station Congo*. New York: PublicAffairs, 2007.

Dommen, Arthur J. *The Indochinese Experience of the French and the Americans: Nationalism and Communism in Cambodia, Laos, and Vietnam*. Bloomington: Indiana University Press, 2001.

Fursenko, Alekxandr and Naftali, Timothy. *Khrushchev's Cold Wars: The Inside Story of an American Adversary*. New York: W.W. Norton & Co., 2006.

Gibson, Richard with Chen, Wenhua. *The Secret Army*. Singapore: John Wiley & Son, 2011.

Hoare, Chris. *Mad Mike Hoare: The Legend*. Durban: Partners in Publishing, 2018.

Lilley, James and Lilley, Jeffrey. *China Hands*. New York: PublicAffairs, 2005.

McCarthy, Roger. *Our Republic in Peril*. Oakland, OR: Red Anvil Press, 2004.

Melton, Alan. *The Champa Flowers: Ivorson in Laos*. Middletown, DE: CreateSpace, 2010.

Mendez, Antonio. *The Master of Disguise*. New York: William Morrow & Co., 1999.

Methven, Stuart. *Laughter in the Shadows*. Annapolis: Naval Institute Press, 2008.

Phillips, Rufus. *Why Vietnam Matters*. Annapolis: Naval Institute Press, 2008.

Rust, William J. *Before the Quagmire: American Intervention in Laos, 1954–1961*. Lexington: University Press of Kentucky, 2012.

Shackley, Ted. *Spymaster*. Dulles, VA: Potomac Books, 2005.

Steigliz, Perry. *In a Little Kingdom*. Armonk, NY: M.E. Sharpe, 1990.

In French

Champassak, Singto Na. *Mon Destin*. Paris: L'Harmattan, 2010.

Deuve, Jean. *La Guerre Secrète au Laos Contre les Communists*. Paris: L'Harmattan, 1995.

In Lao

Rathphangthong, Som. *Public Security for Peace and Happiness.* Vientiane, 1975.

In Vietnamese

Chi, Vien. *55 Năm, Một Chặng Dường* [*55 Years, A Journey*]. Hanoi: Writers Association Publishing House, 2015.
Lich Su Doan Dac Cong Biet Dong 1, 1968–2008. Hanoi: People's Army Publishing House, 2008
Lịch Sử Trung Doàn Không Quân 921, 1964–2009. Hanoi: People's Army Publishing House, 2009.

Government Publications

Ahern, Thomas. *Undercover Armies.* CIA History Staff, 2006.
Asia & Pacific Daily Report, Foreign Broadcast Information Service.
Daily Report, Foreign Radio Broadcasts.
Joint Publications Research Service (JPRS).
U.S. Department of State. *Biographic Register.* Washington, DC: U.S. Government Printing Office.
U.S. Department of State. *Foreign Relations of the United States* [FRUS]. Washington, DC: U.S. Government Printing Office.

Endnotes

Chapter 1

1   Minutes, National Security Council meeting 141, 28 April 1953.
2   Interview with L. Michael Rives, Foreign Affairs Oral History Project, Association for Diplomatic Studies and Training, 25 July 1995.
3   Interview with Ted M.G. Tanen, Foreign Affairs Oral History Project, Association for Diplomatic Studies and Training, 21 September 2000. In the written record of this oral interview, "Korbin" is incorrectly transcribed as "Coburn."
4   As per the Geneva accords, Vietnam had been bifurcated, with the communists given control over the democratic republic in the north and noncommunists controlling a republic in the south.
5   U.S. Department of Defense Intelligence Report, 10 June 1955, Declassified Documents Reference System [hereafter DDRS] 1978, 414D.
6   PAVN was the armed forces of the Democratic Republic of Vietnam.
7   Department of State message from Chargé Rives (Vientiane), 19 July 1954.
8   Seno airbase, located next to the town of Savannakhet, took its name from an acronym for the French points of the compass: *sud*, *est*, *nord*, and *ouest*.
9   The Lao Airborne Battalion jumped into Moung Peun over the course of three days from 8 to 10 July. Messages dated 9, 10, and 11 July 1955, MMF Folder, Box 10 H 5648, French Military Archives.
10   PhD thesis by Milton J. Clark, "Leadership and Political Allocation in Sinkiang Kazak Society," Department of Social Relations for Degree of Philosophy in the Subject of Clinical Psychology, Harvard University, January 1955, p. iii.
11   Coincidentally, an earlier Kazakh refugee column factored into a grim episode in CIA history. In 1947, Douglas Mackiernan joined the Agency at its inception and was posted as vice consul at the remote US diplomatic outpost in Xinjiang. There, making use of his technical background, Mackiernan manned electronic gear to collect atomic intelligence on nuclear tests being conducted across the border in the Soviet Union. Forced to flee from communist Chinese troops advancing into Xinjiang, MacKiernan joined a Kazakh refugee caravan heading toward Tibet. He was shot dead by a Tibetan border guard in April 1950, becoming the first star on the CIA Memorial Wall.

12 Clark PhD thesis, p. 261; Milton J. Clark, "How the Kazakhs Fled to Freedom," *National Geographic Magazine*, November 1954, p. 622.

13 Arthur J. Dommen, *The Indochinese Experience of the French and the Americans: Nationalism and Communism in Cambodia, Laos, and Vietnam* (Bloomington: Indiana University Press, 2001), p. 336.

14 Jean Deuve, *La Guerre Secrète au Laos Contre les Communists* (Paris: L'Harmattan, 1995), pp. 33–36.

15 "Situation in Laos," *Department of Defense Intelligence Report, 10 June 1955, DDRS, 1978, 414D.*

16 *Foreign Relations of the United States* [hereafter, FRUS], 1955–1957, East Asian Security; Cambodia; Laos, Volume XXI, Doc. 344, Memo from Secretary of Defense's Assistant (Special Operations) (Erskine) to the Director of Central Intelligence (Dulles), 13 February 1956; Doc. 349, Memo for the Record by the Special Assistant to the JCS for Mutual Defense Assistance Affairs (Cannon), 4 April 1956; Doc. 351, Memo from the Secretary of Defense's Assistant (Special Operations) (Erskine) to the Assistant Secretary of Defense for International Security Affairs (Gray), 18 April 1956.

17 FRUS, 1955–1957, East Asian Security; Cambodia; Laos, Volume XXI, Doc. 371, Memo of Discussion at 292nd Meeting of the National Security Council, 9 August 1956.

18 Parsons was appointed ambassador in May but did not arrive until late July.

19 William J. Rust, *Before the Quagmire: American Intervention in Laos, 1954–1961* (Lexington: University Press of Kentucky, 2012), p. 49.

20 FRUS, 1955–1957, East Asian Security; Cambodia; Laos, Volume XXI, Doc. 385, Memo from Acting Director of Central Intelligence (Cabell) to the Secretary of State, 27 September 1956.

Chapter 2

1 FRUS, 1955–1957, East Asian Security; Cambodia; Laos, Volume XXI, Doc 412, Telegram from the Embassy in Laos to the Department of State, 8 January 1957; Doc. 420, Telegram from the Department of State to the Embassy in Laos, 1 February 1957.

2 The Yale University president from 1937 to 1951 was Charles Seymour, who was a close acquaintance of CIA Director Allen Dulles. Seymour remained as president emeritus at Yale through the 1950s. As a result of this personal relationship, Yale allowed a large on-campus CIA recruiting presence, to include eminent professors and even the varsity crew coach.

3 Rufus Phillips, *Why Vietnam Matters* (Annapolis: Naval Institute Press, 2008), p. 93.

4 Brought in to coordinate logistical support for CIA programs in the provinces was John William Foley. After a stint in the US Navy during World War II, Foley had gone to college and then worked at a tobacco company before joining the CIA

in 1950. He arrived in Laos during March 1957 for a two-year tour. *Biographic Register*, Department of State, 1959 edition, p. 247.

5   FRUS, 1955-1957, East Asian Security; Cambodia; Laos, Volume XXI, Doc. 420, Telegram from the Embassy in Laos to the Department of State, 15 March 1957.

6   Rust, p. 59

7   Rust, p. 60.

8   *Biographic Register*, Department of State, 1963 edition, p. 197.

9   *CIA and Nazi Criminals*, CIA Draft Working Paper, Chapter 3, p. 31.

10 Draft Laos chapter, provided by Rufus Phillips.

11 FRUS, 1955–1957, East Asian Security; Cambodia; Laos, Volume XXI, Doc. 480, Telegram from the Department of State to the Embassy in Laos, 21 October 1957; Doc. 484, Telegram from the Embassy in Laos to the Department of State, 24 October 1957.

12 FRUS, 1955–1957, East Asian Security; Cambodia; Laos, Volume XXI, Doc. 514, Dispatch from the Embassy in Laos to the Department of State, 16 December 1957.

13 Deuve, p. 56. In July 1956, Souvanna Phouma had ordered SIDASP to suspend surveillance of Pathet Lao officials, only to rescind the order four months later.

14 Interview with Roger McCarthy, 16 May 1997.

15 Deuve, p. 58.

16 James and his sister were distant relatives of Teddy Roosevelt and heirs to the Standard Oil fortune. Correspondence with Alex Fane, 5 December 2016.

17 *Biographic Register*, 1963, p. 223.

18 Fane correspondence.

19 James's arrival came shortly after the departure of Kinloch Bull, who had come down with a serious parasitic infection before being shifted to Bangkok Station in March 1957. *Biographic Register* (Department of State, 1963 edition), p. 61.

20 James's quirks were on full display during his CIA training. Said classmate Jim Sheldon, "He insisted on getting a British cut for his suits and he carried around a gold watch on a fob." Interview with Jim Sheldon, 24 August 2015.

21 Correspondence with Rufus Phillips, 11 January 2018.

22 Deuve, pp. 64, 84.

23 Back in June 1957, senior ANL and police officials—prompted by their French advisors—had held a top-level meeting in which they panned the civic action effort, especially the fact that it was being run by an American coming from Vietnam—Phillips—and that he had brought in Filipinos who did not speak a word of Lao to write the program's leaflets. Deuve, p. 73.

24 FRUS, 1958–1960, East Asia-Pacific Region; Cambodia; Laos, Volume XVI, Doc. 165, Letter from the Deputy Under Secretary of State for Economic Affairs (Dillon) to the Director of Central Intelligence (Dulles), 15 February 1968.

25 The task force was headed by Hugh McCaffrey, who was Sea Supply's chief of operations.

26 Campbell James had visited outlying provinces during the election campaign to observe the conduct of noncommunist candidates. This included a humorous 28 February 1958 incident during an excursion to the northwestern town of Nam Tha. Having been informed that a diplomat from the US embassy would be coming, a delegation from the Lu hill tribe greeted Campbell on his arrival and gave him an ornate document written in Lao and French. The Lu's traditional stomping ground, extending into China, had been taken over by the PRC authorities, and the document implored the US government to accept the Lu homeland as a state in the union. Campbell later prepared a similarly ornate document for the Lu purportedly from President Eisenhower thanking them for the honor but explaining that the United States only admits territories that are a contiguous part of the North American land mass. Fortunately, noted Campbell, Hawaii and Alaska had not yet been admitted. Eugene Pool and Oliver Janney, eds., *A Caviar and Champagne Diplomat, the Memoirs of R. Campbell "Zup" James* (Estate of R. Campbell James, undated), p. 17.

27 FRUS, 1958–1960, East Asia–Pacific Region; Cambodia; Laos, Volume XVI, Doc. 178, Editorial Note.

28 *Bulletin des Amis du Royaume Lao*, No. 3 (October–December 1970), p. 1.

29 FRUS, 1958–1960, East Asia–Pacific Region; Cambodia; Laos, Volume XVI, Doc. 190, Editorial Note.

30 Thomas L. Ahern, Jr., *Undercover Armies* (CIA History Staff, 2006), p. 6.

31 Interview with John Gunter Dean, Association for Diplomatic Studies and Training, Oral History Project, 6 September 2000.

32 FRUS, 1958–1960, East Asia–Pacific Region; Cambodia; Laos, Volume XVI, Doc. 171, Editorial Note.

33 The CIA's Rufus Phillips, who returned to Laos in February 1959 for an additional six-month stint, claims that Hecksher initially had a good relationship with Phoui, which Ambassador Smith then undermined and took over. "Smith hated the CDNI and encouraged Phoui to turn against them," he explained. Correspondence with Rufus Phillips, 12 April 2018.

34 Stuart Methven, *Laughter in the Shadows* (Annapolis: Naval Institute Press, 2008), p. 54. Methven was appointed to Laos in May 1959 but did not arrive in Vientiane until July.

35 *Ibid.*, p. 60.

36 *Biographic Register* (Department of State, 1958 edition), p. 644.

37 FRUS, 1958–1960, East Asia–Pacific Region; Cambodia; Laos, Volume XVI, Doc. 297, Telegram from the Embassy in Laos to the Department of State, 30 November 1959; Doc. 302, Letter from the Ambassador in Laos (Smith) to the Assistant Secretary of State for Far Eastern Affairs (Parsons), 15 December 1959. Said Rufus Phillips, "Smith kept some of his cables away from Hecksher but the relationship between Lao desk officers from State and CIA in Washington was good so [CIA] Headquarters could keep Hecksher informed about what Smith was reporting." Phillips correspondence.

38 In July 1959, the ANL was renamed the Lao Armed Forces (Forces Armées du Laos, or FAL).

39 Hecksher had been scheduled to leave by March 1960. Rust notes that he departed at the end of December 1959, with Jerry Steiner filling in as the acting station chief. Rust, p. 145.

Chapter 3

1 Sisouk na Champassak had joined the Lao Foreign Service in 1954 and was named a liaison officer with the ICC. From 1957–58 he had been the deputy permanent representative of the RLG to the United Nations, then returned to Laos to become one of three CDNI members named to the August 1958 cabinet.

2 FRUS, 1958–1969, East Asia–Pacific Region; Cambodia; Laos, Volume XVI, Doc. 284, Telegram from the Department of State to the Embassy in Laos, 2 November 1959.

3 Ahern, p. 10.

4 *Biographic Register* (Department of State, 1958 edition), p. 651.

5 Interview with Winthrop G. Brown, Oral History Interview, John F. Kennedy Library, 1 February 1968.

6 *Biographic Register* (Department of State, 1964 edition), p. 218.

7 Interview with Kong Le, 2 April 1990.

8 Mathews detailed this ill-fated mission into Cambodia in "Bull Simons, over the Se Khong River," *Gung-Ho* magazine, Vol. 5, No. 47 (April 1985), pp. 22–26.

9 Le Quang Hoi, "Rescuing Prince Souphanouvong," *Quan Doi Nhan Dan*, 12 February 2007. With several guards secretly pledging support to the Pathet Lao, the escape relied on guile rather than force: the prisoners donned military police uniforms and walked out the front gates without being questioned.

10 Interview with Jack Mathews, 30 January 1990.

11 Quinim had run in the tainted April 1960 elections and lost. Over the next four months, he ran a gunsmith shop in downtown Vientiane. Immediately after 9 August, he appointed himself as liaison between the coup troops and the Pathet Lao.

12 In 1959, South Vietnam opened an embassy and the Republic of China on Taiwan opened a consulate.

13 *Battle of Vientiane 1960* (Bangkok: Niyomvithaya Printing Press, 1961), p. 96. Irritated with the excessive reception for Abramov, Souvanna ordered Kong Le to remain under house arrest for a week. Kong Le laughed this off and made a point of attending dinner at Quinim's house that same night.

14 Methven, p. 78.

15 For a week after the August coup, Jack Mathews remained in Vientiane. He met Kong Le on a single occasion, but by then events had progressed too far to reason with the renegade paratrooper. On 14 August, Mathews shifted to Savannakhet. Mathews interview.

16 Correspondence with Arya Panya, 5 April 2020.
17 Alekxandr Fursenko and Timothy Naftali, *Khrushchev's Cold Wars: The Inside Story of an American Adversary* (New York: W.W. Norton, 2006), p. 333.
18 Fane correspondence.
19 Embassy operations were subsequently shifted to the ambassador's residence and the military attaché's house. Interview with Cliff Strathern, 2 February 1991.
20 Lieutenant Colonel Khamouane Boupha, a French-trained commando who was now Phongsaly military commander, had earlier impressed the US embassy and in 1959 was taken on an orientation tour of the United States. However, he had grown disillusioned with the RLG—especially Phoumi Nosavan—following the rigged April 1960 elections; in a telling incident, a plane carrying Ouane Rathikoun to Phongsaly during May was driven off by ground fire (presumably from Khamouane loyalists) on final approach (Strathern interview). By early September 1960, Khamouane had indicated his sympathies were with Kong Le. On 3 February 1961, a Soviet-piloted helicopter flew a PAVN/Pathet Lao delegation to Phongsaly to formalize Khamouane's support for the FAN/Pathet Lao. "Secrets Disclosed After Almost Half a Century," *An Ninh The Gioi* newspaper, 5 August 2019.
21 Methven, p. 23.
22 For example, Thomas L. Ahern, a Notre Dame graduate who had been dispatched to Laos in November 1960 as a desk officer was up-country with the Hmong guerrillas by March 1961.
23 Winthrop Brown oral interview.
24 *A Caviar and Champagne Diplomat*, p. 20. James remained in Luang Prabang through February 1962, but this was not the end of his involvement with Laos. On account of his good rapport with Souvanna Phouma, the CIA dispatched him to Paris as its representative at a September 1964 summit among the Lao factions. While there, James had a private dinner with Souvanna at the Michelin-starred Lapérouse. Perry Steigliz, *In a Little Kingdom* (Armonk, NY: M. E. Sharpe, 1990), p. 103.
25 There is a critical difference between clandestine and covert operations. Clandestine operations must go completely unnoticed; the operation itself must stay concealed. Covert operations, by contract, need only be deniable; if uncovered—which would be inevitable in the case of a large-scale paramilitary operation—only the sponsor must be concealed.

Chapter 4

1 The earlier ICC in Laos had agreed to adjourn in July 1958 but did not cease operations until February 1959.
2 This opened the floodgates to the rest of the Warsaw Pact. In short order, the Hungarian and Bulgarian ambassadors based in Hanoi presented their credentials. The Polish ambassador in Rangoon and Czech ambassador in Phnom Penh followed suit. None of these four, however, were seated in Vientiane.

3   In a forlorn effort to block Beijing, Taiwan's ambassador in Bangkok rushed to Vientiane on 19 July and attempted to present his credentials; they were not accepted. *Foreign Radio Broadcasts Daily Report*, 20 August 1962, p. BBB4. Liu Chun formally presented his credentials on 12 October.

4   *Foreign Radio Broadcasts Daily Report*, 14 November 1962, p. QQQ6.

5   *Quan Doi Nhan Dan* [*People's Army* newspaper], 13 October 2009. Dinh served uninterrupted at the North Vietnamese embassy in Vientiane from 1962 until December 1975. There were two organizations in the North Vietnamese government that conducted foreign intelligence operations. The Research Department (Cuc Nghien Cuu), which fell under the General Staff of the Ministry of National Defense, had a Foreign Intelligence Office which assigned officers to their embassies, such as Dinh, to run intelligence operations. The Ministry of Public Security also dispatched officers under diplomatic or official cover (such as Vietnam New Agency personnel) to conduct counterintelligence and intelligence operations. Correspondence with Merle Pribbenow, 1 June 2020.

6   "Background Information on the Soviet Union in International Relations," Committee on Foreign Affairs, US House of Representatives, 27 September 1961, p. 37. Trushin, the TASS representative in Bangkok, was expelled from Thailand on 7 October 1958 along with a Soviet attaché; *Far Eastern Economic Review*, 15 June 1979, p. 32. A CIA report from the 1960s claimed that up to 80 percent of TASS overseas representatives were affiliated with Soviet intelligence services. CIA Report, "Soviet Foreign Policy and the Roles of the MFA and KGB in Soviet Representations Abroad," p. 4.

7   Deuve, p. 147.

8   Behind the façade of communist solidarity, there was considerable tension between Soviet and North Vietnamese intelligence personnel. This dated back to 1958, when a Soviet intelligence advisory group was stationed in Hanoi to assist the North Vietnamese Ministry of Public Security and PAVN military intelligence department. The next year, an agreement was reached for Vietnamese personnel to receive intelligence training in the Soviet Union. In late 1963, however, North Vietnamese officials became alarmed by Soviet recruitment efforts and called all trainees home. A subsequent investigation of Soviet alumni was known in North Vietnamese circles as the "H Affair." This investigation reached a climax in 1967, resulting in the arrest of more than 300 senior North Vietnamese party and military officers. Correspondence with Robert Destatte, 16 September 1996.

9   The Soviets again opted for an exceedingly direct approach toward a Lao target in the summer of 1966. The RLG ambassador to the Soviet Union at the time was Khamphan Panya, one of the CDNI founders and a former foreign minister. Following a discussion with one of his tennis partners in Moscow, Youri Dementiev, it was agreed to bring the ambassador's son, recent high school graduate Arya Panya, for six months of training southwest of Moscow. When Arya arrived, he found himself in a military-style barracks along with hundreds of Soviet students. The

curriculum focused on basic intelligence tradecraft, as well as paramilitary skills like field-stripping an assault rifle. After less than two months, Arya was hurriedly yanked from the course without explanation and placed on a Scandinavian Airlines flight to Stockholm. Panya interview.

10 When the ICC was quickly reformed in 1961, it had 119 people in its secretariat (117 Indians, 1 Canadian, and 1 Pole), as well as three delegations that would act as field observers. These delegations added another 33 Indians, 27 Canadians, and 39 Poles. "International Commission for Supervision and Control in Laos," Hearing before the Sub-Committee on the Far East and the Pacific, Committee on Foreign Affairs, US House of Representatives, 24 September 1963.

11 Interview with Frank N. Burnet, Foreign Affairs Oral History Project, Association for Diplomatic Studies and Training, 1990.

12 Whitehurst took over as Singapore station chief in mid-1961 following an embarrassing incident one year earlier. This came about soon after Singapore became a self-governing state within the British Commonwealth, leading the CIA to try recruiting a member of the Singaporean Special Branch to give it a separate intelligence stream besides what the British provided. To vet the potential agent, the CIA flew in a polygrapher from Japan. However, when the polygrapher plugged in his machine in a hotel room, he blew out the electricity across the entire building. The polygrapher, potential agent, and another CIA officer were subsequently arrested, with the two Americans facing 12-year prison sentences. The CIA in January 1961 offered Prime Minister Lee Kuan Yew $3.3 million to cover up the incident, but he reportedly wanted ten times that amount. Three months later, incoming Secretary of State Dean Rusk penned a letter of apology to Lee and both CIA officers were quietly expelled. The CIA station chief was subsequently replaced with Whitehurst.

13 Despite the commonly held view that Siho was staunchly loyal to Phoumi, the CIA had been picking up anecdotal evidence for years that Siho had lost confidence in Phoumi and that the two were quietly at odds. See *The President's Intelligence Checklist* (prepared by the CIA), 1 November 1963.

14 The rival was Prince Ekarath Souvannarath, whose father had been prime minister and a deputy head of the King's Council. "Siho was a straight forward henchman," said Deputy Chief of Station Cliff Strathern, who had been assigned as the station's main liaison with Siho. "Ekarath was more intellectually advanced and would have surpassed Siho, so Siho felt he had to be eliminated." Strathern interview.

15 Within the RLG, Siho's DNC was derisively nicknamed the "Lao SS," an allusion to the feared Nazi paramilitary organization. Appropriately, the DNC drove around Vientiane in a fleet of imported Volkswagen Beetles, all painted black. Panya interview.

16 There was a flurry of diplomatic activity from March to May 1965 as various nations tried to arrange asylum for Phoumi and Siho. The United States attempted to send them to Taiwan, the Thai sought to push them to Australia, the British wanted to have Washington accept them in Hawaii, and the French advocated for them to

go to Switzerland. The pair proved too toxic, however, and all these efforts came up short. Telegrams from British Embassy (Vientiane) to UK Foreign Office, 16 March 1965, 22 March 1965, 5 May 1965, and 26 May 1965.

17 "I find [Kong Le] a very odd and rather tiresome little man," wrote British Ambassador Frederick Warner in 1965. "He is a shining light of honesty, but extraordinarily naïve, foolish, vain, and unpredictable. I feel that Lao history is now leaving him behind." British Embassy (Vientiane) to UK Foreign Office, 1 September 1965.

18 After Kong Le spent a month in Indonesia in April and May 1965—where he was feted by President Soekarno—West Germany, France, the UK, and the US all sought to balance Jakarta's influence by inviting him on an extended tour that spanned September and October. He proved to be an especially difficult guest for the British, displaying pronounced indifference during much of his two-week program. An exception came during an evening hosted by the Shell Oil Company, which included a visit to a striptease show at London's Raymond Revuebar. Kong Le had recently divorced his fourth wife, and the show "aroused appetites which his hosts were unable to satisfy." Frustrated as a result, this negatively impacted the latter part of his visit. (Memorandum from Colonel Oliver Berger, Overseas Defense Relations, UK Ministry of Defense, 30 September 1965.) Kong Le's FAN troops revolted against his erratic leadership in 1966, sending him into exile in Indonesia.

19 *Biographic Register* (Department of State, 1968 edition), p. 456; *Department of State News Letter*, August 1965, No. 52, p. 71.

20 Interview with James R. Lilly, Foreign Affairs Oral History Project, Association for Diplomatic Studies and Training, 21 May 1998.

21 Shackley brought to Laos Thomas Clines, David "Pancho" Morales, and Don Stephens. All three had been on the Cuba Task Force; Clines had also been in West Germany. Despite having Foreign Intelligence rather than paramilitary backgrounds, Clines and Morales initially went to Udorn to man desks covering paramilitary operations in northern and southern Laos, respectively. Clines later was sent to head the base in Long Tieng in northern Laos, while Morales became chief of unit in Pakse. Stephens was assigned as a paramilitary officer in southern Laos.

22 James Lilley and Jeffrey Lilley, *China Hands* (New York: PublicAffairs, 2005), pp. 80–83.

23 *Biographic Register* (Department of State, 1964 edition), p. 304.

24 Lilley and Lilley, p. 124.

25 Ted Shackley, *Spymaster* (Dulles, VA: Potomac Books, 2005), p. 33.

Chapter 5

1 Correspondence with Joy Seema, 1 September 2018.

2 Chan's father was Major General Prasan Amattayakul, the deputy director of the staff school under the Royal Thai Armed Forces Supreme Command.

3 James Morrison interview with Pat Dailey, 6 August 1998.

4 Details of the Thai team come from multiple interviews with Albert, Dick, and Tom conducted during 2016 and 2017.

5 *Biographic Register* (State Department, 1969 edition), p. 66.

6 Officially known as the *Monument Aux Morts* (Monument to the Dead), the RLG began building the arc after retaking the city from Kong Le. It misappropriated cement and other building materials that USAID had earmarked for a renovated airstrip at Wattay, leading some to facetiously call the monument "the Vertical Runway." With construction proceeding at a snail's pace, it was not finalized until 1968.

7 In 1958, the Lao intelligence service SIDASP claimed that it recruited a member of the Pathet Lao central committee, whom it codenamed *Tomate*. It was never clear whether this spy was at the Pathet Lao office in Vientiane or in Sam Neua. Despite the fact that the RLG was still allegedly in clandestine contact with *Tomate* as late as 1962, it offered little compelling evidence that its agent could yield any significant information during that entire period. Deuve, p. 137.

8 In October 1963, the DNC allegedly recruited a spy within the Pathet Lao, though it was never clear where this source was physically located. This source was simultaneously supplying information to FAN intelligence officers. The only apparent item of significance from this agent was a list of the central committee members from the Lao People's Party, the clandestine communist party that controlled the Pathet Lao. Deuve, p. 142.

9 Department of Defense Intelligence Information Report, No. 6 856 0371 71, "PW Related Activities at the Office of the Neo Lao Hak Sat Representative in Vientiane," dated 22 November 1971.

10 Grenade attacks are recounted in *Foreign Broadcast Information Service*, Asia and Pacific edition [hereafter, FBIS], 20 March 1967, p. PPP1; 1 September 1967, p. PPP1; and 22 January 1969, p. I1.

11 The harassment, as well as frequent delays in paying salaries, took a toll on the Pathet Lao security force in Vientiane. Of the 58 men who remained in the capital as of 1965, 11 had rallied to the RLG by 1971. *Joint Publications Research Service* [hereafter, JPRS], No. 54692, Translations of South and East Asia, 13 December 1971, p. 14.

12 John Allen's own interactions with his Pathet Lao neighbors were less than cordial. "I was raising chickens," he remembered, "and the Pathet Lao lured them with rice through a hole in our common wall and stole every one of them." Interview with John K. Allen, Jr., 7 June 2020.

13 Larry Devlin, *Chief of Station Congo* (New York: PublicAffairs, 2007), p. 55; *Biographic Register* (State Department, 1967 edition), p. 140.

14 Mike Hoare, who commanded the white mercenaries in 1964–65, later claimed that the CIA indirectly provided their funding during those two years. Chris Hoare, *Mad Mike Hoare: The Legend* (Durban: Partners in Publishing, 2018), p. 107.

15 Several paramilitary officers who served in the Congo during Devlin's tenure also came to Laos. This included Russ Lefevre, a Maritime Branch expert who had helped coordinate the use of Swift boats on Lake Tanganyika, and Rip Robertson, who had led eighteen Cuban commandos at the head of the column that pushed its way into Stanleyville to liberate the US consulate. In Laos, both of these officers worked with trail-watching teams in the southern panhandle. Another Congo paramilitary alumni, Don Courtney, arrived in mid-1970 and was assigned to Savannakhet Unit. The Congo "mafia" in Laos extended to Ambassador G. McMurtrie "Mac" Godley, who overlapped with Devlin on both Congo tours, and two other senior State Department diplomats in the political section (Monteagle Stearns) and USAID (Charlie Mann).

16 The North Vietnamese embassy was trying not just to win over the local Vietnamese community, but also to salt intelligence operatives in it. In late 1958, the Research Department dispatched two agents to Vientiane, codenamed N1113 and N114. The former, whose real name was Tong Van Trinh, got fake identity papers and took a job at the vehicle registration office in Vientiane's Public Works Bureau. Later in 1963, he became the chief accountant at Veha Akhat airline. He remained in Laos through December 1975, during which time he helped infiltrate two other North Vietnamese agents into the city. Trinh would send his intelligence reports back to Hanoi either in hard copy using invisible ink (likely via the North Vietnamese embassy) or in encrypted radio transmissions. Years after his retirement, public accounts of his alleged intelligence coups—which border on the fanciful—were widely published. See Phan Dinh, *Cuộc Vượt Ngục Kỳ Diệu* [The Amazing Prison Break] (People's Army Publishing House, Hanoi, 2008), p. 174; "The Intelligence Agent Who Obtained the Plan for the Route 9–Southern Laos Operation, *Kien Thuc* newspaper, 13 November 2009; "Declassifying Espionage File No. 113," *An Ninh The Gioi* newspaper, 27 May 2014.

17 In December 1971, the North Vietnamese embassy was even visited by entertainer Bob Hope, who offered to make a $10 million donation to a children's charity in an unsuccessful bid to win the release of American prisoners of war.

18 A fictionalized version of the swamp operation is found in Alan Melton, *The Champa Flowers: Ivorson in Laos* (Middletown, DE: CreateSpace, 2010), p. 32.

19 Beed and the Michigan operation were exposed in an April 1966 story in *Ramparts* magazine.

20 As of October 1969, the Special Branch totaled 6 civilians, 44 police officers, and 140 policemen. USAID, "Evaluation of Public Safety Program," November 1969, p. 62.

21 According to a memoir by Vien Chi, who headed the North Vietnamese Ministry of Public Security's Dispatched Agent Department, the department recruited an officer in the Special Branch who had family roots extending into Vietnam's Nghe An Province. See Vien Chi, *55 Năm, Một Chặng Đường* [55 Years, A Journey] (Hanoi: Writers Association Publishing House, 2015), p. 122.

22 Interview with Huong Baccam, 16 May 2020; interview with Baccam Seum, 18 May 2020.

23 FBIS, 19 January 1968, p. JJJ1; 23 December 1968, p. K1; 24 March 1969, p. K3.

24 FBIS, 28 August 1968, p. I1.

25 Interview with Mike Magnani, 6 July 2016.

26 FBIS, 18 October 1967, p. PPP1.

27 The car accident did not happen in a diplomatic vacuum. During July 1969 cabinet meetings, Souvanna Phouma had been hinting of an impending settlement after North Vietnam floated to him a proposal to withdraw its troops in exchange for a bombing halt and RLG support for the communists at the Paris peace talks. There was growing fear that Souvanna, exhausted by years of war, would fall for this hollow promise and opt for something akin to Cambodia's left-leaning neutrality. Ahern, p. 321.

28 FBIS, 22 August 1969, p. I4.

29 *Daily Report, Foreign Radio Broadcasts*, 27 August 1969, p. K1; 28 August 1969, p. K2.

Chapter 6

1 CIA Intelligence Information Cable, "Emergence of Japan Committee for Investigation of War Crimes in Vietnam as Dominant Japan Organization Supporting Bertrand Russell War Crimes Tribunal," 29 December 1966.

2 CIA Intelligence Information Cable, "North Vietnam's Reservations Concerning the Planning for the Bertrand Russell 'War Crimes' Tribunal and its Intention to Coordinate with the JCP on Collection of Evidence," 23 February 1967.

3 CIA Intelligence Information Cable, "Collection of 'Evidence' of Japanese Collaboration with US in Vietnam by Japanese Leftists," 31 January 1967.

4 CIA Intelligence Information Cable, "Activities and Plans of the Japan Committee to Investigate War Crimes in Vietnam Delegation to North Vietnam," 13 February 1967.

5 CIA Report, "Differences in the Theoretical Objectives of Bertrand Russell and the Japan Committee to Investigate War Crimes in Vietnam," 1 February 1967.

6 FBIS, 28 July 1967, p. JJJ1; 1 August 1967, p. JJJ6.

7 CIA Intelligence Information Cable, "Japanese Communist Party Evaluation of the Copenhagen Session of the International War Crimes Tribunal," 15 December 1967.

8 FBIS, 7 January 1969, p. K11.

9 Haase's background was in paramilitary operations. From 1954–57, he was a Sea Supply advisor based out of Udorn. In 1957, he participated in the CIA's short-lived effort to support the rebellion on Sumatra against Indonesia's central government. Haase next went to Korea, but was sent to Laos on temporary duty in 1961–62 to train road-watching teams. From 1964–67, he was back at Udorn in support of counterinsurgency efforts in northeastern Thailand. In mid-1969 he

was posted to Vientiane with the External Branch in his first foreign intelligence assignment.

10 McCabe took over a slot in the External Branch left vacant by Fred K., a young case officer with the Thai surveillance team who was summarily expelled from Laos in July 1970 after he got into a bar fight with a FAR officer over the affections of a woman.

11 The lieutenant colonel, a Muslim Cham named Les Kosem, had been the senior officer within the Royal Cambodian Armed Forces who acted as liaison with the Chinese shipping company that brought in weaponry destined for communist forces in South Vietnam. After the change in governments in Phnom Penh in April 1970, Kosem went to Vientiane and allowed Evans to debrief him over three days. Alan, the case officer who handled the Tai Dam team, sat in on the meetings to translate from French. Correspondence with Alan, 19 July 2020.

12 Correspondence with Richard Lammon, 1 February 2018.

13 The orange bomb was almost certainly a BLU-24 submunition the size and color of an orange. The spider bomb was probably the BLU-42; the mine contained therein released eight tripwires that resembled spider legs.

14 Daily Report, *Foreign Radio Broadcasts*, 10 December 1970, p. K9.

15 *Mainichi Shimbun*, 10 December 1970, p. 18.

16 For their efforts during this operation, Jim Haase later held a ceremony in which Albert and Dick were presented with "Flying Squad Certificates of Appreciation," along with engraved cigarette lighters from Udorn airbase.

17 FBIS, 7 December 1970, p. J1.

18 "Don Eric," 44, was a Korean War veteran who played tackle at Amherst during his college days. He was reportedly the basis for the hulking character in *Quin's Shanghai Circus*, a surreal 1974 novel written by CIA veteran Edward Whittemore.

19 Mendez gives an account of his participation in this operation, with the date incorrectly given as November 1968. Antonio Mendez, *The Master of Disguise* (New York: William Morrow, 1999), pp. 100–107.

20 Tsuyoshi, who also held a position in the Vietnam-Japan Friendship Association, had been in Hanoi since October 1970. FBIS, 21 October 1970, p. K1.

21 FBIS, 8 December 1970, p. C2.

22 Funazaki's paper was entitled "Adverse Effects on the Human Body of Brutal Weapons used by the US in Vietnam as seen by the Medical Point of View."

23 FBIS, 30 March 1971, pp. J1-J2.

24 CIA Intelligence Information Cable, "Negative Japanese Response toward International War Crimes Tribunal Overtures to use Tokyo as an Alternate Site after New York for a Third War Crimes Tribunal," 23 June 1972.

Chapter 7

1 Correspondence with Domenic Perriello, 5 May 2020.

2 Ahern, p. 306.

3   Correspondence with Steve Murchison, 14 February 2015. The situation had gotten so bad that Souvanna Phouma said in May 1970 that he would forgo his annual "rest cure" in Grasse on the French Riviera.

4   Penco had been created by Air America in June 1965 as a subsidiary to design and supervise airport construction in South Vietnam. Beginning in 1971, the same company was used as cover for CIA personnel heading to Laos.

5   The majority of contract paramilitary officers were brought to Laos under the IUJEWELL program, which recruited college graduates with prior military experience. Besides filling the need for paramilitary officers, IUJEWEL acted as an audition of sorts to identify those officers deemed eligible for conversion to career staff.

6   FRUS, 1969–1976, Vol. VI (Vietnam), Document 98, Kissinger to Nixon, 19 July 1969; Vol. VII (Vietnam), Document 37, Helms to Kissinger, 10 March 1972.

7   James Morrison interview with Malcolm Kalp, 12 May 1997.

8   Kalp interview.

9   "The B-52s were About to Die…But They Did Not Know It," *Quan Doi Nhan Dan* [newspaper], 24 December 2012; "Vietnamese Intelligence's Legendary Attacks Inside Thailand," *Soha* [newspaper], 22 April 2014.

10 *Lich Su Doan Dac Cong Biet Dong 1, 1968–2008* (Hanoi: People's Army Publishing House, 2008); "Attacking B-52s Right on their American Air Force Bases," *An Ninh The Goi* [newspaper], 22 December 2015; FBIS, 11 January 1972, p. J1.

11 Kalp interview.

12 Magnani interview; interview with Boutsy Bouahom, 4 August 2016.

13 In September 1971, Souvanna Phouma went to Washington and met with President Richard Nixon. The prime minister told Nixon that he had tried to penetrate Pathet Lao cave strongholds to determine whether there were American prisoners being held, but he had failed in his attempts. FRUS, Vol. VII, Vietnam, July 1970–January 1972, Document 264, Memorandum of Conversation, 30 September 1971.

14 CIA Intelligence Information Report, "Description and Location of PL/NLHS Offices, Officials, and Activities in Ban Nakay Neua, Sam Neua Province, Laos," 14 April 1972.

15 In 1968, the Pathet Lao began issuing their own currency in 100-, 200-, and 500-kip denominations. In late 1970, they started issuing smaller notes in 10-, 20-, and 50-kip denominations. All were printed in China. As a psychological warfare operation, the CIA printed and distributed fake Pathet Lao 200-kip notes in March 1970, but with the That Luang temple on the front replaced with a portrait of Ho Chi Minh; this was done to suggest that the Pathet Lao were beholden to the North Vietnamese. *Xat Lao*, 11 January 1971, p. 1; FBIS, 7 April 1970, p. I3.

16 A good case in point was when Arya Souphanouvong, the eldest son of Prince Souphanouvong, was murdered on 23 December 1967 under mysterious circumstances while visiting Vieng Xai after earning an engineering degree from Moscow. Word of this incident slowly went from Sam Neua to Hanoi and finally

to Moscow, where fellow Lao students held a memorial for him in August 1968. This was picked up by the RLG ambassador in Moscow, who belatedly notified Vientiane. During an October 1969 Senate hearing, former Ambassador to Laos William Sullivan, now the deputy assistant secretary of state for East Asian Affairs, said the US government was still having trouble getting any details about the murder. "Hearing of the Subcommittee on US Security Agreements and Commitments Abroad," Senate Foreign Relations Committee, 20 October 1969, p. 379.

17 In late 1969, 3,000 refugees were evacuated prior to a battle for control of Muong Phine, a village close to the Ho Chi Minh Trail. They were sent to Seno and given land adjacent to the airbase.

18 Bouahom interview.

19 The North Vietnamese Air Force headquarters ordered up to eight MiG-21s to be prepared for Laos incursions in late November 1971. *Lịch Sử Trung Đoàn Không Quân 921, 1964–2009* (Hanoi: People's Army Publishing House, 2009), p. 100. As the incursions grew more frequent in late December 1971 and garnered criticism from the RLG, the Pathet Lao office in Vientiane laughably claimed that the jet fighters belonged to the Pathet Lao and were flying from hidden airfields in Sam Neua. *Xat Lao*, 30 December 1971, p. 1.

20 See, for example, a Radio Pathet Lao broadcast from 5 January 1972 in FBIS, 10 January 1972, p. I2.

Chapter 8

1 CIA Document, "The Soviet Mission Abroad," pp. 19, 75. The document as archived on the CIA website does not have a date, but is apparently from the late sixties.

2 Interview with "Rob," 6 May 2020.

3 Chiriaev is identified as an intelligence officer in "The KGB in Asia: Society of Subversion," *Far Eastern Economic Review*, 3 January 1975, pp. 25.

4 "The Soviet Mission Abroad," p. 38.

5 Shackley, pp. 34–35.

6 *Khao Pacham Van*, 8 April 1972, pp. A1. From 1960 to 1964, forty scholarships to Lao students were given by the Soviet Union, fifteen from Czechoslovakia, ten from Poland, ten from Hungary, and five from East Germany. These figures do not include Pathet Lao candidates dispatched from Sam Neua.

7 *Berkeley Barb*, Vol. 7, Issue 24 (13–19 December 1968).

8 Correspondence with Maya Velesko, 18 April 2020.

9 Correspondence with Terry Wofford, 25 February 2017.

10 By the time O'Connor took over the Newell case, the couple's young son, George Newell, had been accepted as the only American to enroll in Russian language lessons at the Soviet Cultural Center. There, Elena Gretchanine, the GRU colonel's wife, acted as his tutor. Interview with George Newell, 4 November 2019.

11 In one case, the CIA was unknowingly sharing a source with the Thai. Years later while stationed at Udorn, Kenning met a Royal Thai Army intelligence officer who admitted he had held a clandestine meeting with a FAR intelligence officer at the latter's Vientiane house in the early seventies. As the meeting went long, the FAR officer's CIA handler had arrived before the Thai could depart. Not wanting to be exposed, the Thai officer hid in a closet for the duration of the CIA officer's meeting. Interview with George Kenning, 2 October 2019.

12 "The KGB in Asia: Society of Subversion."

13 The Hard Target wing later tried turning the young FAR intelligence officer against the Soviets, though the approach made little headway. In something of a missed opportunity, the wing did not give more attention to using the Soviet stable of agents as conduits for disinformation.

14 Ibid.

15 FBIS, 25 September 1972, p. 12.

16 "Soviet Embassy Employee Defects," *Houston Post*, 16 September 1972.

Chapter 9

1 Poppy cultivation on a small scale continued at isolated Hmong strongholds such as Bouamlong. In May 1970, for example, Royal Lao Air Force H-34 helicopters were called to Bouamlong allegedly to help haul out the poppy harvest. *The Royal Laotian Air Force 1954–1970* (Project Checo Report), p. 145.

2 "The US Heroin Problem and Southeast Asia," Committee on Foreign Affairs, US House of Representatives, 11 January 1973, Appendix B. British embassy telegrams written at the time mostly corroborate Ouane's account that a small Thai Airways plane crashed on takeoff from a makeshift Lao strip in May 1955. Lao authorities killed the Thai pilot when he resisted arrest, jailed eight others, and seized the narcotics aboard. Richard Gibson and Wenhua Chen, *The Secret Army* (Singapore: John Wiley& Son, 2011), p. 176.

3 "The US Heroin Problem and Southeast Asia," Committee on Foreign Affairs, US House of Representatives, 11 January 1973, pp. 26–27.

4 Drug dealing was not Ouane's only vice. A serious gambler, Ouane was reportedly obsessed with winning the Thai lottery. According to a CIA officer, Ouane purchased half of all the tickets for one drawing—but still lost. Magnani interview.

5 In 1958, Laos suspended all licensing requirements on the movement of gold and thus became a major legal importer of the precious metal in Asia. The gold trade became a significant source of national income for Laos, though smuggling from the kingdom declined somewhat in 1968 after introduction of a two-tier world gold market caused speculative demand for gold to drop. "The Declining Gold Trade in Laos," CIA Intelligence Memorandum, September 1968, p. 3.

6 *The Royal Laotian Air Force 1965–1970*, p. 60.

7 Muscled out of his monopoly, Sacda manager Ts'ai Kuang-Jung retreated from Laos to Chiang Mai by 1971.

8 Related to his drug dealings, Ouane was also suspected of profiting from the trafficking of US weaponry via Laos to the Koumintang and other Burma-based insurgents. As late as 1970, US military advisors reported planes from Taiwan transshipping rifles in Savannakhet that were apparently earmarked for the Golden Triangle. "The US Heroin Problem and Southeast Asia," p. 21.

9 In Congressional testimony, Hsing's name was transliterated as Huu Tim Heng. "Foreign Assistance and Related Programs Appropriations, Fiscal Year 1973," Subcommittee of the Committee on Appropriations, US Senate, 92nd Congress, 29 February 1972, p. 701.

10 Letter from BNDD Director John Ingersoll to Rep. Charles Gruber, 27 May 1971.

11 Ouane was not the only senior RLG official immune from accountability. In April 1971, Prince Sopsaisana departed for Paris to become the new Lao ambassador to France. But caught upon landing with 60 kilos of heroin (allegedly provided by a French Corsican in Vientiane), he was sent packing back to the kingdom—only to be named the speaker of the National Assembly.

12 "RLAF Ad Hoc Committee Report," Deputy Chief JUSMAG, March 1975, p. 40; *The Royal Laotian Air Force 1954–1970*, p. 144.

13 *The Royal Laotian Air Force 1954–1970*, p. 60.

14 FBIS, 30 June 1971, p. I2.

15 A CIA assessment from July 1971 described Bounpone as "not highly regarded in military or personal affairs." Weekly Summary, CIA Directorate of Intelligence, 16 July 1971.

16 "Elements of Non-Communist Politics in Laos," CIA Directorate of Intelligence Weekly Summary, 31 December 1970, p. 8.

17 Though not seriously tainted by drug smuggling like Ouane, Bounpone was tied to at least one incident in late 1971 when two C-47 transports transited Pakse en route to South Vietnam. US embassy officials in Vientiane implored the recently promoted regional commander, Brigadier General Soutchay Vongsavanh, to impound the two planes. Upon learning that the aircraft were carrying drugs on behalf of Bounpone and Prince Boun Oum, Soutchay refused to take on the FAR commander in chief. "I told [the embassy officials] it was not my job to arrest the plane crews," recalled Soutchay; "it was my job to fight the North Vietnamese." Correspondence with Soutchay Vongsavanh, 2 August 2020.

18 FBIS, 4 August 1972, p. I11; FBIS, 25 September 1971, p. I1.

19 "Overseas Chinese Involvement in the Narcotics Traffic," CIA Intelligence Memorandum, January 1972, p. 6.

20 In 1968, the Bureau of Narcotics and Dangerous Drugs (BNDD) was formed within the Department of Justice. As this bureau did not yet have overseas personnel and networks to conduct effective counter-narcotics operations, the CIA filled the gap. In 1973, the BNDD was replaced by the Drug Enforcement Administration.

21 Prior to mid-1971, CIA paramilitary officers in northwestern Laos were far more preoccupied with staging intelligence-gathering forays than with counter-narcotics concerns. Said George Kenning, who was handling Mien tribal teams at the time, "Basically, we were told to make sure drugs were not on the planes. That was about it."

22 Ibid, p. 24.

23 American officials in Laos reportedly discussed the possibility of bombing Houei Tap in mid-1971. "CIA Reported Shifting Attention in Laos from Communists to Opium," *Baltimore Sun*, 7 March 1972.

24 As of late 1970, the CIA suspected that the king received payoffs from Ouane for drug and arms smuggling. The king also earned income from real estate, two large farms, and the Royal Teak Forest, as well as from a small annual grant in the annual budget. "Elements of Non-Communist Politics in Laos," CIA Directorate of Intelligence Weekly Summary, 31 December 1970, p. 4. A Thai businessman reportedly paid the king $2 million a year for the teak forest concession. Arya Panya interview.

25 This was actually the second time that the RLG had an intelligence agency with this name. In December 1958, the earlier intelligence body known as SIDASP had been rebranded as the CND. This name was retained until it was absorbed into Siho's Directorate of National Coordination at the start of 1961.

26 "World Drug Traffic and its Impact on US Security," Committee on the Judiciary, US Senate, 18 September 1972, p.266.

27 Interview with James Sheldon, 24 August 2015. Paisone Bannavong hailed from a relatively wealthy Lao family. His sister, Rochana Kirkland, had achieved notoriety when she was convicted, along with her Lao boyfriend and a third Lao accomplice, of murdering her husband—an American national working as the deputy chief of Air America's Vientiane office—in July 1973 during a staged robbery at their Vientiane residence. Sentenced to ten years by a Lao court, Rochana was given permission to leave prison in 1974 for specialized medical attention in Bangkok, then refused to return from Thailand. *Vientiane News*, 14–20 January 1975, p. 10.

28 By the second quarter of 1973, as domestic cultivation plummeted, it was believed that Laos had gone from a drug exporter to a net drug importer solely to satisfy the local addict population. "Report on Tri-Country Narcotics Meeting in Vientiane, 26–28 April 1973," US Embassy in Vientiane to Bureau of East Asian and Pacific Affairs, 7 May 1973.

Chapter 10

1 There had been a team member code-named Jack—since deceased—in the first Thai surveillance team. As the two teams were kept strictly segregated from each other, there was no chance of confusion over members on different teams with the same nicknames.

2   JPRS 56392, dated 29 June 1972, p. 36.

3   FBIS, 15 August 1972, p. J1.

4   Journalist John Barron claimed that Soviet Ambassador to Laos Valentin Vdovin (who arrived in late 1972 after the Sorokin defection) was a KGB officer with prior experience in France and French-speaking Africa. In hindsight, Vdovin's alleged KGB affiliation was almost certainly not the case. John Barron, *KGB: The Secret Work of Soviet Secret Agents* (New York: Reader's Digest Press, 1974), p. 411.

5   O'Connor was briefly sidetracked by one other issue. In 1972, it became apparent that the Soviets in Laos were quietly trying to set up an AT-1 telescope with an automatic camera system to track and position their satellites optically. The Soviets had openly positioned these telescopes in sixteen countries around the world, mostly from the Warsaw Pact and allied communist nations such as North Vietnam. In other countries where permission was not assured, they had resorted to guile to erect their telescopes. In Rangoon, for example, they had concealed one in a water tower on the embassy grounds. In Vientiane, the External Branch had gotten word that the Soviets were modifying the top floor of their embassy with a removable section of roof to accommodate the telescope. O'Connor eventually buzzed the compound in an Air America helicopter to photograph the construction.

6   George Kenning, also a tennis buff, was often crossing paths with Vorobiev on the courts. Their actual affiliations had become an open secret around Vientiane, to the point that a cheeky sports club manager took it upon himself to reserve courts in the name of "George CIA" and "George KGB."

7   The US air attaché, Colonel Albert DeGroote, described Vorobiev as a "slick, intelligent KGB operative who spoke English like a native of Dayton, Ohio." Continued DeGroote, "George's M.O. was to introduce himself [at diplomatic functions] to any new arrival as 'George,' hoping that the new arrival would assume he was an American and give him some useful information. Albert DeGroote, *A Flight through Life* (lulu.com, 2013), p. 217.

8   The Polish ICC commissioners mostly hailed from their Foreign Ministry. On a single occasion the commissioner was a known intelligence officer. That officer, Jerzy Kowalski, served in Vientiane from June 1969 to August 1970. "Secretive Spies or Ordinary Clerks? Polish Communist Intelligence Services in Brussels, 1975–89," by Idesbald Goddeeris, *Dutch Crossing*, Vol. 39, No. 3, November 2015.

9   Correspondence with David Jenkins, 12 August 2020.

10 Police Colonel Som Rathphangthong, *Public Security for Peace and Happiness* (Vientiane, 1975), p. 112.

11 US State Department telegram 021636, "PRC-DRV Relations in Laos: Cooperation or Competition?" 1 February 1974.

12 FBIS, 6 August 1970, p. I1. Relations between China and the Soviet Union were especially tense during this period, to include border skirmishes in March 1969. The assignment of the New China News Agency correspondent to Laos was seen as an effort by Beijing to counter the TASS correspondent at the Soviet embassy. "The KGB in Asia: Society of Subversion."

13 "China and Southeast Asia: A Gentle Rapprochement," CIA Intelligence Memorandum, 15 November 1971, p. 6; FBIS, 12 February 1969, p. I8.

14 Weekly Summary, CIA Directorate of Intelligence, 16 July 1971.

15 "China and Southeast Asia: A Gentle Rapprochement," p. 6.

16 FBIS, 29 September 1971, p. J4.

17 Arya Panya interview.

18 Correspondence with Roger McCarthy, 17 June 2002.

19 The failure to afford Ben USAID cover in Laos is all the more curious given that he already had USAID cover while in Jakarta.

20 Perhaps to help him expand these contacts, Ben was listed as an investor in a Chinese restaurant in Vientiane.

Chapter 11

1 Physically, the two branches were kept segregated. Whereas the External Branch was based at the USAID compound and given USAID cover assignments, Internal Branch officers were all stationed at the embassy building (or the annex located across the street) and given cover assignments within the Political and Economic sections.

2 The President's Daily Brief, 11 October 1966.

3 Lilley and Lilley, p. 119.

4 The President's Daily Brief, 3 January 1967. After the election, Ambassador Sullivan referred to Deputy Station Chief Lilley as Mr. Tammany Hall, an allusion to the New York City vote-getting machine in the late 19th century. Lilley and Lilley, p. 120.

5 "Elements of Non-Communist Politics in Laos," p. 9.

6 "Some Thoughts on a Rightist Takeover of Laos," CIA Office of National Estimates, 18 March 1971, p. ii.

7 Interview with Richard C. Howland, Foreign Affairs Oral History Project, Association for Diplomatic Studies and Training, 26 January 1999.

8 The results of the January 1972 elections were nearly identical to 1967, with the vast majority of winners loyal to regional military commanders. One of the rare exceptions was in the southern province of Sithandone, where a left-wing candidate surprisingly beat out a military favorite. Receiving threats to his life from local troops, the leftist politician had been forced to take refuge in the provincial information service office on Khong Island in August 1972. Unfortunately for him, the crew of a US Air Force AC-130 gunship, incorrectly believing it was over Cambodia, opened fire on the office building and destroyed it. The legislator escaped with his life—barely—but no doubt thought the attack was no accident. Memorandum from G.A. Carver (Vietnam Affairs Staff) to Director CIA, 15 August 1972.

9   The President's Daily Brief, 12 August 1972.

10 Correspondence with Dan Arnold, 10 September 2018.

11 Document 162, Memorandum from Kissinger to Nixon, 18 May 1972, FRUS, Vol. VII, Vietnam, January–October 1972.

12 Document 181, Memorandum from Special Assistant for Vietnam Affairs, CIA, to Richard T. Kennedy of the National Security Council Staff, 31 May 1972, FRUS, Vol. VII, Vietnam, January–October 1972; Document 196, Memorandum Kissinger to Nixon, 8 June 1972, FRUS, Vol. VII, Vietnam, January–October 1972.

13 Arnold correspondence.

14 Document 188, Memorandum Kissinger to Nixon, 12 June 1972, FRUS, Vo. VII, Vietnam, January–October 1972; Ahern, p. 353.

15 Central Intelligence Bulletin, 9 July 1971, p. 1.

16 Document 222, Minutes of a Washington Special Actions Group Meeting, 27 July 1972, FRUS, Vol. VIII, Vietnam, January–October 1972.

17 Document 227, Minutes of a Washington, Special Actions Group Meeting, 4 August 1972, FRUS, Vol. VIII, Vietnam, January–October 1972.

18 Among his many hats, Souvanna Phouma was officially the foreign minister. But since he could not devote sufficient time to that role, he named a minister-delegate to head the Foreign Ministry. The minister-delegate in effect became the acting foreign minister.

19 Besides Player, there had been two other African American officers in Laos, both of whom had tragic deaths. Edward Johnson, who had a previous tour with Sea Supply in Thailand, was a paramilitary training officer visiting forward guerrilla bases in northwestern Laos when he died in a helicopter crash on 20 August 1965. Wilbur "Will" Greene was serving as chief of paramilitary operations at Savannakhet Unit when he fell ill and died during a gall bladder operation at Udorn on 28 August 1972.

20 FAR began a night curfew in Vientiane on 31 January 1972 due to the deteriorating security situation around the kingdom.

21 Correspondence with Walter McIntosh, 10 March 2020.

22 Mendez, pp. 116–119.

23 In November 1972, Souvanna Phouma confided during a cabinet meeting that a Lao settlement would not be possible until Washington and Hanoi first came to a definitive agreement on Vietnam. The President's Daily Brief, 27 November 1972.

Chapter 12

1   Interview with Jack Mathews, 15 February 1998.

2   Interview with Roger McCarthy, 16 May 1997.

3   In 1962, during his second tour in Taiwan, McCarthy helped organize Taiwanese paramilitary support in South Vietnam's Mekong Delta.

4   In hosting the Thai surveillance team at his residence, the case officer no doubt weighed the risks. The benefit of bonding with the team was seen as outweighing the chance of exposure, especially since villagers from the immediate area were also invited to the movie showings so as not to focus attention on the team. Still, by early 1974 it was known within the embassy that the Pathet Lao were actively compiling lists of locals working for the US mission (Vientiane 02285, 20 March 1974, Whitehouse to SecState) and were alternately harassing domestic workers and appealing to them to conspire against their American employers.

5   FBIS, 20 February 1973, p. I1.

6   FBIS, 6 July 1973, p. I1.

7   FBIS, 16 July 1973, p. I1.

8   Interview with Hawkeye, 14 December 2017.

9   FBIS, 13 June 1968, p. I1.

10 FBIS, 18 December 1970, p. I1.

11 *Peking Review*, No. 36, 4 September 1964, p. 17.

12 FBIS, 9 April 1971, p. I1; FBIS, 12 April 1971, p. I1; FBIS, 19 April 1971, p. I8.

13 Thao Ma had been given political asylum in Thailand in September 1967 (FBIS, 8 September 1967, p. vvv1). The RLG sentenced him to death in absentia in 1968.

14 The T-28 pilots had been in Thai exile with Thao Ma since 1966. Lt. Col. Pany has been in Thailand since the failed coup that resulted in the dissolution of the DNC in 1965.

15 In May 1973, Phou Khao Khouai, a mountain redoubt 40 kilometers northeast of Vientiane, was designated as a retraining site for CIA-sponsored guerrilla forces prior to being formally integrated into the FAR. Vang Pao's guerrilla regiments were being rotated through the base every five weeks for this purpose. The presence of Hmong troops at Phou Khao Khouai apparently gave rise to the mistaken belief that Vang Pao had maneuvered forces near Vientiane to support Thao Ma.

16 Brigadier General Khamhou, whose office was located near the radio station, mobilized members of his anti-narcotics GSI to help retake the station.

17 The three—including Bounleut's Saycocie's nephew—landed their plane on a stretch of road adjacent to the Asian Institute of Technology in Bangkok. They then abandoned the plane and disappeared in the busy Thai capital. They were granted political asylum in Thailand the following month. FBIS, 28 September 1973, p. I2.

18 Roger McCarthy, *Our Republic in Peril* (Oakland, OR: Red Anvil Press, 2004), p. 80. Pany was executed at dawn.

19 "Lao Weekly Sitrep—November 8." Telegram Amembassy Vientiane to Secstate DC, 8 November 1973.

Chapter 13

1   A curfew beginning at midnight was instituted in January 1972, then expanded from 1900 to 0500 hours after the Thao Ma coup.

2   The three were Joe Murphy, Howie McCabe, and James C. When Bernie D'Ambrosio and John LeClair departed in mid-1971, McCabe temporarily acted as case officer for the original Thai surveillance team through mid-1972. He was occasionally assisted by Mike Van Quill, a Penco case officer who spent most of his Laos tour assigned to an interrogation center at Pha Khao in northeastern Laos.

3   DEA Special Agent Seema was killed during an undercover operation in Los Angeles in February 1988.

4   The CIA's relationship with the Tai Dam had grown complicated over time. In August 1971, a notional resistance front targeted against the DRV was disbanded when half of the Lao-based Tai Dam leadership was polygraphed and found to have had, or continued to have, ties to the Pathet Lao and North Vietnamese. Also in 1971, the CIA recruited a battalion of Tai Dam from the refugee community around Vientiane. Intended to be used for POW rescue missions, the battalion was given extensive commando raider training at four sites in Thailand and Laos. By the time instruction was finished, however, serious doubts were being raised about the mettle of the troops. The battalion, as a result, was quietly disbanded, with many of its members used as fillers for predominantly Hmong guerrilla battalions in northeastern Laos.

5   The female trainee was a heavyset Thai army sergeant who was nicknamed *Noi* (Thai for "small"). The two male trainees were call-signed Youngblood and Tony (a repeat of the pseudonym used by the team leader in the Kangaroos). All three were gone by 1974.

6   Frank Sommers, the last head of the Hard Target wing, remained impressed by the depth of Vorobiev's awareness of American culture, especially after he laughed immediately and appropriately at a Howard Cosell reference. Correspondence with Jane Sommers-Kelly, 10 September 2020.

7   DeGroote, p. 217.

8   Correspondence with John Wood, 24 January 2017.

9   "Chen Shu-Ling was an older guy who spoke only Chinese," recalled US air attaché DeGroote. "He was shadowed at all times by a much younger officer who spoke fairly good French and who, in my opinion, was the guy in charge." Correspondence with Albert DeGroote, 7 November 2016.

10 Following President Nixon's February 1972 visit to the PRC, there was sporadic contact between the US and Chinese embassy in Laos. US military attachés were invited to dinner by their PRC counterparts on a couple of occasions in 1974, invariably followed by what the Americans called "Chinese movie torture": hours of Chinese propaganda films in Chinese with no subtitles. DeGroote correspondence.

11 Som Rathphangthong, p. 113. The PRC's fixation against Taiwan was overkill. As of 1973, the Taiwanese presence consisted of only a small garrison and a radio relay outpost along the far western border of Laos, as well as a tiny liaison office in Vientiane. These were all manned by personnel from the Intelligence Bureau of Taiwan's Ministry of National Defense. The RLG had also allowed Taiwan to tacitly control the Chinese schools in Luang Prabang, Pakse, and Vientiane. In neighboring Thailand, Taiwan maintained a radio relay outpost in Chiang Rai province, as well as a larger radio intercept station adjacent to the CIA paramilitary headquarters at Udorn Royal Thai Air Force Base. FBIS, 9 May 1973, p. J3; correspondence with Fred Rustmann, 27 January 2015.

12 Correspondence with Dennis Obermayer, 25 August 2020.

13 The Soviets had been drip-feeding the Pathet Lao transport planes since early 1973. By September 1974, the Pathet Lao inventory included two An-2 biplanes, one An-24B, one An-26, and one Yak-40 passenger jet. This last aircraft had been a point of contention, as the Royal Lao Air Force for years had been lobbying the US for jet planes. In 1974, Washington finally agreed to transition four Lao officers in the T-38 jet trainer at Randolph Air Force Base, Texas. Although the four completed instrument pilot certification, the Soviets beat the United States to the punch by delivering the Yak-40.

14 "Biographic Sketches of Members of the New Coalition Government," Telegram from Amembassy Vientiane to Secstate DC, 9 April 1974.

15 The lone paramilitary officer, Jim Sheldon, was stationed on the top floor of the embassy in Vientiane to handle residual paramilitary issues.

16 Staunch US ally Thailand had also noticed the changing geopolitical landscape and started to question openly its close relationship with the CIA. This was compounded by an ill-conceived CIA operation in December 1973 in which a case officer at the up-country Sakhon Nakom office (who had previously served in Savannakhet Unit) sent letters to the Thai prime minister and five Thai newspapers. The letters were purportedly from a senior Thai Communist Party member asking for a truce in exchange for autonomy in its "liberated" zones. The letters were exposed as hoaxes because the office boy at the CIA office in Sakhon Nakom, ordered by the case officer to mail the letters to Bangkok, had registered them under his own name. The reaction to the CIA meddling was intense, including a massive protest in front of the US embassy on 9 January 1974. Even Lt. Gen. Vitoon Yasawasdi, who had led CIA-sponsored Thai forces in Laos, publicly commented that Thailand should "deal [the CIA] a painful blow" (FBIS, 14 January 1974, p. J4). Three months later, the head of the Thai Police Special Branch, which had long harbored close ties with the CIA, negatively commented on the number of CIA officers in Thailand and stated that he was "authorized to wreck, arrest, and deport foreign spies" (FBIS, 5 April 1974, p. J5).

17 McCarthy, p. 76. Station Chief Dan Arnold was somewhat more understanding of Souvanna's predicament: "With the cards that he had to play, how could he have done better?" (Correspondence with Dan Arnold, 4 September 2020)

18 FBIS, 19 July 1974, p. I2.
19 *Berkeley Barb*, Vol. 20, Issue 13, 11–17 October 1974.
20 Correspondence with Jack Huxtable, 31 October 2017.
21 Interview with Jim Shelton, 20 January 2015.
22 Huxtable correspondence; *Vientiane News*, 7–13 January 1975, p. 3.
23 In October 1966, Whitehouse was the deputy chief of mission in Guinea when that country's foreign minister was detained in Ghana during transit. The Guinea government placed Whitehouse and the rest of the US embassy under house arrest for a week as a bargaining chip to secure the release of their foreign minister.

Chapter 14

1 Daniels, a former smokejumper, had arriving in northeastern Laos in 1965 as a 24-year-old junior paramilitary officer.
2 FBIS, 20 January 1975, p. I5. DeGroote was never able to arouse enough interest in Washington to generate a reconnaissance flight (DeGroote correspondence).
3 The seven Soviets had carried a large supply of caviar and vodka when they departed, but they refused to share. The entire convoy, totaling more than 500 expatriates in 26 trucks, reached the Thai border on 3 May.
4 From 28 April to 4 May, as part of the reconciliation process, the king visited the Pathet Lao headquarters in Sam Neua. Plans called for him to undergo his long-delayed official coronation ceremony in December 1976.
5 National Intelligence Bulletin (CIA), 12 May 1975.
6 Decades earlier Khamouane had been an American favorite, and CIA analysts had been slow to acknowledge the Phongsaly warlord's tilt toward the communist camp. In September 1961, for example, a CIA memorandum claimed that Khamouane was "above suspicion," though other members of the Boupha clan had Pathet Lao ties. A 1973 CIA document claimed he had not shifted loyalty to the left until his ranks were infiltrated by the Pathet Lao in 1963 ("The Lao Communists," CIA Intelligence Memorandum, 12 March 1973, p. 6). In hindsight, Khamouane had pragmatically sided with the communists by 1961.
7 As of 11 May 1975, there were 11 American officials and 11 dependents in Luang Prabang, plus 2 more officials in nearby Xieng Ngeun.
8 USAID's Jack Huxtable noted that in 1971 secure radio rooms with reinforced steel doors had been built at USAID compounds in Ban Houei Sai, Luang Prabang, Savannakhet, and Pakse to support counter-narcotics operations. Added Huxtable, "I am sure these rooms were the subject of many conversations before, during, and after our departure." (Huxtable correspondence)
9 Correspondence with Peter Flynn, 2 November 2017.
10 Ster and Pearcy lived in the Phoumi Nosavan Compound, so named because a decade earlier it had been the residential complex of General Phoumi.

11 Correspondence with Dan Ster, 4 September 2020.

12 Wilson kept a low profile a little too long for the liking of Station Chief Arnold. In March 1975 when the student uprising first started, Arnold sent him a brief classified message. When Wilson took it to his communications vault and decrypted it, he found haunting words: "Your reporting is conspicuous by its absence, PSM." Said Wilson, "The most dreaded phrase in Station terminology was 'PSM,' meaning 'Please See Me.' It meant drop whatever you are doing and go to Dan's office for an ass chewing. That afternoon I was on a plane to Vientiane to get my butt chewed!" Correspondence with Rex Wilson, 31 October 2017.

13 On 11 May, the US Embassy had distributed an evacuation handbook entitled *Operation Bend with the Wind*. With Pathet Lao antiaircraft units taking up position around Wattay, two US Marine officers flew to Vientiane the following week to discuss heliborne evacuation contingencies. However, because Marine assets were too far removed (afloat in the South China Sea) and US Air Force CH-53 Knives at Nakhon Phanom had taken heavy losses during the 15 May Mayaguez incident off the Cambodian coast, no satisfactory plan was ever developed.

14 Several of the banners denounced an alleged CIA officer named "Bob," even though there was no CIA officer at the station by that name. Other banners accused Frank Sprage, the head of the compound's guard force subcontractor, Trans-Air Protective Services, of being a "CIA bandit."

Chapter 15

1 As soon as Soutchay departed, one of his trusted subordinates, Major Phouthone Phouthavong, grabbed power in Pakse. A French-trained logistics officer who graduated at the top of his military academy class, the opportunistic Phouthone attempted to ingratiate himself with the Pathet Lao; his efforts failed and he was soon cast aside without portfolio. Correspondence with Soui Sananikone, 7 January 2018; Singto Na Champassak, *Mon Destin* (Paris: L'Harmattan, 2010), p. 96

2 A similar scene had unfolded at the house of Frank Sommers, the last head of the Hard Target wing. A truckload of Pathet Lao soldiers showed up while he was out to dinner. He had no choice but to seek alternate accommodations for his final days before evacuating at the close of May. Sommers-Kelly correspondence.

3 McCarthy, p. 84.

4 For his role in rescuing more than 500 key indigenous personnel from Laos, Sheldon received a commendation in 1976 from then-CIA Director George H. W. Bush.

5 In July 1971, Chao Sinh was concurrently named deputy commander of FAR's Military Region One headquartered in Luang Prabang. In late 1974, he was promoted to FAR chief of operations.

6   In September 1973, Thao Ly was named FAR chief of intelligence. He replaced General Etam Singvongsa, who was named to the vacant (and nearly identical) post of FAR deputy chief of staff for psychological warfare and intelligence.

7   FBIS, 4 September 1975, p. 14.

8   On 10 May, Khamhou had fled to Thailand. Five days later, it was announced that Colonel Khamphai Latsavongthong, a Pathet Lao officer, would take his place as head of the National Documentation Center. Another week after that, the government announced that the center was being permanently abolished. National Intelligence Bulletin (CIA), 27 May 1975.

9   On 27 November, Arya Panya, serving as the palace's chief of protocol, had a final audience with the king. During that opportunity, he handed over the case left by General Thao Ly with the roster of Savannakhet soldiers. Drained of energy, the king set it aside without looking. Three nights later, Arya and the king's youngest son fled across the Mekong. In March 1977, the king and remaining members of the royal family were sent to reeducation in Sam Neua; they died from the effects of hard labor and malnutrition the following year.

10 One day prior to this incident, Anders and McCarthy had ventured to Wattay to discreetly watch a UN-chartered plane transit Laos on the way to Bangkok. On board were fourteen foreign nationals whom PAVN had captured during the final weeks of the Vietnam War. Among them was Jim Lewis, a former CIA paramilitary officer who had served with guerrilla units on the Bolovens. Lewis had been captured on 11 April in South Vietnam and then marched north and subjected to torture and malnourishment. Lewis and his wife were killed in April 1983 when a suicide bomber detonated a bomb at the US embassy in Beirut.

11 McCarthy, p. 87.

12 Fitting for the times, the smooth KGB *rezident* George Vorobiev in late 1975 was replaced by the far more overbearing Yury Shimanovsky. Recalled MI-6 representative Mark Scrase-Dickins, "Yury would tease me that when he became Commissar of Southern England he would see us okay!" Correspondence with Mark Scrase-Dickins, 27 April 2020.

13 Team member Tim died an untimely death in mid-1977 when he was shot in the head while driving his car in downtown Bangkok. It was later learned that he had embezzled a large amount of money from a company sending Thai laborers to the Middle East and had paid for the indiscretion with his life.

14 Bangkok Station persisted with the hijinks against the Soviet embassy in January 1982 when it posted letters purportedly from the new Soviet press officer demanding that Thailand cease "collaboration with US and Chinese imperialists." The Thai deputy foreign minister summoned the Soviet ambassador to admonish him over the "rude, undiplomatic notes." FBIS, 12 January 1982, p. J1.

Chapter 16

1   BAKIN Case File, "Vladimir Piguzov." Information on Piguzov's time in Indonesia is gleaned from this file, which was accessed during research for the author's book *INTEL* (Jakarta: Equinox Press, 2004).

2   "CIA Turncoat," *Washington Post*, 2 November 1980, p. A1.

3   Correspondence with Jack Platt, 2 December 2005.

4   Statement released by Senator Daniel Inouye, 29 October 1980.

5   In 1994, the Red Banner Institute was named after Yuri Andropov, the largest-serving KGB chief from 1967-82.

6   The CIA later arranged to smuggle Piguzov's widow and children out of Russia.

Index